*The Heritage of
the English Library*

The Heritage
of the
English Library

RAYMOND IRWIN
M.A., F.L.A.

Professor of Library Studies in The University of London
Director of The School of Librarianship and Archives,
University College, London

HAFNER PUBLISHING COMPANY

New York

1964

PRINTED IN GREAT BRITAIN
in 12 on 13 point Bembo type
BY C. TINLING AND CO. LTD
LIVERPOOL, LONDON AND PRESCOT

To I. S. I.
with love

FOREWORD

In 1958 *The Origins of the English Library* was published. Its purpose was to provide, not a new history of our libraries, but studies of certain aspects of that history which might give vitality to the often rather meagre facts, and set them in perspective against the development of our civilization. The present work attempts to carry these studies still further, adding in one or two cases further discussion of points briefly raised in the *Origins*, but for the most part exploring fresh ground in the story of our subject. When the details in the foreground are scanty, a knowledge of the background becomes even more important than usual if the few surviving facts are to be properly interpreted. No apology is needed therefore if some of these studies relate mainly to the background, and especially to the spread of literacy and the habit of reading. With an illiterate public, it would be rash to expect libraries of any significance, but as literacy and education expand, their existence can often be assumed whether it is confirmed by the few records or not. There is still a wide field open for research, both in background and foreground, and it is to be hoped that new explorers will be tempted to venture into this most rewarding territory.

A few of the chapters in the present work are based on articles that have appeared in various periodicals, and I am grateful to the editors of *The Library Review*, *The Library Association Record* and *The Private Library* (the quarterly journal of the Private Libraries Association) for allowing me to make use of this material; also to University College, London, for allowing me to reprint part of the lecture entitled *The Golden Chain*. I would like to thank many good friends for help and advice, especially Dr A. N. L. Munby of King's College, Cambridge, Mr C. H. Roberts of Oxford, and my colleagues at University College London. My special thanks are due to Miss Mary Piggott who has not only helped with proof reading but has given much time to the compilation of the index.

R.I.

University College, London
January 1964

CONTENTS

CHAPTER I

The Written Word

I N the history of libraries we are concerned not only with their purpose and content, but with the social background which produced them. This leads us, therefore, both into the history of scholarship in its narrower sense, and into the wider field of the history of human civilization and culture and literacy. Three achievements in particular mark the first appearance of human civilization in primitive times.[1] One is the gathering of men into cities, with all the social organization that belongs to urban life. Another is the growth of the religious idea, expressed by means of holy places (whether they be grove, stone circle, sacred hill, shrine, temple or church) which serve to bind the urban population into a unit. The third is the development of the art of human communication, and in particular of the much more significant art of *recording* communications, which in its true sense is found only amongst human beings. Animal communication is in the main an instinctive stimulus evoking a reflex response in other animals. It appears perhaps in its most highly developed form amongst the social insects, and especially amongst the bees, which are apparently able to pass on messages involving indirect responses to absent stimuli (e.g. the direction and distance of a particular patch of flowers); bees have of course a highly complex social organization, and indeed a 'city life' in which communication is a necessarily important factor. In general, however, animal communication is limited to the satisfaction of immediate wants, and there is no biological need for them to be recorded, in any way comparable to human records. They can be recorded on the memory, so that similar calls produce similar responses, but there are no true external records.[2]

---

[1] On this, see J. Z. Young, *Doubt and Certainty in Science*, 1951.

[2] Animals which communicate with one another by the sense of smell may be said to produce external records, but these are transitory and accidental, rather than deliberate.

The art of recording communications, which thus distinguishes the human race, is the art of writing. This essentially human achievement gives added significance to the other two developments of the religious idea and of urban life. The authority of religion over the tribe or city is exercised partly by the power of the holy places in which it finds expression; partly by traditional ceremonies and ritual (as Dr Johnson noted in his Hebridean tour), but even more by the apparent magic of the art of writing; so much so indeed that books (and therefore libraries) have always been closely associated with temples or churches from the most primitive times. And the complicated pattern of urban life, with its specialization of functions, the administrative activity of the state, and the commercial activity of business life, are almost impossible without the use of written communications. These are the conditions which called forth not merely the art of writing, but, in due course, all the arts which grace our civilization: the arts of story-telling, of epic and lyric poetry, of history and criticism; the arts of the theatre; and of painting, sculpture, architecture, and music.

To primitive man, and perhaps to modern man also, the magic of the art of communication consists not merely in the knowledge possessed by the scholars who have mastered this mysterious art, but in the fact that by its aid man has conquered both time and space. It is this, indeed, more than anything else, that distinguishes recorded communication from the immediate and instinctive communications of social insects such as the ants and bees. And note, by the way, that animal communication reaches its highest development in the social (i.e. urbanized) insects, bearing further witness to the truth of Aristotle's association of culture with urban life.

Man's conquest of time by the art of writing enables him to hear the words of his forefathers through untold generations, and to speak to his children's children in generations to come. His conquest of space carries his words over land and sea, so that the soldier on Hadrian's Wall could speak to his friend on the Euphrates, the pilgrim in Jerusalem could converse with his family in England, and farthest east can talk to farthest west. Wherever, indeed, man travels in the wide world, the written word can travel too; and the only effect that modern science has had on this marvel is to increase the speed at which a message travels, except of course that the telephone does away with the written word: sometimes, but not always, an advantage. The history of libraries is in brief the history of this conquest of space and time. 'To read,' says a modern Chinese writer, 'is to escape from the prison of the here and now.'[1]

The social life of a human city depends utterly and completely on the faculty of communication by means of a standardized language, familiar to everyone and able to satisfy all social needs; a language which can be put into writing, taught to children and employed in all human intercourse. The primitive demands of sex, hunger and danger still remain. They are the foundation from which any human system of communication must grow, and their importance survives in the recorded communications which we call our literature. But urban life produces a whole series of new needs which are only indirectly concerned with these primitive instincts, and could only appear in an organized community of human families. They are for the most part needs arising from the partial specialization of functions in human society, and from the organization and administration on which business life, industry and manufacture depend; for all of which not only communication, but the ability to record communications, is essential. And such communication is much more complex than the simple expression of love or hunger or fear in primitive man and the animals. It involves communication of detailed information, methods, plans, policies such as the animal never achieves. It involves references to the records of the past, and preparation for the distant future. Urban life demands also the organization of social amusements, games and entertainments, developing ultimately into all the various branches of literature, music, drama and art. Again it demands the arts of government in both peace and war, thus bringing into being military as well as political and economic science. Every one of these social activities—education, business, manufacture, entertainment, art, government, war, and eventually social welfare, rests firmly and entirely on the basic faculty of communication between man and man, and on the recording of communications in some more or less permanent form. It is noteworthy that the first workable

[1] Lin Yutang, *The Importance of Living*, 1938.

alphabet in the West was introduced by the merchants of Phoenicia to facilitate their trade and commerce. From this there sprang in due time the Hebrew as well as the Greek and Latin alphabets. Early Minoan documents seem almost exclusively to have been of a commercial character. In urban life the art of communication must overcome the problems of time and space by methods more accurate than memory can provide. Memory itself is, within its limits, a tool of quite remarkable efficiency in the recording of information. Indeed it is an indispensable tool in human thought and learning. Its purpose is to give intellectual continuity to the life of the individual. By its means, facts are as it were digested and related to the rest of our particular experience. It is not primarily a device for recording facts, but rather for interpreting them and giving them significance. It has not the mechanical infallibility of the printing press in reproducing ideas, simply because it is a much more marvellous machine than the printing press. It records nothing without absorbing it and making it its own. That is to say, it records nothing without altering it and itself being altered by it, if only to a slight degree. Thus it does more than record; it learns and thinks and creates. But this, however wonderful, is not what we require of an instrument for recording communications. We do not want such an instrument to alter our communications, or to be affected by them. We do not want it to think. We do not want it to vary in its efficiency with different people and at different times, as the human memory does. We want it rather to turn out exact and unerring copies of the information we entrust to it.

An oral message may be passed down a line of men from mouth to mouth. It will never arrive exactly in the form in which it starts, and the longer the distance it travels, the greater will be the error. The reason for the error is simply the fallibility of the mind as a recorder and transmitter; at every step the message is slightly altered by the filter through which it passes. Similarly an oral message may be passed down through time from father to son. We call this tradition; and we know that it is an extremely fallible method of handing down historical fact. It may of course be useful in checking the validity of written records, especially if these are for any reason suspect; for oral tradition is less easily influenced by those who set out deliberately to tamper with history, while the written record can be falsified or forged.

Although oral tradition may thus be untrustworthy, it is nevertheless one of the most primitive of all forms of recorded communication. The early history of nearly every race or country is permeated by traditional legends and stories, passed on from one generation to another by bards or minstrels who, though they habitually introduce topical elements into their tale, nevertheless often transmit the essentials of their story with remarkable faithfulness. When such a tradition is handed down in the form of an exact religious ritual, it may assume even greater accuracy. 'Legends,' said Dr Johnson in the *Journey to the Western Islands*, 'are the only records of a nation that has no historians ... Their only registers are stated observances and practical representations. For this reason an age of ignorance is an age of ceremony. Pageants and processions and commemorations gradually shrink away, as better methods come into use of recording events and preserving rights.'

Pageants and processions do not in fact shrink away as Dr Johnson imagined, for they serve other needs than the recording of events. Indeed, being part of the machinery of propaganda by which society shepherds and controls the individual they tend to become more elaborate as the power of society increases. Sooner or later however the written record comes into use, more enduring and less fallible than memory or legend or tradition. In Kipling's *Just So Stories* Tegumai, busied with his little daughter Taffy in designing the first alphabet, cries 'I believe we've found out *the* big secret of the world'. Which indeed they had, for the emergence of written characters has proved, as we have already suggested, the key to the conquest of time and space, and the most powerful of the weapons which man wields against man. With the art of writing (as Carlyle said) the age of miracles began. By its means the accumulated wisdom of the community is set before children at school. By its means countries are administered, scientific research is carried out and scientific discoveries are recorded and handed on. By its means the chronicles of the race, the stories of its warriors and the songs of its lovers are made immortal on stone or parchment or paper. These are the records on which civilization rests, and it is with the care of these that libraries are concerned.

The relation between civilization and urban life was noticed long ago by Aristotle. The connection between the growth of libraries and urban life with its specialization of functions is a natural corollary. Government and administration, trade and industry, social activities and entertainment, all demand literacy; literacy creates letters, documents and books; books create libraries. It is no accident that our Western civilization in all its phases and periods has been founded on organized city life. Athens, Alexandria, Rome, Constantinople, Paris, London and a score of other cities have in succession provided the stimulus for that flowering of letters which is the mark of civilized life. There is scarcely any exception to this rule. The Roman scholar in Imperial times may have done much of his work in the peace of his country villa, but Roman villa life would have been impossible without Rome at its centre. The monastic libraries of medieval times were often housed in remote and lonely places, but again they had Rome at their centre; and when the universities grew up in the twelfth and thirteenth centuries, scholarship was drawn from the monasteries to the new academic centres of Bologna, Paris, Chartres, Orleans, Oxford and Cambridge.

There may be a possible exception in the civilization of Ireland in the fifth and sixth centuries. There were no towns in the Ireland of that day, and scarcely any villages; all the Irish towns were Norse in origin. There was however a quite remarkable amount of literacy and artistic activity, and an equally remarkable number of important libraries, at the many monastic foundations scattered through the country. These were based on local tribal organization, not on the normal organization of the Church through bishops and dioceses. The diocesan organization was largely built on the system of Roman provincial administration, and Ireland of course had never been part of the Empire. In some degree the Irish monastic communities (some of which were of considerable size) provided a kind of urban life of their own. But though their contact with Rome was for a long period tenuous, there seems to have been at all times some traffic between Ireland and Bordeaux; Ireland had provided a sanctuary for refugees from Britain, Brittany, Southern Gaul and Galicia, and Irish scholarship may have been largely drawn from this source.

Nevertheless the traditions of literacy and the vigorous missionary endeavours of early Ireland were less obviously based on urban life than is usual elsewhere. In general the rule holds good: libraries prosper most in busy and populous centres, and the existence of a prosperous city implies almost inevitably the existence of the libraries on which its prosperity in part depends.

The religious element in library development is perhaps even more interesting and remarkable, and it is indeed strange that so few writers have studied it or even noticed it. The part played by the holy place or sacred mountain in the history of primitive peoples is well established. It served as a focus for the life of the tribe and a centre where the leaders might take counsel and issue orders which would derive some of their authority from the sanctity of the place in which they were made. The dwelling place of the tribal god thus served as a channel of communication between governors and governed. Stonehenge and the Manx Tynwald are obvious examples; others are the mountain shrines of Olympus, Cretan Ida, Sinai, Carmel, Mount Moriah and Saphon. A. C. Bouquet describes[1] how natural objects such as a grove or hill become conventionalized in the pyramid and temple, and how the 'arborescent look of lofty Gothic aisles' may well prove to be a real reminiscence of Central European forests. Frazer in the *Golden Bough* quotes Grimm's argument that the derivation of the Teutonic words for 'temple' suggests that amongst the Germans the oldest sanctuaries were natural woods. The whole thesis of the *Golden Bough* is of course built on the rites associated with the grove at Nemi.

Sooner or later then the grove or hill develops into a temple, or in Christian days into a church or cathedral; and if enquiry were made, it would be found that a quite remarkable number of medieval churches and religious houses were built on sites already hallowed by pre-Christian traditions. Whatever our private views may be, a holy place of this kind gathers to itself, by custom or inspiration, an atmosphere of sanctity and awe that compels our reverence. J. Z. Young tells how one Sunday afternoon in Paris he went to the cathedral of Notre-Dame. 'As I looked up at the tremendous vertical lines of the nave I found that there were tears

---

[1] *Comparative Religion*, 4th ed., 1956, p. 33. See also J. Z. Young, *op. cit.*, pp. 89-99, and C. H. Gordon, *Before the Bible*, 1962, p. 232.

in my eyes. Why is it that one is sometimes moved in this way by a great church? When I left Notre-Dame I walked around the outside and looked at the mountain of stone, supported by its flying buttresses. Then, sitting in the sun, I speculated on this extraordinary human habit of making great buildings. As a biologist I naturally considered, first, what may be its significance for human survival, and secondly, why do such works move us in this way.'[1] There will be few of us who have not had this kind of experience, and have not wondered at the power that such a holy place can exercise over our feelings and emotions. In London, S. Paul's commands our devotion as a national shrine; and the proximity of the Abbey Church of S. Peter's to the Palace of Westminster is full of significance.

It is no surprise therefore that libraries have from the earliest times been closely associated with holy places. Almost without exception every great library from the days of Aristotle, with his school and library in the grove of Apollo Lyceius and the Muses at Athens, right down to the Age of Reason, has been built on holy ground. The Platonic Academy was in a grove sacred to the hero Academus. The Alexandrian Museum was in the precincts of the royal palace; and it must be remembered that any royal foundation shares some of the divinity attaching to the king. It was ruled and administered by a president-priest. The daughter library founded under Ptolemy III was in a temple dedicated to Serapis and Isis; and when the Patriarch Theophilus destroyed both temple and library AD 391, he erected the church of S. John Baptist and a monastery in its place, thus incidentally preserving the holiness of the site. The rival library at Pergamum was in the precincts of the temple of Athena, and a statue of the goddess stood in the centre of the largest surviving room of the library. All the known libraries of Rome were in temples: Pollio's foundation in the Atrium Libertatis, the Octavian Library in the temple of Juno and Jupiter, the Palatine library in the temple of Apollo, the Bibliotheca Pacis in the temple of Peace, the Ulpian Library close to the temple of Trajan, and there were libraries also in the temple of Asclepius and in the Pantheon. Of the two Imperial libraries in Athens, one was dedicated to Athena and Trajan, and the other was in the mag-

[1] *op. cit.*, p. 89.

nificent temple of Panhellenian Zeus. Evidence is lacking about the many known to have been scattered through the provinces of the Empire but some at least certainly,[1] and most of them probably, were associated with temples. Julian the Apostate even attempted to counter Christian propaganda by encouraging the establishment of temple libraries. A letter from himself as Supreme Pontiff to his provincial vicars suggests a code of rules for their formation, and an *index expurgatorius*; priests are instructed to acquire true histories and orthodox philosophy, including Pythagoras, Plato, Aristotle and the Stoics, but they are forbidden to read the works of the Epicureans and they must utterly reject frivolous comedies, licentious novels and the writings of the Jews and the Galileans.[2]

Christianity was from the first a religion of congregational worship and intense missionary effort. This means that unlike any of the pagan religions with which it came into conflict, it was vitally dependent on books.[3] Wherever the Church penetrated, she brought books with her: the scriptures, the writing of the Fathers, service books of every kind, devotional works for the faithful, and books on grammar and rhetoric for the schools. It was indeed the emphasis that the Church placed on reading, copying and teaching, that stabilized the Greek language in the East and Latin in the West, and preserved an interest in classical literature through the centuries till the humanist revival.

The special character of Christianity involved an immediate interest in books, and therefore in libraries. There were great Christian libraries in the East, at Caesarea and Jerusalem, in the third century AD; and by this time it must have become usual for every Christian church to possess its own collection of books. In the fifth century the last of the Imperial libraries at Rome, the Ulpian, held Christian books, for Sidonius Apollinaris, Bishop of Auvergne, tells with pride how his portrait and his works were installed there.[4] The systematic development of ecclesiastical libraries begins however with Cassiodorus and S. Benedict in the

[1] e.g. Tibur, in the temple of Hercules; Thamugadi, where the library contained a statue of Minerva; Prusa, where the library had a statue of the deified Trajan.

[2] Julian. *Works* (Loeb ed.) 2. 295.

[3] The dependence of the Jewish religion on its written records is confirmed by countless passages in the scriptures; the significance of its archives and libraries is well depicted in 2 Maccabees 3. Similarly Buddhism depends closely on its scriptures.

[4] *Ep.* 9. 16; *Carm.* 8. 7. See p. 83 *infra*.

sixth century. From that time onwards to the Renaissance there were no libraries in Western Europe that were not ecclesiastical in origin and purpose. Some were episcopal: those of Isidore of Seville in the seventh century, Grosseteste in the thirteenth and Richard de Bury in the fourteenth century are famous examples. Some were primarily educational such as that of Alcuin at York in the eighth century, or those of the great cathedral schools of France and England in the twelfth century. From S. Benedict however till the thirteenth century the only libraries that could boast stability and permanence from one generation to another were those of the monastic institutions. With the rise of the universities and the coming of the friars, monastic influence on education and book-production declined; but the new universities were quite as firmly rooted in the Church as the monasteries, and their libraries were no less part of the armoury of the Church. Indeed, though the curriculum of the student was widened by the change, the control of the Church over his studies tightened, as Oxford found when Wyclif's books were burnt at Carfax. It is important to remember that until the fifteenth century, the whole educated world was directly within the fold of the Church. The man who could read and write fluently was almost automatically a *clericus*, at least in minor orders. This meant that the country depended on the Church not only for its education but for its civil service; from S. Dunstan to Wolsey all our chief administrators were churchmen. They were indeed the only people who had mastered this new magic, the art of letters.

In the fifteenth century, as will be seen later, the lay scholar appears on the scene. Wealthy humanists were importing books from Italy and building up collections of a new sort, and middle-class business men and landowners were gathering small libraries of their own. Perhaps the first English layman to amass a real working collection of substantial size was Sir Thomas More.[1] The tragedies of the sixteenth century interrupted the course of humanism and destroyed or mutilated English libraries everywhere. But when the work of salvage had been set on foot and

---

[1] Chaucer's library may well have been substantial for his period. There were doubtless many notable lay collections in the Italy of Petrarch, Boccaccio and Marsiglio of Padua, but there was nothing comparable in England.

universities had been re-organized and new libraries and schools founded, the control of the Church still remained, though her authority now came from Whitehall rather than from Rome. The story of the religious aspect of libraries is wrapped up sadly in the history of heresy and persecution. Diocletian, the Council of Ephesus, Wyclif, Henry VIII: a long procession of names are concerned with the destruction of books, and the list could be extended to the present day. Few people in medieval days thought of books primarily as the means of education or enjoyment. They were the weapons of God, the aggressive and defensive armament of the Church; and in religious strife, the contestants felt impelled to destroy the weapons of the foe. There was an old saying that a monastery without a library was like a castle without armour. This meant logically that the works of a heretic were the tools of the devil and must be thrown to the flames. Why should truth tolerate error? Nor did the Reformation change this attitude, at least for two centuries more. Richard de Bury regarded his great library as a bulwark against heresy and false teaching, just as Sir Thomas Bodley thought of his new library at Oxford as a rampart of Protestantism. 'My hope was and is,' Bodley wrote, 'that the greatest part of our Protestant writers will be given: but whether they be or no, they all shall be had, before the place is frequented.' So also Archbishop Parker sought desperately to recover the historical records which Cromwell had wantonly dispersed: records which he regarded as the foundation stones of Church and State alike.

Until the eighteenth century, all the English institutional libraries, whether at the universities, at the newly founded schools, at the cathedrals and at the many parish churches where small libraries were established, were in effect part of the ecclesiastical machinery. This is largely true also of the early town libraries at Norwich, Bristol, Ipswich and Leicester. The new parish libraries for which Dr Thomas Bray, the Rev James Kirkwood and the SPG were responsible in the eighteenth century were definitely religious institutions, and even Samuel Brown's scheme for county libraries in Scotland in 1817 required that half or two-thirds of each box of fifty books should be religious. It is worth remembering that Oxford and Cambridge were exclusively Anglican universities till Gladstone's Test Act in 1871. Apart from the British Museum and the scientific libraries, the first non-sectarian collections were those of the eighteenth century; and many of the proprietary libraries owed their existence either to Anglican, or more often to Nonconformist, inspiration. Dr Williams's Library (1716) was of course wholly a nonconformist foundation, and nonconformity made itself felt strongly in the various educational movements that gathered pace at this time; the influence of Wesleyanism on popular literacy was for example considerable.

We rightly value our intellectual freedom today, but we sometimes forget that it is based far more on expediency than on principle. Toleration begins when a single dominant church is replaced by a number of competing sects of roughly equal influence. In such circumstances the price of freedom for one sect is freedom for all. In the totalitarian state there is no such balance of power, and heresy (re-christened 'deviationism') again becomes, as it always was till the eighteenth century, treason.

Although religion is no longer an active factor in the control of the general library, the magic of the written word remains as potent as ever. The State has taken the place of the Church as the dispenser of education and welfare. Our universities and libraries have, it is true, an honourable tradition of independence. But even in our own country the State wields as great a power over the hearts of men as was ever exercised by the medieval church. In some other countries we have in our own day seen this same power exalted to the level of divinity, much as the Roman Emperors were deified. Man is by nature born to worship the source of power; and if one religious organization is disestablished, another is created to take its place. But the weapons of authority remain the same, and power is still wielded mainly by all the arts of the written and recorded word. Thus the age of miracles which was heralded by the discovery of the art of writing still progresses; and though some of the traditions and ritual which are its machinery have been secularized, its magical element persists. A religious focus is still demanded for civilized life. We need not press too closely such words as miracle and magic. They represent something that excites in us wonder and awe; something that binds us to a power greater than ourselves. Nobody can read the history of the Chosen People without realizing the power that was vested in the scribes, from Ezra onwards. They were the copiers of the Law, and therefore its interpreters; and because with the Hebrews the Law and theology were equated, their authority was all but unquestioned. Today the keys of knowledge may be in other hands; but the link between this miracle which is the art of record, and our religion, our social and political behaviour and our government, is as strong and as significant as ever.

CHAPTER II

The Golden Chain

THERE need be no apology for the title of this chapter. The Academy at Athens maintained by its 'golden chain'[1] a continuous tradition of teaching and an 'apostolic' succession through the long centuries from Plato and Socrates to Proclus and the Neo-Platonists: all but a thousand years. We can by a fair analogy adopt this term for the equally golden links that have handed on our tradition of scholarship and libraries from the beginnings of Western civilization in classical Athens to the present day. Plato, Aristotle, Plotinus, S. Augustine, S. Thomas Aquinas; the Lyceum, Alexandria, Rome, Constantinople, Paris, Oxford: the chain is there for all to see, both in human learning and in the books and libraries in which it is enshrined. It is as wise to stress the unbroken continuity of the chain in the history of our libraries as it is in the history of scholarship. With such a heritage, to forget our yesterdays would be to lose the significance of today.

This golden chain of written record is indeed the conquest of time and space of which we have spoken. By its magic (and it is not extravagant to use the word 'magic') its links have been forged. Before we study any of the links in detail, let us think for a little of the means by which this conquest of space and time has been achieved. All kinds of materials have been used by man for his messages to distant lands and future generations. They may be light and flexible; they may be rigid or brittle; they may be ponderous and immovable; they may be fragile and perishable; they may seem as enduring as time itself. Some of these materials and their peculiarities we shall be studying presently. Here we are

---

[1] The phrase has of course been used in other senses. In Jeremy Taylor it stands for the link between God and the penitent sinner. In Homer however its meaning is less lofty. Zeus (*Il.* VIII 19–30), in order to prove his power proposes a sort of tug-of-war between himself on Olympus and the rest of the gods and goddesses on earth, each side pulling on a rope of gold.

concerned only with the fact that some have successfully survived their devious journeys through time and space, so that we can read in London today the words men wrote in Athens over two thousand years ago.

We are faced at once by a curious paradox. Of all possible materials, something hard such as stone or metal would at first sight seem the most enduring. The makers of the Dead Sea Scrolls evidently supposed that copper sheeting would be suitable for a document of special importance on which was recorded the hiding places of buried treasure. Their faith in the copper was misplaced, for corrosion and oxidation proved it less durable than the parchment rolls in the same library, and much skilful and delicate laboratory work was required before it could be deciphered.[1]

Stone therefore might seem the first choice for a message intended for future ages. It carries an inscription clearly, and we still use it for any memorial that we hope will endure for ever. Nothing gives so readily the impression of solid and unyielding permanence. It is the hard stuff of the earth itself, and as lasting therefore as the world on which we live. Indeed it has always been looked upon as the symbol of everlasting stability: rock of ages; upon this rock I will build my church; the house founded upon a rock. We think perhaps of the pyramids; or of the Sphinx which Kinglake describes in one of his purplest and most noble passages as 'bearing awful semblance of Deity—unchangefulness in the midst of change—the same seeming will and intent for ever and ever, inexorable'. And he reminds us how it has gazed on keen-eyed travellers—'Herodotus yesterday and Warburton today'—with the same earnest eyes and the same sad tranquil mien, and will go on watching with the same tranquil mien everlasting. But bear this in mind: the Sphinx, whatever its mysterious purpose, may have conquered time, but it has not conquered space. It is rooted immovably in the sands of the desert, and unlike those fragments of papyrus that the same sands have yielded in rich measure, it cannot be transported from place to place. The written word must be portable.

Bear also in mind another thing. Even stone is perishable. Man can destroy it with ease; but if he spares it, time in the end will

[1] J. M. Allegro, *The Dead Sea Scrolls*, 1956, App. IV.

erase its message and lay it low. We may recall that scene on Sinai when Moses carried down the two tables of stone, engraved with the writing of God and how at sight of the golden calf and the dancing he cast them from his hand and shattered them to pieces. Or the reader of Juvenal may remember how he answered the question 'What is fame?' by pointing to a gravestone that had been fractured by the upthrust of a young fig tree.[1] Pericles perhaps gave a more positive answer to the question when he spoke of 'the grandest of all sepulchres, not that in which their mortal bones are laid but a home in the minds of men'. 'The whole earth', he said, 'is the sepulchre of famous men.'[2] And Horace was even more explicit. It is right to assume that he meant exactly what he said when he made his proud boast: *Exegi monumentum aere perennius*. And he added that this monument of his will overtop the pyramids: neither rain nor wind nor the unending procession of the years will destroy it. '*Non omnis moriar*,' he cries; 'I shall not wholly die, and a great part of me will escape the tomb.'[3]

If ever a boast were justified, surely this one was, for no poet has for so long been read and memorized and studied with such loving care. It was not, of course, the tablets on which Horace first wrote his odes, nor the papyrus on which they were published, that were to outlive brass and stone. Very far from it. The wonder is that the poet was prepared to entrust his immortality to substances so fragile. The papyrus was merely the necessary vehicle of his creation, as the human body is the vehicle of the soul. But few of the substances used by man for his writing are as perishable as the papyrus in common use for nearly a thousand years of Graeco-Roman civilization. Any of the hazards which Horace mentions—rain, wind, and the lapse of time—would be fatal to it, but nothing will probably destroy it so quickly as the mere handling of it by the reader; and a roll cannot be read without every part of it being handled. The only safe way to preserve papyrus is to keep it, not merely dry, but untouched, unused, and unconsulted. So kept, it may endure almost as long

[1] Juvenal X. 143–5.
[2] Thucydides 43. 3.
[3] Shakespeare was equally explicit in Sonnet 55:
      'Not marble, nor the gilded monuments
      Of princes shall outlive this powerful rhyme.'

as paper or even parchment, but this is not the kind of endurance
we expect from a book; and in any case you will rarely find a
dry enough atmosphere outside Egypt. The prose works of
Philodemus, disinterred from the tufa at the Piso villa in Herculaneum after seventeen hundred years, were barely legible. And
if Matthew Paris's story of the rolls found by Abbot Eadmar in
the armarium of a ruined villa at Verulam in the eleventh century
is correct, these must surely have been of parchment; papyrus
would scarcely survive a year of the English climate under such
conditions. The Emperor Marcus Claudius Tacitus, who succeeded Aurelian AD 275, choosing to imagine that he was
descended from the great historian whose name he bore, was
inspired to order that ten copies of the historian's works should
be made each year and placed in the libraries of Rome.[1] This at
least suggests that the Emperor had little faith in the survival value
of Roman library books. It also implies that papyrus rolls were
still being used by the Roman libraries at that date, for not even
an Emperor would think of publishing a new parchment codex
edition of Tacitus every year. And yet, as I say, Horace was prepared to entrust his immortality to this most perishable of
materials.

The secret of course is this, that the very fragility of papyrus
guaranteed its survival, if the text it bore proved worth survival.
Folding cracked it, handling disfigured it, damp and mould
destroyed it, worms devoured it; and the patient owner was
compelled to copy and re-copy and re-copy whatever he valued
among his books. So the possessor of a collection of any size,
such as Cicero or Atticus, kept his copyists constantly at work in
his private scriptorium; much as the great Renaissance collectors
kept their scribes, and some later collectors, such as Horace
Walpole and Sir Thomas Phillipps, their printing presses. Under
such conditions there can have been but small demand for the
ready-made book; large editions were not published at one time,
and the Roman bookshops in the Argiletum dealt mainly in
small pieces newly issued: Martial's poems, for example, and the
keepsakes and gift books he describes. Good editions (as Cicero
tells his brother Quintus[2]) were hard to come by without the

[1] Vopiscus, *Tacitus*, 10. 3.
[2] Cicero, *Q. Fr.* III. 4. 5.

help of an agent, and the owner of wealth and taste employed scribes to prepare his own volumes. So also in medieval times when parchment volumes were expensive, the university student had to borrow an exemplar and make his own copies of the texts he needed; while even a family of moderate wealth such as the Pastons would occasionally employ a jobbing scribe. In the days before printing, copying was an unending chore that must proceed constantly, year in, year out. When parchment was the material in use, it would be a regular winter occupation, using the skins from the cattle that had been slaughtered and salted down in the autumn.

This, as much as anything, made for the survival of what we value in our literary heritage; by the constant reproduction on perishable material of the texts that mattered the links were forged in the golden chain that reaches out to us today from fifth-century Greece and earlier. The stone memorials we erect seem everlasting; we engrave on them the words *in perpetuam memoriam*, and nobody troubles to copy the inscription because it is there for ever—or few at least did till the antiquarians began to collect and record the relics of the past, and to edit their great *corpora inscriptionum*. But if the manuscripts in your library were on papyrus, you had to re-copy them or lose them; and if they were on parchment, and therefore longer lived, you still had to copy to increase your supply of them. So, in a garden, the annual flowers, sowing themselves freely, may survive when the longer lived perennials die out.

This constant reproduction of texts throughout the classical and medieval periods was rarely, if ever, based on any long-term views of preservation for posterity. There is a possible exception in the great international collection, organized with oriental magnificence by Greek scholars under the Ptolemies, and the establishment of the Alexandrian Canon tends to confirm this. Sometimes preservation was sought for the authorized texts of particular writers: at Athens, the texts of Aeschylus, Sophocles, and Euripides were carefully guarded; the Peripatetics attempted to do the same for Aristotle; and the Church similarly protected the approved version of the scriptures. Even after the Renaissance, the collecting zeal of Matthew Parker and the Elizabethan antiquarians was grounded on religious or political motives, rather than any zeal for pure scholarship. The disinterested preservation of texts for their own sake is largely a development of the eighteenth century, when all things antiquarian acquired a value of their own.

(Generally speaking, in all earlier periods, copying followed immediate demand; and the fact that so much of what matters has come safely down to us is in no small measure due to the steady and continuing demand for school and university texts. Education has indeed been the great stabilizing force in western civilization. The teaching of rhetoric in particular served for centuries to stabilize the Greek language in the East, and the Latin language in the West, and the teaching of literature (always a necessary preliminary to rhetoric) has helped to keep alive in reasonable purity the texts of classical authors. (It is noteworthy that few kinds of book are, even today, as profitable to both author and publisher as the school text book which has won general acceptance in scholastic circles.) Such losses as have occurred are in the main due to man's interference with the received tradition. The fashion for summarizing and epitomizing, for example, caused losses in the Byzantine period[1] and again in the later medieval period in the West.[2] The failure of English monastic libraries in the Norman period to give hospitality to Anglo-Saxon vernacular poetry caused regrettable losses in this field.[3] Neglect, indifference, and the accident of fire have at various tims ccaused other losses, while the deliberate destruction of English books in the period 1536 to 1550 was a grave disaster. Such losses have become less likely now that the printer has replaced the scribe, and the copyright libraries are carrying out their duties efficiently. The books most likely to become lost, in the absence of systematic preservation, are those which are at once popular and ephemeral, being quickly replaced in popular favour by new works of the same kind. As Miss Husbands has shown, half the English novels issued between 1770 and 1800, and therefore the mainstay of the circulating libraries of that time, have apparently disappeared.[4] One should add that scholars

[1] Especially under Constantine Porphyrogenitus. See Sandys, *History of Classical Scholarship*, I (1903), p. 426.

[2] V. H. Galbraith, *Historical Research in Medieval England* (1951), pp. 30–1.

[3] R. W. Chambers, 'The Lost Literature of Medieval England', in *The Library*, 4th ser., V (1925), pp. 293–321.

[4] R. W. Chambers, *op. cit.*

are not wanting who complain that far too many books have come down to us, and too few have been lost; Sir Thomas Browne certainly held this opinion,[1] and I believe that Dr Gilbert Norwood and Lord Grey of Falloden have been tempted to agree with him.

Let me mention here one other aspect of the literary tradition which sometimes escapes notice. The word 'reproduction' may sound ominous to the artist or to the musician. The art of letters is in fact one of those arts in which reproduction has no effect, either good or bad, on the original creation of the artist; that is, in this case, of the writer. In painting, however skilful be the work of the reproducer, the original creation is always in some degree altered, and generally for the worse. In architecture, especially in those forms that depend for their value on the movement of light and shade, such as for example the curved Byzantine mosaics, photographic reproduction can give but a partial and imperfect reflection of the original. A work of music is capable of a two-fold reproduction. Like a book intended only for reading aloud, the score has first to be interpreted by the players, and this may be done well or ill. But the interpretation can be reproduced mechanically, and this again may mar the original creation. The typographical reproduction of a book, however (or indeed its hand reproduction by a scribe), has no more effect on the original work than the printing of a piece of music has on the original composition. True, the reproduction may be inaccurate, and in this case there is work for the bibliographer and the textual critic in establishing the authority of the original text, with any revisions made by the author. Or the book may be well or badly printed, and may thus be pleasant or unpleasant to handle. Poor typography is an obstacle interposing itself between reader and writer, but one that can be surmounted by the patient reader in a way that the obstacle of a badly reproduced picture can never be surmounted. Ideally, perhaps, the physical book should as nearly as possible be a transparent screen through which the reader can see the author without interruption or distortion. But the writer's message is not materially altered by the obscurity of the screen, as an artist's message is altered by a poor reproduction of his painting. The

[1] *Religio Medici* XXIV.

only process which may genuinely distort an author's composition takes place in the mind of the reader; that is, in his aesthetic re-creation or appreciation of the original. And unless the book is being read aloud, this distortion, being in the reader's mind and not in the book, affects nobody but the reader himself. The reader may, for example, have not learnt to read intelligently, or he may be unfamiliar with the terms used by the writer; and he is then in the position of a man without artistic training looking at an original painting and failing to understand it.

Note that there is an ambiguity in our use of the word 'reproduction'. The manuscript or printed page is not in itself a reproduction of the original creation. It is merely an arrangement of conventional symbols of commonly accepted meaning, intended to serve as a key to the interpretation of the original. The symbols as arranged by the writer can therefore be 'reproduced' or copied by any means *ad infinitum*, without changing the author's original intention. Only if the symbols are themselves changed, by translation for example, or abridgement, is the original creation distorted. If, of course, the typographical design is part of the original (as for example in Blake's *Songs of Innocence*, or on a different level, the mouse's tale in *Alice in Wonderland*) then the original may easily be marred by the printer. Blake's illuminated printing is all but impossible to reproduce faithfully, and the same difficulties are experienced with a finely illuminated manuscript, for this is a work of art in itself, and something more than a book in the ordinary sense of the word.

Printed or written symbols serve therefore to 'fix' and stabilize the author's composition, and it remains unchanged as long as the symbols can be correctly interpreted. The only other possible medium open to the author is that of oral tradition—the medium of the ballad singers, the Irish bards, the rhapsodists, and the Arabian story-tellers; and here the composition is anything but fixed, every fresh recital producing its interpolations and alterations. The library therefore is essentially the repository of fixed compositions which have been stabilized symbolically, and the librarian is their guardian, or in the common term their curator or keeper.

It must not be supposed that the reproduction of particular works constitutes more than a part of the literary tradition. The 'golden chain' has indeed other strands, more important, more significant, perhaps, and much more complicated than this. The genealogy of scholarship and letters is as complex as any family tree. Books have their ancestry and their descendants like any human being; and though we cannot unravel every strand in the web, we can often distinguish particular threads which throw light on the character and significance of a writer.

It is helpful in considering this to retain the analogy of the family tree, and to think of books as living things. Indeed this is more than a mere analogy, for there is a real sense in which a book is in very truth a living thing, an embodiment of vitality, a kind of re-incarnation of its author that gradually gathers to itself an independent life of its own: independent, in some degree, of its author, and curiously independent, too, of its physical embodiment, for no human being (fortunately perhaps) can be reprinted like a book, and yet remain the same being. But the true significance of the analogy lies in the fact that every book has its own parentage, and some at least have their own offspring.

The principal agent in the production of a book is, of course, its writer, the author of its being. But the author never works *in vacuo*, and, to a greater or lesser degree, his literary offspring are always the result of a marriage between his own mind and the communicated experience of other minds, either contemporary or in past time. And since this communicated experience is, in the main, received through the medium of books, the conception and birth of the new book commonly take place in the author's library.[1] It is, indeed, the prime function of a library to be the scene of such marriages; and the genealogy of scholarship, or of a particular book, is the tracing of its parentage and offspring. It is fair to add, of course, that the offspring may take some other form than books. A man may collect mainly in order to preserve, as Sir Robert Cotton did, or Sir Thomas Phillipps. Or a man may be a great teacher, and yet write nothing, though he may contribute by his teaching indirectly to the works of his pupils. Or the marriage may lead to physical action, rather than further writing; it may bring relaxation, rather than further study; it

---

[1] A new scientific work may be born in the laboratory, but this, after all, is the scientist's study and workroom. Science, even more than humanism, depends on the interchange of recorded communications.

may even be sterile and barren. But whenever a new book appears, its parentage may be sought in its author's library, and its value may be assessed from its breeding and its inherent fruitfulness. Good breeding counts for as much in the production of books as in the production of human children.

Sheila Kaye-Smith wrote in her autobiography 'I am mentally as much the books I have read as I am chemically the food I have eaten; their sequence too is very much the sequence of my life'.[1] There is, of course, a definite, but complicated, relationship between intake and output in this sort of production. It is obviously not a quantitative relation; no argument can be drawn from the sixty thousand volumes in Lord Acton's library, the seven thousand volumes from which the *Decline and Fall* was produced, or the handful of books to which a writer such as John Bunyan was indebted. But we can note that both indigestion and starvation are to be avoided; and of these two evils, indigestion and over-feeding is by far the commoner. It was a favourite dictum of Thomas Hobbes that if he had read as much as other learned men, he would have been as ignorant as they were; and with a similar purpose, Hazlitt observed that the idle reader reads twenty times as many books as the learned one.[2] If it is true that never were so many books being read by so many people as today, this is not necessarily a matter for unqualified congratulation. On the other hand the contrary evil is not unknown. Kinglake, in *Eothen*, describes Lady Hester Stanhope's régime. Milk was her only food, and 'her abstinence from food intellectual was carried as far as her physical fasting: she never, she said, looked upon a book nor a newspaper, but trusted alone to the stars for her sublime knowledge'. But an exclusively astral diet is unsustaining to the mind, and we may justly ascribe some of Lady Hester Stanhope's oddities to this peculiar self-denial.

The interest of this type of enquiry comes when we analyse the reading of particular writers. The field here is endless, and I can give only one or two illustrations. Such an analysis is simplest of course when the author's reading has been severely restricted. Blake, Bunyan, and John Clare are good examples of this. The absence of any classical studies in Blake's life (at least till William

---

[1] Sheila Kaye-Smith, *All the Books of My Life* (1956).
[2] To reverse Bacon's dictum, reading, on occasion at least, maketh an empty man.

Hayley at Felpham tried to read the *Iliad* with him in the original, with the help of Cowper's translation) had its effect, for good or ill, on the quality of his work. Similarly, Sir Walter Scott's failure to acquire any Greek at school may have had its effect on his writing; one of his biographers has suggested that 'some acquaintance with the Greek masterpieces, some tincture of the Greek spirit, might have trimmed that prolixity which was to be his besetting sin'. On the other hand, Scott knew his Latin well enough; and his profound knowledge of the Border ballads, dating from earliest childhood, did much, it has been said 'to purify his taste and to weaken—unfortunately it did not destroy— the dominance of the bad models of his youth. It was an education in directness, in economy of speech at moments of high drama, in the simplicities of great passion'.[1]

An extreme example of restricted reading is found in the library of the peasant poet, John Clare. This consisted only of a copy of Thomson's *Seasons*, which he bought in Stamford market; the price was 1s 6d, and he found considerable difficulty in raising the money. Here the effect is seen plainly in Clare's verse, and it was on the whole a bad effect, for Thomson was scarcely the right model for Clare's rustic talents.

In a different field the eighteenth-century physician, Sir William Browne (1692–1774), thrice happy, as Sir William Osler called him, made shift with a pocket library which was sufficient for all his needs: a Greek Testament, which was the source of his divinity; the aphorisms of Hippocrates, from which he derived his medical knowledge; and an Elzevir Horace, from which he drew his good sense and vivacity.[2] This was presumably one idea of a liberal education in the age of reason. Sir William Browne is also said to have ascribed his vivacity in old age to the fact that he had then neither wife nor debts; but his will directed nevertheless that his Elzevir Horace should be placed reverently on his coffin.

Let us note two further examples on a bigger scale. The first concerns the Venerable Bede. Bede's resources can be assessed, not, indeed, with certainty but with considerable probability, from an analysis of his own works. There are, of course, risks in

---

[1] John Buchan, *Sir Walter Scott* (1932), pp. 31, 42.
[2] Sir William Osler, essay on 'Books and Men' in *Aequanimitas* (3rd ed., 1939).

drawing conclusions from quotations and references, but the risks are greater in the later medieval period, when ready-made quotations were common currency. And Bede is so careful and conscientious a historian that we can trust him with more than average confidence. An analysis of his probable sources not only reveals the width and depth of his reading, but gives us the only evidence of the size and importance of the very great library which Benedict Biscop had collected for Monk Wearmouth.[1] Bede never travelled far from this library. He was a faithful exponent of that wise Benedictine principle of stability (*ubi stabilitas, ibi religio*) which the feverish world of today chooses to forget; he would, indeed, have agreed heartily with that comment of Petrarch's: 'It is a strange madness, this desire to be for ever sleeping in a strange bed.' This fact enables us to link Bede all the more closely with the Wearmouth library. We can feel certain that there was at that time no greater library in Western Europe (including even Italy, if Cassiodorus' library at Vivarium had by then been dispersed); and none that was so nobly justified by its fruits. And if in the following generation Alcuin's library at York was equally outstanding (as seems very possible), we can be proud of the beginnings of English scholarship.

The Benedictine ideal of stability is worth emphasizing here. Of all the conditions that favour the growth of libraries, stability and security of tenure are perhaps the most important. If this is true of the monastic or academic libraries, it is doubly true of domestic working libraries; there were, for this very reason, few such collections in England before the fifteenth century. The lord whose life is spent in migrating from manor to manor is rarely drawn to collecting books, particularly if his manors contain no private living-room for the lord and lady outside the great hall. There is a record of a thirteenth-century bishop of Hereford, Richard de Swinfield, who in one period of 296 days moved his household eighty-one times. This included stays of a month or more at three of his manors, and a visitation tour of fifty-one days, during which he slept at thirty-eight different places: an extreme example, perhaps, but significant enough. Such

---

[1] On this, see the chapter by Ramona Bressie in J. W. Thompson, *The Medieval Library*, 1939 (reprinted with supplement, 1957); also M. L. W. Laistner, 'Bede as a Classical and Patristic Scholar' in *Trans. Roy. Hist. Soc.*, 4th ser., XV (1933), 69–94.

a life must surely discourage the most serious student from collecting books.[1] There were, in fact, no episcopal collections of any size in that period, excepting only that of Richard de Bury; and if any bishops were the authors of books, their writing was mostly done before their consecration.

For a second example, and a very neat one, let us come down to the nineteenth century; a time when the reading of most writers is growing so discursive, and resources are, in general, so abundant, that it becomes more difficult to identify single threads of any significance. If we can judge the value of a collection by its immediate fruit, then the libraries collected by Edward Gibbon and Lord Acton, which I mentioned a moment ago, might be quoted as significant examples. But a more curious one can be found in the work of Coventry Patmore.

Patmore's special interest in theology, philosophy, and mysticism separates him completely from all the other literary figures of his day. There are few other writers in any age whose intellectual life was so systematically and consistently founded on their reading. His intellectual diet began with Plato, Aristotle, Emerson, Coleridge, and Wordsworth; passed on to Swedenborg; and in due course embraced S. Thomas Aquinas, S. Bernard of Clairvaux, S. John of the Cross, S. Teresa of Avila, S. Augustine, S. Catherine of Genoa, S. Ignatius Loyola, S. Francis de Sales, S. Catherine of Siena, and finally Dante and Newman. A careful analysis of his writing, such as that recently made by J. C. Reid,[2] reveals this plainly. To some extent, of course, he used the British Museum library while he was on its staff; but, for the most part, he relied on his own books. Almost all these writers were well represented in his own library, and its catalogue confirms to a quite remarkable degree the analysis of his sources. Whether Patmore justifies so careful an analysis may be a matter of opinion; but at least his work illustrates admirably the genealogy and provenance of a man's writing.

I am tempted to add one more illustration in a lighter vein. The records of Imperial Rome speak of various large private collections of books; none larger, however, than that of a certain

---

[1] *A roll of the household expenses of Richard de Swinfield, Bishop of Hereford, during part of the years 1289 and 1290*, ed. John Webb, Camden Society, 2 vols. (1854–5). See also J. R. H. Moorman, *Church Life in England in the Thirteenth Century* (1945), pp. 176–79.

[2] J. C. Reid, *The Mind and Art of Coventry Patmore* (1957).

prolific writer named Serenus Sammonicus, who was murdered by Caracalla, AD 212. His library of 62,000 volumes was inherited by his son, a poet of the same name, who was a friend of the Emperor Gordian I, and the tutor of Gordian II. This large library was bequeathed by the poet to his imperial pupil; and Gibbon celebrates the result in characteristic fashion. 'Twenty-two acknowledged concubines, and a library of sixty-two thousand volumes, attested the variety of his inclinations, and from the productions which he left behind him, it appears that the former as well as the latter were designed for use rather than ostentation.' There is here a typical footnote which explains that each of his concubines presented him with three or four children, and his literary productions were by no means contemptible. Even if the results of imperial fruitfulness, intellectual and physical, have largely perished, we can still, while marvelling at the ability of any man to combine two apparently full-time occupations, accept the story as reinforcing the analogy we have already employed. An author's books are the children of his mind, born of a marriage between his own spirit and the recorded experience of others. That marriage normally takes place in his library; there these children of his are conceived, and there they are born and live, surrounded by their ancestors and their relatives in every degree of proximity. For a man's library is a family or community of books, with a reality greater than the sum of the individual volumes. And in that community, the children of his mind will find, if long life be their portion, their crown of wild olive, *aere perennius*, more enduring than bronze.

The golden chain, therefore, is an interweaving, not so much of the lives of single books, as of the living communities of books which are our libraries. In that chain, some of the strands are short, appearing and then disappearing into the general stream. But some are persistent, giving a quite remarkable continuity to the thread that binds past, present, and future together. Horace is one such strand. Callimachus, two and a half centuries earlier, set going another persistent strand; the more notable because so much of his influence is indirect, surviving in the vitality of his imitators and translators. And Callimachus was a bibliographer as well as a poet, taking us back to the great, organized community of books that was the Alexandrian Library.

Some of the strands from Callimachus were gathered up and transmuted by Ovid, who set going a strand of his own that has proved as enduring and as pervasive as Horace's; his two-thousandth anniversary was celebrated not many years ago. Another thread, even older and more persistent than these, leads us straight back to Aristotle, almost 2,300 years ago, and to the research institute which he founded at his Lyceum—the first systematic plan to collect, record, and preserve man's knowledge of himself and the world about him. There were, of course, far earlier writers than Aristotle; but there is no earlier example recorded, in Western civilization at least, of that living and organic community of scholars, researchers, students, and books which constitutes a great library. And no writer has permeated the whole of man's knowledge so completely during two millennia; the Aristotelian threads are interwoven in every link of the chain from his day to ours.

There are other notable threads: Virgil, Homer, and, perhaps most notable of all, the Bible itself, than which no work has, I suppose, been copied and re-copied, translated and re-translated, with more zealous and unfailing care. Its Greek translation, the Septuagint, was one of the fine achievements of the first great library in our history, that of the Ptolemies at Alexandria; and the recent finds by the Dead Sea confirm its continuing interest to scholarship. In between we have to acknowledge its massive influence on English culture and literature as well as religion. It has appropriated the Greek name for a book, and the Greek name for a library also in medieval days, when 'bibliotheca' signified the Bible. In later times it was often the first book which the ordinary English home came to possess. It can, indeed, still claim to be the dominant thread in our heritage. Regarded in this light, a library becomes something much more than a shelf of books, or a press, or even a great book-lined reading room. Without its owner, without its users, it is dead. And so it is true to define a library as a community in which both reader and writer meet, to which both contribute something of value, mutually forging the links of the chain as it passes from mind to mind and from generation to generation. At the centre of this community, if the library be a great one, is the librarian. He has two main duties. First, he is the keeper or curator, charged with the task of preserving for future readers the books in his care. Secondly, he is the centre of the organic community which is the library, caring not merely for his books, but for the needs of every member of that community, and for the chain of recorded tradition which day by day is being handled, corrected, re-moulded, strengthened, added to, and passed onwards. That these special responsibilities have not been explicitly recognized, at least till recent times, is beside the point. The idea of preservation for posterity is, as we have seen, comparatively modern. Gabriel Naudé, who collected and arranged the Bibliothèque Mazarine in 1642 and was the first to propound a theory of library economy,[1] scarcely mentions it. His guiding purpose in library organization was the practical convenience of the library for scholars—itself a new principle at that date—and his careful explanation of the librarian's duties foreshadows admirably our second requirement: that he should be the centre and heart of the organic community held together by the library. The same points were made with even greater clarity in another early statement of the duties of a librarian: that of the Abbé Cotton des Houssayes in an inaugural lecture celebrating his appointment as librarian of the Sorbonne in 1780.[2] This concept of a library as an organic community is a useful one. It stresses the significance of what might be called in biological language the ecology of the book; the study of book associations and habitats, as plant associations and habitats are studied by botanists.

The over-riding belief that we must at all costs preserve our heritage for posterity has arisen with the establishment of national libraries to house the national and international collections of the world, and strangely enough it is grounded not on any scarcity of books or their threatened destruction, but rather on their abundance; the mass-production of printed material is piling up the volumes almost beyond counting. The belief has however resulted in the concept of the sanctity of literary and archival records, comparable almost to the sanctity of human life: nothing must be destroyed. This concept is not supported by any sanction except that of expediency. Unwilling to trust to our critical judgment, aware of the inconstancy of literary fashions and ever

[1] *Avis pour dresser une Bibliothèque*, 1627.
[2] J. L. Thornton, *Classics of Librarianship*, 1957, pp. 26–31.

uncertain as to which is chaff and which grain, we choose to leave the winnowing to Time. This may be wise; but the provisions of legal deposit at our national libraries tend to nullify the process of winnowing, and there gathers at these libraries therefore a vast and rapidly growing accumulation of chaff which is cherished with all the devotion due to works of merit. The good sense of this policy is perhaps questionable, and a bolder solution of the problem might be recommended. The danger however lies not so much in any carelessness of the curators as in the meddling of politicians, and these are more likely to lay their hands on the grain than on the chaff. Some at least of the chaff could be spared as expendable; its loss would be our gain, for it is not part of the true literary heritage. History surely gives us cause for faith and hope in this matter. By good luck or by providence the golden chain has preserved its integrity through the storms of more than two millenniums; and looking back on the hazards of its long story it seems almost as though a guiding hand had, in the midst of insecurity, held it securely and led it on its way.

Nevertheless preservation and not destruction must always be the main care of the curator of books. Time will destroy what it must; he will preserve what he can. The two factors which we have discussed—the preservation of the written records, and the building up of a community to which every member, readers, writers, and things written, contributes a due share—together form the forge out of which the heritage, that I have called the golden chain, is fashioned. It is more than a heritage, more than a remembrance of things past; for it looks forward as well as backward, binding together both yesterday and tomorrow, and impressing the stamp of today on the links as they pass through our hands. The true history of our libraries is the history of this magic chain, more lasting than bronze, which the art of writing enables us to unfold as the days and the years go by.

CHAPTER III

Circumstantial Evidence

RECORDS of the existence of libraries in the early period of Western civilization are scanty and unilluminating, and to get a true picture of the part they played in the beginnings of our history, we must to some extent fall back on probability to supplement the recorded facts. A study of the special conditions which are likely to favour the collection and preservation of books in libraries will be helpful; and it will be seen that in certain circumstances we can safely argue from these conditions to the libraries themselves. We have seen that the initial impulse may be provided by the growth of religious organization in an urban population, but beyond this there are five special conditions which point to the likelihood of the existence of libraries, and may justify the argument from the one to the other.

(1) *The Economic Factor*

There must be abundant supplies of writing materials of a reasonably durable nature. The importance of this condition must be underlined, for it has a direct effect on the production of books and on their publication and preservation in libraries. Abundance and ease of handling is more important than mere durability, and in Western civilization only three materials have filled the requirements satisfactorily, namely, papyrus, parchment and paper. The link between the abundance or scarcity of these materials and the output of literary activity is remarkable; if writing material is plentiful, people will write readily. The introduction of paper into Western Europe had at least as great an effect on the literature of the Renaissance as the introduction of printing from movable type. The import of papyrus from Egypt into Greece rose substantially in the sixth century, BC, and was followed immediately by the great outpouring of Greek literature in the fifth century. The Nile valley was the only important centre of the papyrus industry, and the trade began to decline in the third or fourth centuries AD, partly perhaps because the plant had been harvested too plentifully. The recognized substitute for papyrus was the prepared skin called 'parchment' (*charta Pergamena*) which had been a familiar material for records for a long time in the cattle and goat raising districts of Asia Minor and Syria, where it was comparatively cheap. It began to replace papyrus for Christian literature in the second and third centuries AD, and for pagan literature soon afterwards. As we shall see, it has certain definite advantages over papyrus; it is more durable in a wet climate, and it folds easily into the gatherings needed for the codex form of books. But its expense, even where cattle were plentiful, must have limited both book production and literary activity. The skin of one sheep is needed for two leaves of a folio book; the medieval term *pecia*, denoting a gathering, was a technical term borrowed from the tanners signifying one sheepskin. The production of a whole book in folio therefore might require the skins of a considerable flock of sheep. The dependence of the medieval period on parchment curbed its literary activity to no small degree, and its book collections were by modern standards few and very small; only in Constantinople were really large libraries to be found. Though the Western monastic libraries were small, they became in the later centuries congested and ill-organized; there were various reasons for this, but one must have been the cost of parchment which made copying expensive, invited reliance on palimpsests, and encouraged editors to cut down their texts into epitomes—a most unfortunate practice which caused the disappearance of original texts not only in the West, but in Constantinople in the tenth and eleventh centuries. These difficulties were surmounted when paper came into use as a writing material in the fifteenth century. Its appearance released a flood of literature: personal, such as the letters of the Paston, Cely and Stonor families; religious, upholding either the old faith or the 'new learning'; literary, in the creative work of the Elizabethan period.

The expense of parchment had its effect also on the development of book hands and the appearance of the manuscript page. Rustic capitals and uncials gave way to the neater but less spacious script of the Carolingian minuscule,[1] and for still further economy, scribes began to use subscript letters and to abbreviate almost every other word, thus saving time as well as space. As a result the page tended to become overcrowded. This fault is particularly noticeable in the work of Irish scribes, and the congested page and the use of palimpsests was especially common at the Irish foundations of S. Gall and Bobbio.

The introduction of paper in the fifteenth century made the writer's raw material plentiful, whereas previously it had been hard to come by, and the introduction of printing made book production a far easier process. The resulting increase in the quantity of books brought into being new libraries of greatly increased size, and raised new problems in the storage and arrangement of books which first began to demand solutions in the seventeenth century.

(2) *The Literary Factor*

This follows from the first requirement, and has indeed already been implied. There must be a corpus of national literature of such extent and importance that it is valued and preserved by the educated part of the population. That is to say, if public and private libraries are to exist and flourish, there must be an abundance of books which justify collection and storage; as we have seen, this is itself directly related to the supply of writing material. These conditions obtained in Greece from the fifth century BC, onwards; in Alexandria from the beginning of the third century BC; in Rome from the first century BC; in Constantinople from its foundation in the fourth century AD; and in Western Europe from the Renaissance onwards. In all these periods libraries were necessarily active. Only in classical Athens is there any scarcity of historical evidence of their activities, but even here we are justified in assuming their existence. On the other hand the libraries of medieval Europe were few and small in size precisely because these conditions were not adequately met.

Wrapped up in this factor and implied by it is the basic requirement of literacy. In general books are written in order that they can be read, and the production of books necessarily implies a degree of literacy in the population. A marked increase in

[1] See for example Plates 112 and 113 in *Medieval England*, ed. A. L. Poole, vol. II, 1958.

literacy such as took place in England in the fifteenth century, and again in the eighteenth century, always precedes an increase in library activity; and we can with reasonable safety argue back from book production to literacy. In the first stages of literacy, books tend to be written for public declamation or reading aloud, rather than for private study. This stage can be detected in classical Athens and Rome, and in England in the circulation of the Wyclif translations and in later periods also. It is always however a transitional stage; the reading aloud of a book means that one person at least is literate, and as has been noticed elsewhere, reading is an infectious habit which tends to spread.[1]

(3) *The Social Factor*

Given this background of writing materials, literacy and book production, it is safe to say that libraries of some kind will develop. If corporate (as opposed to private) collections are to appear, there must be in existence institutions engaged partly or mainly in intellectual pursuits, and these should have a continuing identity secured by some type of recognized constitution, and should own property where their work is carried out, with endowments for their maintenance. Any institution which fills these conditions will almost necessarily develop a library of its own. The modern university and the twelfth century Benedictine monastery offer equally good examples of such an institution. Under this head however we can include almost any school or college; any learned society with buildings and endowments; any important business or administrative organization; any large ecclesiastical building, whether church, cathedral or monastery; and in the ancient world, most pagan temples and royal palaces of any size and importance. The existence of corporate libraries in medieval and modern times is usually well documented, but in the classical period evidence is often lacking. In the early period however we can argue with fair probability from the existence of an institution of this type to its library. This assumption can for example be made about most of the Greek and Roman universities. There is confirmation of this only in one or two isolated cases, but the probability in the others is too strong to be overlooked. In making the assumption, the nature of the teaching at

[1] *Origins of the English Library*, 1958 (hereafter cited as *Origins*), pp. 191–213.

the institution must of course be taken into account. Rhetoric for example required little or no reading of books though it was always grounded on a knowledge of literature. On the other hand the work at the Lyceum at Athens and the Museum at Alexandria needed the support of their libraries, and the same must surely have been true at the law schools of Constantinople, Berytus and Rome, and probably also of the medical schools of Cos, Alexandria and Rome. The great sanctuaries of Asclepius at Epidaurus, Cos and Pergamum were equipped with theatres, gymnasia and baths, and probably with libraries also. Equally it would be hard to imagine that no libraries were associated with later universities such as, for example, Carthage (it is known that Carthage had a learned library in the time of Apuleius,[1] and we can surely guess that one still existed in S. Augustine's day) or Bordeaux (even though Ausonius does not mention it in so many words).[2] The tools of teaching are books, and its workshop is a library.

(4) The Book Trade

The existence of private collections of books in the classical period must be deduced in the main from circumstantial evidence. No contemporary account of libraries has survived, and the evidence from letters (always a valuable source in reconstructing the social or personal background) is restricted to those of Cicero and the younger Pliny. The absence of other evidence of this type (with none at all from Greece) is probably due to the habit of using waxed tablets for correspondence, by its nature an impermanent medium.[3]

The private collection requires two special conditions if it is to flourish. First there must be in existence an active publishing and book-selling trade. It is true that the wealthy collector might have his own private scriptorium. This was done for example by Cicero and Atticus in Rome and by Origen in Caesarea; rich Byzantine

---

[1] Apuleius, *Florida* 18.

[2] The main subject taught at Bordeaux may well have been rhetoric, but the twenty-five professors commemorated by Ausonius cannot all have been rhetors. Ausonius himself taught literature there as well as rhetoric, and a library is a not unreasonable assumption.

[3] The Oxyrhynchus fragments include many letters on papyrus, but they are not very revealing on domestic life. See Jack Lindsay, *Daily Life in Roman Egypt*, 1963.

collectors probably had their own scribes in Justinian's time, and later in the time of Photius when Arethas' manuscripts were being copied. Richard de Bury had his staff of copyists in the fourteenth century, and there were many private scriptoria in Renaissance Italy. So also in later days Horace Walpole and Sir Thomas Phillipps had their private presses. But these were exceptional. All of them moreover acquired books freely from external sources, in addition to those produced at home. The collector on a humbler scale would presumably obtain most or all of his books from booksellers, though he might occasionally, like Sir John Paston, employ a jobbing scrivener. Unless therefore there are shops and salerooms where books can be acquired, the private collector is not likely to be very common. The existence of bookshops in Athens and Rome is well established, but after the fall of the Empire they disappeared from history till the Renaissance. They reappear in Western Europe in the thirteenth century at the new university cities of Bologna, Paris, Oxford and Cambridge, under the name of *stationarii*; in the fifteenth century some, such as Vespasiano's establishment in Florence and perhaps John Shirley's publishing house in London, acquired a considerable reputation. Meanwhile, books were being sold at country fairs such as those of S. Giles and Stourbridge, and pedlars were carrying them in their packs. Facts such as these can rightly be adduced as evidence of private collecting in classical times, and in Western Europe from the fifteenth century onwards. Contrariwise, they confirm the disappearance of private collecting (except in monastic and episcopal quarters) between the time of Cassiodorus and, say, Petrarch. In both Roman and Renaissance times there is of course direct evidence of private collections. In Greece there is a dearth of such evidence, at least before the first century AD, when a villa library of the Roman type at Athens is mentioned;[1] there are however many indirect pointers to their existence in Greek literature; and these, combined with our knowledge of the Athenian book trade, may confirm their existence.

The second requirement for the emergence of private collections is the existence of domestic houses large enough to provide accommodation both for the storage of books and for their study,

[1] Aulus Gellius I. 2.

occupied by men possessing sufficient education and taste to desire books, sufficient wealth to acquire them, and sufficient leisure to enjoy them. This applies especially, of course, to the larger private collection which has made a name for itself in history, but in a measure it is true of all collecting; there must be a place to keep the books and a place to read them, as well as time and opportunity to devote to them. These conditions have not always obtained. Classical Greece cannot have had many houses of this type. The educated Greek spent his leisure time not at home, but outdoors, in the market place or the gymnasium with his fellow citizens; home life as we know it played little part in his daily round. This must have limited the development of collecting, though it certainly did not preclude it altogether; it did not for example prevent the young Euthydemus from trying to build up a large library.[1] On the other hand, the Roman view of family life produced the country villa in which a private library became part of the necessary equipment, sometimes for use, sometimes for display as a mark of gentility. With the fall of the Empire these conditions lapsed in Western Europe. In the more stable atmosphere of Constantinople private collecting continued right through the Byzantine period. In the West however it ended with Boethius and with the villa libraries of Southern Gaul in the fifth century AD, re-appearing with Petrarch and Chaucer a thousand years later.

In fifteenth-century England the castles and fortified manors were being replaced by more settled and peaceful country houses, and both these and the town houses of prosperous merchants were being equipped with some of the comforts of life. Comparatively small manors such as those described in the Paston letters began to accumulate not only the records and archives inseparable from the ownership of land and the administration of justice, but small collections of books used by the family as a whole. At the same time the castles and palaces of the great nobles were being enlarged and provided with luxuries that would have seemed strange to the Norman barons. Establishments such as those at Kenilworth, or the Savoy in London, or that of the fifth Earl of Northumberland described in the *Northumberland Household Book*, were not merely great administrative organizations,

[1] Xen. *Mem.* 4. 2.

but schools of chivalry and manners where boys and girls of high birth received their training. The Northumberland staff for example included a dean and ten priests, of whom one was a grammar master. Such an organization must have had, in addition to its administrative papers and archives, a collection of books—school books, devotional works, legal, medical and agricultural books, and romances, in Latin, French and English.

By comparison the intervening period was barren and dark, so far as domestic houses were concerned. The light shone in the monastic cell rather than the private house, and literacy was all but a clerical monopoly. This was a time in which reading and writing were 'infra dig', for the noble class, as Professor Galbraith has pointed out.[1] Few of the kings were literate; even Charles the Great's literacy is doubtful, and the only certain exceptions were the learned Aldfrith, and Alfred and Otto III; all of these possessed royal libraries, that of Aldfrith being the earliest in this country. Professor Galbraith makes the point that royal illiteracy cannot be equated with ignorance. If the king did not read or write, this would be because he had others to do this for him; it was only after Henry I that men came to realize that 'Rex illiteratus asinus coronatus'.

Nevertheless the association of letters with the royal court and the feudal castles, though it varied considerably, must usually have been close. The administration of royal courts and feudal estates was in the hands of clerics, as was all the education of the children. They provided an educated background to aristocratic illiteracy; and it was from this background that the humanism of the classical revival eventually sprang. The patrons of humanism were not the universities, but the princes and leaders of church and state; most of the English humanists of the fifteenth century for example were aristocrats who could collect their books in Italy and bring them back to English libraries—not so much to their own homes, however, as to the libraries of universities, colleges and cathedrals.

The really important English private collections had to await the more spacious days of the seventeenth and eighteenth centuries: the age of wealth and stability, of big landed estates and of stately mansions that had to be filled with books and furniture and

[1] *The Literacy of the Medieval English Kings*, 1935.

paintings. It is under conditions of stability, prosperity and leisure that the private library becomes substantial and magnificent. In the medieval period, even where prosperity and leisure were present, stability was usually absent. Royal courts and nobles and bishops tended to be peripatetic and almost nomadic; rolling stones that gathered no books in their progress. The private library is above all an ornament of the stable home, rooted in the soil.

(5) *The Evidence of Research*

There is still one important source from which we can deduce the existence of libraries in earlier times. This is the appearance of books which evidently entailed literary research for their compilation. The evidence of these is all the stronger if they are indeed what we now call 'scissors and paste' compilations rather than works of creative scholarship, for not only are such works more completely dependent on research in a library, but the actual contents of the library can often be guessed. For such evidence we can look especially to histories and chronicles based on source material, encyclopaedias, lexicons, commentaries, variorum editions, anthologies, florilegia and most works supplied with bibliographies or lists of authorities. The earliest Greek encyclopaedic works in the Hesiodic age may no doubt have been based on oral tradition, though even at that early date there were temples and probably temple archives. In later centuries however when books were a common commodity the deduction is much more certain. Some examples will make this clear. The elder Pliny, in the introduction to the *Historia Naturalis* gives a list of his sources and explains that in collecting material for this great work he consulted 2,000 volumes and compiled 20,000 references from 100 principal authors. These are round figures of course, and actually 473 authors are cited in the course of the work. Quite obviously this involved research in a good library, and in Pliny's case it was probably his own private collection on which he depended in the main. Or consider the great Byzantine lexicon known as Suidas, produced in the tenth century. It is based on a wide range of earlier lexicons, histories, biographies and scholia, and it includes a vast amount of biographical and bibliographical information. It could not have been compiled without the aid of

51

a large library; in this case probably the Imperial Library at Constantinople. Or take two productions of a much later age: Montaigne's *Essays* and Burton's *Anatomy of Melancholy*. Both are plainly the work of men writing in their own libraries, with all their references at hand. Evidences of the actual use of libraries, whether corporate or private, constitute perhaps the most profitable and interesting part of the history of libraries: a neglected part too, for although there is little else we can discover about the story of some of the earlier libraries, the clues provided by their use in research have been followed up only here and there and for brief, isolated periods. Illustrations of the importance of studies of this kind can be found in J. W. Thompson's *Medieval libraries* (1957); we have already noted[1] for example his analysis of the works used by Bede, whose sources (apart from the information he obtained from Albinus, Nothelm and one or two other correspondents) must have been located almost exclusively in the library at Wearmouth; we know that Bede travelled scarcely at all, and the evidence is the more valuable for this reason. There are of course dangers in arguing from sources and quotations to the contents of libraries, especially in the medieval period when so much second-hand knowledge was in circulation. But the attempt is often worth making, and it will usually offer probable clues as to the kind of library the writer was using, and indeed sometimes to the very existence of libraries, when no explicit records of their existence have survived.

It is well to bear all these five or six points in mind in tracing the development of early libraries. To summarize them, we look for the publication of works involving research in libraries, the existence of an active book trade, the occupation by people of education and leisure of houses large enough to provide accommodation for books, the existence of corporate institutions with a recognized constitution and sufficient endowments, devoted to educational or literary pursuits, the existence of a sufficient corpus of national literature, and abundant supplies of writing materials.

The dependence of libraries on literary output, and of literary output on abundance of writing materials, is very evident on reflection, and is confirmed by the history of libraries in the

[1] *Supra*, p. 37.

classical and post-classical period. Striking illustrations can however be found in other periods. The dependence of art and letters on economic factors in the history of Iceland has been described elsewhere.[1] The absence of materials for the decorative arts, the comparative abundance of skins for parchment and the long Northern winters gave the settlers time and opportunity to develop the art of writing, and a rich store of manuscripts of history, poetry and saga was produced. In the words of the thirteenth-century Danish historian Saxo Grammaticus, *Inopiam ingenio pensant*, they made good their penury by their wit.[1] It is remarkable that this should have taken place in an island with scarcely any more urban development than Ireland had in its early period; its links with Scandinavian culture were of course close, as were those of Irish culture with that of Southern Gaul. It is worth repeating that it is nearly always the popular, much used books that are most apt to perish and often fail to survive. The unpopular, less used, book has a much better chance of survival. A striking instance of this can be seen in the English popular novels of the first period, 1750–1800; a very large number of these have disappeared, and comparatively few are in the British Museum.

A different, but equally pertinent, example can be found in the scarcity of paper that prevailed all through the Spanish Colonial period of South American history. This, together with the censorship imposed by State and Church, restricted the production of books severely, and though printing presses were set up at an early date, their output was meagre till the nineteenth century. Economic factors of this kind are always worth investigation in tracing the origins of literacy and scholarship and libraries in any region.

---

[1] See *Origins*, p. 121; G. Turville-Petre, *Origins of Icelandic Literature*, 1953.

CHAPTER IV

Hellas

THE effective history of Greek libraries begins with the Athenian schools of philosophy; in particular with Aristotle. There were of course books in abundance in Athens long before Aristotle's day, and possibly even before the great flowering of Greek literature in the fifth century. It is known that the import of papyrus from Egypt into Greece increased very considerably about the middle of the sixth century BC, and the connection between this fact and the outpouring of literary work in the fifth century is evident. But the art of writing goes back much earlier than this; not merely to the Homeric and Hesiodic age, but to the Minoan scripts that were the precursor of Greek, and of which evidence is found at Mycenae and Knossos and at most of the great shrines of the Mycenaean civilization. Professor Webster, in summarizing the transition from the Mycenaean to the Homeric age,[1] gives two conditions which had to be realized before the Iliad and the Odyssey could be composed: (1) the achievement of prosperity, so that there was both the leisure and the will, not only for the privileged aristocracy to hear the poets in their houses, but also for a wider section of the population to hear them at the great festivals. These are indeed much the same conditions that had to be met in England before the medieval period could give way to the Renaissance, though declamation had by then been replaced by the written book. And (2) the introduction of alphabetic writing, which made possible the change from the short song of the solo singer, to prolonged recitation by a team of rhapsodes. This alone could make possible full appreciation of the lengthy and complex unity of the Iliad and the Odyssey. It was about 850 BC, that alphabetic writing replaced the earlier syllabic writing; the change reduced the

---

[1] *From Mycenae to Homer*, 1958. Mycenae was sacked *c* 1100, and Homer is dated *c* 800.

54

number of signs used very considerably, and brought an immense gain in precision.

As with the earlier Mycenaean shrines, most of the larger Greek temples and oracles must have had their collections of records; rudimentary collections sometimes no doubt, but not necessarily so. Temples were religious foundations with a regular succession of officers and a tradition of complex ceremonial and ritual which had to be handed down. Often the ritual included the recitation of poems which would have to be learnt or read from written documents. The inscriptions associated with temples included literary as well as historical material, and must be regarded as forming part of the temple library or record repository; many are indeed historical documents of the first importance. Many temples assumed the function of record repositories. At Athens for example the institution of public archives began in the fifth century BC, and temples were employed for the purpose, though the particular temple used seems to have varied from time to time. All kinds of documents were accepted, including private papers and registers of landed property; the deposit of legal documents became compulsory. Literary works were apparently admissible. As early as 500 BC the philosopher Heraclitus of Ephesus is said to have deposited his magnum opus in the temple of Artemis, this being his chosen method of publication. In the fourth century BC under a decree of Lycurgus the Athenian record office was entrusted with the official copies of the plays of Aeschylus, Sophocles and Euripides as a check on textual corruption by the producers. These were the authorized texts which Ptolemy is said to have borrowed on a deposit of fifteen talents for the Alexandrian Library, though he retained the originals and returned copies, thus forfeiting his deposit.[1] Some temples on the other hand specialized in certain branches of knowledge, such as the arts, genealogy, medicine or even banking. The temple treasury at Ephesus acted as bankers for kings and cities as well as private persons, and the Parthenon was the safe deposit for the city funds at Athens. There is a parallel here with medieval days when cathedral chapters, religious houses and sometimes even church-wardens lent money at high rates of interest and sold annuities.[2]

---

[1] Galen *In Hippocratis Epidem* 3. 2. ; Sandys, *Hist. of Class. Schol.*, vol. I., p. 58, 111.
[2] R. H. Tawney, *Religion and the Rise of Capitalism*, 1937, Pt. I.

There is no reason to doubt that the more important temples were the first corporate institutions in the Greek world to organize and preserve collections of books and documents, even though these are largely unrecorded.

It is certain that by the last half of the fifth century, the age of Sophocles, Euripides, Herodotus, Thucydides, Aristophanes, Xenophon and Plato, there was an amply sufficient corpus of literature, not merely to justify but indeed to compel the collection of books into libraries either by private people or by institutions. Athens had become a centre of the book trade for the whole of the Aegean and Xenophon refers incidentally to the export of books from Athens to the Pontus.[1] New tragedies and comedies were being produced year by year at the Athenian festivals. Acting copies must have been needed for these, and the plays were apparently sometimes published before production, or at least in the hands of the audience during production.[2] No estimate is possible of the annual production of new works, but the great number still extant either whole or in part must represent only a fraction of the total. In the circumstances the existence of libraries seems inevitable, though the records are meagre.

Let us consider first the question of corporate or institutional libraries. State libraries can be dismissed briefly. They could have been foreign to the principles of Athenian democracy, which, though it provided gymnasia as educational and sports centres, preferred to leave education and similar services to private enterprise. This is true at least before the latter part of the fourth century. Two royal libraries have however been recorded by late and not always very trustworthy writers, namely Athenaeus and Aulus Gellius.

The first is said to have been founded by Polycrates, who was tyrant of Samos in the Aegean c 540–522 BC.[3] He turned the island into a considerable naval power, developed its industries and gathered round him a circle of poets and artists. The most famous Samian of this period was Pythagoras, who however removed to Croton in Italy c 531, and it was possibly at Croton that his major studies in mathematics and music (which would

[1] Xen. *Anab.* 7. 14.
[2] Aristoph. *Frogs* 52.
[3] Athenaeus 1. 3.

presumably need the help of a library) were carried out. The second was a public library founded by Pisistratus, who was tyrant of Athens 560–527 BC. He had been a pupil of Solon, and his reign was enlightened and benevolent. He is said to have been the first to establish a library where books were on display for public reading.[1] The Athenians maintained and increased the collection, but Xerxes carried it off to Persia in 480 BC. Later Seleucus Nicator (the first of the Seleucid line, c 358–280) returned it to Athens.

In the absence of other evidence these two stories have often been doubted, but on the face of it there is no reason why they should not be grounded on fact. The library at Samos would be a royal palace library, such as would come naturally into being whenever a literary circle was gathered around a ruler who was well disposed towards the arts. Thus at a later date the royal palaces at Antioch, Macedonia, Alexandria and Pergamon were all directly or indirectly associated with libraries. Again, the court of Hieron I at Syracuse, c. 475 BC, was the centre of a distinguished circle of scholars and poets, including Aeschylus, Pindar and Epicharmus, and the existence of some kind of royal library seems at least probable.

The story of Pisistratus' library at Athens was widely believed in the ancient world, but is now generally doubted. S. Jerome even linked it with the Alexandrian library, and implied that Origen and Pamphilus in founding the great Christian library at Caesarea were hoping to outshine these two famous libraries of the ancients.[2] S. Jerome doubtless relied on Aulus Gellius; Isidore, possibly quoting a lost work of Suetonius, calls it the first Greek library, and adds the details about Xerxes and Seleucus Nicator.[3] Against this is the fact that the story is not mentioned by Herodotus or Thycydides or any writer of the classical period. Nevertheless it is not an impossible tale, nor perhaps one that would be likely to have been invented. Pisistratus was a mild, liberal and able ruler, with a marked interest in the literary heritage of Athens. He is known to have ordered an official recension of the text of Homer to be carried out by four

---

[1] Aulus Gellius 6. 17. 'Libros Athenis disiplinarum liberalium publice ad legendum praebendos primus posuisse dicitur Pististratus tyrannus.'

[2] *Ep.* 34 *ad Marcellum.*

[3] *Orig.* 6. 3. 4.

experts, partly in order to establish an authorized Athenian version and to correct the corruptions that were creeping into the popular recitals of the text, and partly to delete some of the worst blots on the Greek character as shown for example in the story of Achilles. It is recognized that the *Iliad* was the work of a philo-Trojan under Minoan influence, and that it is in essence a veiled attack on the Olympian religion of the northern barbarians. Pisistratus was also accused of interpolating passages for political ends. The *Iliad* was accepted not merely as a national epic, but as an authority in Greek territorial disputes; Pisistratus for example used Ajax's connection with Attica to claim Athenian sovereignty over Salamis, and was said to have inserted lines to support this. The outcome was the end of the Olympian religion as a serious cult, and the failure of the Greeks to evolve a worthy moral code.[1] The relevance of this is that major editorial work of this kind presumes not merely the use of books, but care and interest in their preservation, and can fairly be adduced in support of the story of Pisistratus' library. It is at least possible, even perhaps likely, that he founded a rudimentary state library in which the literary heritage of his day could be deposited for sake keeping. There is however no independent evidence for its theft by Xerxes and later return by Seleucus Nicator. Seleucus was the ablest and most powerful of the successors of Alexander, and the founder of the two cities of Seleuceia and Antioch. There was certainly a state library at Antioch, if not at both cities; and it seems improbable that Seleucus would have returned the books to Athens at the very time that the Ptolemies were seizing books from Athens and elsewhere for their own new library at Alexandria.

We are on more certain ground when we turn to the later educational institutions of Athens and their libraries. Note first that the Athenians were a highly educated people; this is indeed true in some degree of most of the Greek city states. All free-born Athenians, most of the foreigners in the city, and a fair proportion of the slave population, were well grounded in the national literature, reading easily and with enjoyment, knowing by heart the famous passages of their poets and dramatists, and loving passionately to talk about them, for they were famous talkers.

[1] See Robert Graves, *The Greek Myths*, 1955, sections 163, 165, and references there quoted.

Their instinct for social life and intellectual discussion in the
gymnasia and the Stoa encouraged the development of literary
taste, just as the clubs and coffee houses and dinner parties did in
eighteenth-century England. There was little home life as we
know it, or even as the Romans knew it; once a boy had passed
the nursery stage, hardly any of his education took place at home.
This is not to say that family affection did not exist; it could
indeed be very strong, as is shown by the story of the little
Autolycus in Xenophon's *Banquet*.

In Athens education was largely a matter of private enterprise
till the fourth century BC. Schools were plentiful, at least from
the time of Solon, and possibly earlier. At their primary schools
boys of six or seven years upwards learnt their reading, simple
arithmetic and μουσική which included literature and the arts in
general as well as music, in addition to athletics and games in a
private sports arena or palaestra. About the age of fourteen the
boy went to a secondary school, provided his parents were well-
to-do, and his time was devoted to studies in literature and grammar, mathematics (including geometry, the theory of numbers
and harmony) and the new subject of rhetoric, as well as more
physical training. Technical or vocational training formed no
part of his course. All the recognized leaders of education in
Athens viewed with disfavour any training which aimed at
money-making; those whose parents could not afford the fees
for secondary education would be apprenticed to a craftsman or
trained by the father. There are arguments both for and against
this view, but only a nation which relied on slave labour for its
industries and manufactures could afford to plan its education on
these lines.

The hard core of all Athenian education, and the essential basis
for all later studies in rhetoric, was a thorough knowledge of the
national literature. This was imbibed by every boy at the hands of
his γραμματιστής at the primary school and the γραμματικός or
professor of literature at the secondary school, so that after three
or four years at his secondary school he had a very sound knowledge indeed of his country's poetry, history and drama. This
fact alone confirms (if confirmation were needed) that the schools
would be equipped with some sort of library or master collection
of books; teaching would be partly no doubt by dictation, which

would supply a ready means of copying passages on tablets or papyrus. No doubt the pupils would sometimes possess copies of essential works; the young Alcibiades is said to have assaulted his schoolmaster because he was without his copy of Homer. Supporting evidence comes from one or two school library lists on Egyptian papyrus fragments, and a vase painting of a schoolroom showing rolls in baskets hanging on the wall.[1]

More important for our purpose are the libraries of the universities and the schools of philosophy. At the age of eighteen the young free-born Athenian became an ἔφηβος or undergraduate-conscript, and undertook two years' military service under the control of state commissioners and army officers, one year being spent on garrison duty at the frontier and one year in the city itself. Throughout he underwent a rigorous discipline of athletic and ethical instruction as well as military training. When Athens lost her independence, the rigour of the system was relaxed. The course was reduced to one year; teaching in literature, rhetoric and perhaps philosophy was included; and foreigners were admitted. These changes began to operate about 300 BC, and the ephebic college gradually assumed the status of the University of Athens. With the Macedonian victory of 322 BC civic life in Athens was abruptly transformed. She was no longer the political centre of the Aegean, nor a military power, and in its place she was gradually changed into a quiet university city: vacuas Athenas was Horace's description of her.[2] By the first century BC she had outlived the supremacy of Alexandria in the world of scholarship, and had become the Oxford of the Mediterranean world. The young Roman citizen completed his education at Athens and Rhodes, much as we in our day graduate in Oxford or Cambridge; Cicero, his son Marcus, Ovid, Horace and many other famous men of letters were among her alumni, though in the first century AD her popularity seems to have waned. Strabo speaks of students being drawn away from Athens by the sophists and philosophers of Marseilles, and he declares that both Athens and Alexandria were surpassed by Tarsus in liberal studies.[3] A

[1] See Freeman, Schools of Hellas, 1907; Amer. Journ. of Archaeology, 1948, p. 340; and Gueraud et Jouguet, Un Livre d'Ecolier (L'Institut français d'Archéologie Orientale, Cairo, 1938), which is a study of either a pupil's notebook or a teacher's master-copy.

[2] Ep. 2. 2. 81.

[3] J. W. H. Walden, The Universities of Ancient Greece, 1913, p. 70.

revival came at Athens during the second century however when, under Hadrian and the Antonines, chairs were endowed for sophists, grammarians, physicians and philosophers. Marcus Aurelius gave chairs to all the four Athenian schools of philosophy, and established the constitution of the University on more formal lines, with the sophist Herodes Atticus acting as a sort of Chancellor.[1] After this period however her reputation began once more to fade, losing itself finally in the mists of Neoplatonism, and in AD 529 with the rescript of Justinian she finally closed her doors.

The university as we understand it today was essentially a medieval innovation, and many have questioned the propriety of giving this name to the academic institutions that sprang up all round the Mediterranean in post-classical times. It is true that they apparently lacked any written constitution, and offered no formal qualifications, but they had nevertheless a continuing identity, with endowments from the state or elsewhere, and they must have owned property. They were engaged in higher education, and they served as a nucleus to which both individual teachers and students could be more or less loosely attached. Professor Knowles however objects that they were not universities in the modern sense of the word, as neither science nor philosophy formed part of the curriculum.[2] These disciplines, he points out, had come together temporarily under Aristotle, but parted company almost at once, both developing separately in the hands of specialists, while law and medicine were also taught by their own professional experts. On the other hand university teaching today is suffering from so much fragmentation and specialization, that it would seem scarcely just to deny some sort of academic status to these institutions of the ancient world: either to law schools such as those at Berytus, Constantinople and Rome, or to medical schools such as those at Epidaurus, Pergamum or Cos, or (at a later date) Salerno, or to more general academies such as Athens, Rhodes, Carthage and Bordeaux, or a research institution such as the Alexandrian Museum, and perhaps Origen's Christian university at Caesarea. If Bologna was, as Professor Knowles

---

[1] Walden, op. cit., p. 92.

[2] Knowles, The Evolution of Medieval Thought, 1962, p. 62–3. Chapter V of this work offers the clearest short account of education in the classical period.

maintains, the first fully-fledged university,[1] it is well to remember that it was itself an almost accidental assemblage of independent schools of Roman law, canon law, arts, medicine and theology. Too precise a definition of the term is perhaps unwise. Obviously it would not mean the same thing to Cicero as it does to us, but Athens nevertheless was Cicero's Oxford, and we can recognize her as such.

If therefore we can with any propriety speak of the University of Athens (and as an academic institution it had a longer life than Oxford has yet achieved) we should, remembering the conditions specified in the preceding chapter, expect it to have a university library. That it did possess a library is confirmed by a single inscription. A custom arose in the second century BC whereby each ephebic year contributed a hundred books to the library, and a fragmentary inscription of the first century BC gives part of the list of books purchased during the year or possibly part of the library catalogue.[2]

It is relevant to mention at this point that rather similar inscriptions testify to the existence of ephebic libraries at Cos and perhaps Rhodes. At Cos, an inscription dated 200–175 BC, on the wall of the gymnasium (where ephebic lectures would be given) records contributions of 200 drachmas, or that sum with 100 books, from certain named people who might be either students or citizens; this would be either an ephebic subscription, or a voluntary levy ($\epsilon\pi i\delta o\sigma\iota s$) of the kind that was common in Greek cities.[3] At Rhodes a similar inscription of the same date announces a decision of the popular assembly to form a library and to appeal for subscriptions and books; a list of names follows.[4] Another inscription from Rhodes appears to be part of a catalogue of a university library or similar institution. It is dated not later than 100 BC, but the authors specified belong to the fourth and third centuries. They are: Demetrius of Phalerum, Hegesias, Theodectes and Theopompus. It is arranged alphabetically, and the topics lie within the field of politics and rhetoric, so that it

[1] Knowles, op. cit., pp. 115, 163.
[2] Daremberg et Saglio, Dict. des Antiqu. Grecques et Romaines, Tome deuxième, 1892, p. 632; A. H. M. Jones, The Greek City from Alexander to Justinian, 1940, pp. 224, 352; H. I. Marrou, Histoire de l'Education dans l'Antiquité, Paris, 1948, p. 259.
[3] Louis Robert, Bull. de Correspondence Hellénique, 1935, 59, pp. 421–25; W. A. Oldfather, Library Quarterly, 1938, 8, p. 287.
[4] Library Quarterly, 1938, 8, p. 287.

might be part of a subject catalogue. The interest of this inscription lies in the fact that the titles are followed by numbers indicating, not the number of books in the work, but the number of rolls containing it. For example the τέχνη of Theodectes, which is in three 'books', is marked τέσσαρα, i.e. in four rolls; on the other hand a work of Demetrius in five 'books' occupies five rolls, one to each book. This would indeed seem almost essential information for catalogue entries of papyrus rolls.[1] A third inscription from Rhodes announces a popular decision that certain works were to be registered in a library, and confirms that this has been done; this is referred to the second century AD. The three inscriptions imply library activity in the important commercial and university city of Rhodes over a period of three or four centuries. If any credit can be placed in the gossip of Athenaeus, there was a library in Rhodes at an even earlier date, when Ptolemy Philadelphus was collecting works for his new Alexandrian library.[2]

The University of Athens, if this high title is deserved, was nevertheless a loosely knit organization to which many individual teachers and schools were attached by interest and convenience rather than by any formal ties. From the fourth century onwards the sophists and rhetoricians, with their strictly practical aims of good citizenship and its attendant qualities of leadership, urbanity and eloquence, tended to dominate the academic scene. Rhetoric however was largely in the hands of private teachers, the first and greatest being Isocrates, and none of them founded any school or institution which could own a library. Moreover a library would scarcely have been needed, for students did not *read* rhetoric; they *heard* it (ἀκροᾶσθαι) from a particular teacher, and practised it themselves. The teaching was nevertheless always based on a sound preliminary training in literature, music and mathematics, and it was here that a library would have been necessary. It is possible that the need for books in the study of rhetoric increased as the subject grew more artificial and fell from its first high standards. The last of the great sophists, Libanius, complained, in the fourth century AD of the cost of academic life at Athens, where he studied rhetoric; and in addition

---

[1] Powell and Barber, *New Chapters in Greek Literature*, 2nd series, 1929, pp. 83–87.
[2] See *Origins*, pp. 27–38.

to fees, board and lodging he mentions the cost of books.[1] And Quintilian, it will be remembered, devoted a whole book of his *Institutio oratoria* to his discussion of the importance of reading and to his bibliographical guide to the Greek and Latin works which the student would need to study.

Nevertheless the schools of rhetoric, though they formed the basis of higher education in the classical period, are an unprofitable field in which to look for libraries. More important for our purposes were the schools of philosophy. There were four major schools at Athens: the Academy, the Lyceum, and the schools of the Epicureans and the Stoics. It will be recalled that one of the conditions for the existence of a library which we laid down was that the organization concerned should own property where it could be housed, with endowments for its maintenance. Of these four schools, only one had no property of its own; this was the school of the Stoics, whose teachers used the Stoa Poikile with its public hall and colonnade for their work. It had a long history, with a continuous succession of heads from Zeno *c.* 300 BC to the third century AD, but there was apparently no definite constitution, and no library was accumulated. In the circumstances the long life and the far-reaching influence of the school is remarkable.

Epicurus opened his school at Athens in 306 BC, in his house with its famous garden. The school with its garden and library was bequeathed in his will to his pupil Hermarchus of Mitylene, with funds for its maintenance.[2] Little else is known of the library, but it must have been substantial if, as Diogenes Laertius states, Epicurus' own works occupied 300 rolls. The influence of the Epicureans (as of the Stoics) remained vigorous till Roman Imperial days, when, as the main focus of 'free thought' and atheism, it aroused the hostility of the early Fathers.

Plato established his school at the gymnasium known as the Academy and in his garden at Colonus about 385 BC. The Academy had a longer life than any of the schools; its somewhat chequered and shadowy career extended to AD 529 when, after the final flicker of Neo-Platonism under Proclus, it was closed down by Justinian. It was justly proud of its 'golden chain'—its

[1] Libanius 2. 289. 9; *Ep.* 1192.
[2] Diogenes Laertius 10. 21, 26, 27.

apostolic succession, as it were; and though for much of this time it was living on its capital, nevertheless a corporate existence for over nine hundred years is a worthy achievement for any cultural foundation.

Although the Academy is exactly the type of institution which inevitably collects its own library, the records are silent about it. The headship of the school passed, on Plato's death in 347 BC, to his nephew Speusippus, and it can be assumed that the library preserved the official copies of Plato's works, and probably also the works of Speusippus, who was a biologist and a prolific writer, though he survives only in a few fragments. Equally it can be assumed that it possessed the works of the Pythagoreans; not only of Pythagoras himself, but of Alcmaeon and Philolaus, and of Archytas the mathematician whom Plato visited at Tarentum, where doubtless the Pythagorean school had a library of its own. According to Diogenes Laertius, Plato was not without wealth; he was subsidized by Dionysius II of Syracuse to the extent of 80 talents (perhaps £20,000), and he is said to have used 100 minas (say £400) in the purchase, through the agency of his friend Dion in Syracuse, of three Pythagorean volumes from Philolaus.[1]

There was a theory that appealed to those of the earlier Christian writers who were anxious to rescue their readers from the temptations of pagan literature, that Plato disapproved of books. He did indeed object to the abuse of books: to their use, that is, as substitutes for thought or for purposes of display. His teaching, and that of Socrates also, was based on the method of discussion and debate, of question and answer, rather than on the private and solitary study of other men's writings. Thus he hoped to induce first-hand thought rather than the second-hand borrowing of other men's thoughts. On the other hand, the dialectic of philosophical research which formed the climax of the teaching at the Academy and in some degree also of the system of education expounded in the Republic,[2] was built squarely on a long preliminary discipline of reading and study in literature and music and mathematics (especially geometry), followed by hard physical

[1] Diogenes Laertius 3. 9.

[2] The preliminary reading in *The Republic* was heavily censored for ethical reasons; the 'guardians' were indeed to be deliberately indoctrinated, to fit them for their duties. This is at least a tribute to the power which books can exercise.

training and experience in civil administration. The system thus goes beyond the recognized goal of good citizenship to the higher ideal of knowledge and wisdom needed by the immortal soul. Again and again Plato and Socrates underline the need for this preliminary discipline of study; always they assume that their students are soundly versed in their national literature.[1] Moreover, the special need for books in certain callings such as medicine, architecture, astronomy, mathematics and poetry is recognized.[2] And at the trial of Socrates we hear of the cheapness of books in Athens. Copies of the works of Anaxagoras were being sold in the market for a shilling or less, and everyone can be presumed to have read them.[3] Plato was addressing not merely a literate, but an educated, population; and if the Academy did not teach through books, this was because the students were abundantly disciplined in book-learning before admission. It is said that over the entrance to the Academy was written 'Let no one ignorant of geometry enter'. In Athens there would have been no need to extend the prohibition to other subjects such as literature.

The fourth of the schools under notice was Aristotle's Lyceum. Aristotle, the son of a physician at the Macedonian court, entered the Academy at the age of seventeen and continued his studies there till Plato's death in 347 BC. Both he and Speusippus were interested in biology, and when Speusippus became head of the Academy, Aristotle, not content to work under his colleague, left Athens and carried on his researches in various islands of the Aegean, partly with Theophrastus in Lesbos. In 342 BC he went to the court of Philip of Macedon to act as tutor to the young Alexander. On Philip's death in 336 he returned to Athens and opened his own school in the north-eastern suburbs of the city, in the garden of Apollo Lyceius and the Muses. The buildings which he rented for his college (as it may justly be called) became famous by reason of the περίπατος, the colonnade or ambulatory from which the Peripatetics took their name. Aristotle drew up a written constitution for his college, provided a refectory for the students, and arranged a monthly symposium which must have been a general assembly of faculties or departments to discuss

---

[1] See for example Plato, *Protag.* 326; Xen. *Mem.* 1. 6. 14.
[2] Xen *Mem.* 4. 2.
[3] Plato *Ap.* 26d.

reports of progress in the various fields of study. There were several departments engaged in research, such as constitutional history, music, philosophy and biology. Theophrastus, who later succeeded Aristotle, was in charge of the biological research. In 323 BC the death of Alexander caused a revulsion against Macedonian rule in Athens; and Aristotle, possibly fearing a repetition of Socrates' trial, handed over the college to Theophrastus and retired to Chalcis, where he died the following year.

The Lyceum may have been a larger institution than the Academy; under Theophrastus it is said to have had as many as 2,000 students.[1] Its central purpose was something new to the world of that time, namely, scientific research: the collection, organization and recording of knowledge for its own sake. Such work inevitably demanded the support of a library, and both this and a scientific museum were provided. One of the patrons was Alexander, who subscribed 800 talents (a very large sum indeed) to the funds of the college.

Theophrastus took charge of both the college and the library on Aristotle's retirement. As has been said, his interests lay in the field of biology, and his two treatises on botany and plant physiology, which represent a worthy attempt to construct for the first time an organized system of botany, were doubtless based on his researches with Aristotle in Lesbos and on the work of his students at the Lyceum. On his death, Theophrastus bequeathed the college to Straton of Lampsacus (*ob.* 268 BC) who himself bequeathed both the college and his books to Lycon (*ob. c.* 225 BC);[2] and with Lycon the work of the college began to decline. Theophrastus in his will however expressly left all his books to Neleus, who was one of his executors.

For the rest of the story we must turn to Strabo and Athenaeus. The latter, writing five hundred years after the event and anxious to glorify the origins of his beloved Alexandria, chose to forget all earlier stories and announced that Ptolemy Philadelphus purchased all the Peripatetic books from Neleus, and brought them to Alexandria, together with other books he had procured at Athens and Rhodes.[3] There is ample evidence of Ptolemy's acquisitive instincts in building up the Museum library, and it is

[1] Diogenes Laertius 37.
[2] Diogenes Laertius 5. 62.
[3] Athenaeus 1. 3.

at least likely that Demetrius of Phalerum was able to obtain some of Aristotle's books for him. There is no reason at all to believe that he secured them all; and we can guess that what he did obtain were transcripts of Aristotle's treatises and lecture notes, not the master copies: if these were purchased, the transaction was fair enough in the circumstances. It may be noted that there is no other evidence of a library at Rhodes as early as this; Athenaeus is not in any case to be trusted as a historian. It is noteworthy that nothing of Aristotle has survived on papyrus fragments from Egypt.

Strabo is a safer authority, and his version is more circumstantial.[1] Neleus (he says) took the library back to his home at Scepsis in the Troad. There in due course it was left to his heirs who were plain, simple folk, vaguely aware of its value but ignorant of the careful treatment it needed. They locked it away in chests, and forgot it. Later, fearing that the authorities at Pergamum (in whose territory Scepsis lay) might impound it for their own library, they buried it underground. Eventually their descendants dug it up, and sold it to the bibliophile Apellicon of Teos (ob. 84 BC) for a large sum, though it was greatly damaged. Apellicon tried to repair and edit the defective manuscripts, but lacked the scholarship to make a success of the task, and the texts remained corrupt. After his death Sulla carried off the library to Rome, where c. 40 BC they were edited and arranged by Andronicus Rhodius and Tyrannio the Elder, and an authorized edition, the basis of all our present texts, was published. Soon afterwards Andronicus went to Athens to become head of the Peripatetic school. With the restoration and revision of Aristotle's lost treatises and lecture notes, there was a revival of interest in the field of metaphysics and logic, the most important of the new commentators being Alexander of Aphrodisias, who began lecturing at the school AD 198. Later the school seems to have lost its separate identity to some extent, becoming merged in the Academy. Commentaries continued throughout the Byzantine period, but the Peripatetic contribution to medieval scholasticism was largely made through the channel of Neoplatonism, in the work of Plotinus and S. Augustine.

[1] On this see Colin Roberts, *Buried Books in Antiquity*, 1963; W. Jaeger, *Aristotle: Fundamentals of the History of His Development*, 2nd ed., 1948.

On the whole it seems likely that the Alexandrian Library cannot have been successful in acquiring any considerable part of Aristotle's work for its collection; nor did much remain at the Lyceum between the time of Straton and the editorial work of Andronicus. The question occurs as to why Theophrastus, though he left the school to Straton, separated the library in his will and bequeathed it to Neleus, who presently returned home with it to the Troad. Did he himself have no faith in the continuity of the school? We can at least say that Sulla achieved nothing of such memorable and far-reaching importance as his recovery of Neleus' manuscripts from Apellicon.[1] For this we may even forgive him for cutting down the trees in the Academy and the Lyceum to supply his engines of war, and even overlook his massacre of the population of Athens.[2]

As has been noted elsewhere, there is a wealth of information about private libraries in Rome. By contrast there is surprisingly little information about private collections in Greece, partly perhaps because no Greek letters have survived comparable to those of Cicero and the younger Pliny,[3] and partly because of the rather different social background of Athens which drew people away from their homes into the market place and the gymnasia. Nevertheless, with books circulating in quantity from the fifth century BC onwards, private collections must have existed. There are evidences that a few famous Athenians had their own libraries, as indeed we should expect them to have. A passage in the Frogs[4] implies that there was a topical joke about Euripides and his books, and Athenaeus refers to the collection of Euripides, and also of a certain Nicrocrates of Cyprus and of Euclid in Alexandria.[5] Plutarch tells how Alexander carried books about with him on his campaigns, including Aristotle's edition of Homer (the 'Casket Iliad') which he kept with his dagger under his pillow at night.[6] The story that Xenophon recounts[7] of the encounter between Socrates and Euthydemus, who was building up a great library of the poets and the sophists

---

[1] On this see especially C. H. Roberts, op. cit.
[2] Plutarch Sulla 14.
[3] O.C.D. s.v. Letters (Gk. and Lat.).
[4] Aristophanes Frogs 1407.
[5] Athenaeus 1. 3.
[6] Plutarch, Alex. 8.
[7] Xen. Mem. 4. 2. 8.

rings true, and, such collections in Athens cannot have been unfamiliar. Lucian refers to Demosthenes' interest in fine book production and mentions his 'eight magnificent copies of Thycydides, all in his own handwriting'.[1] In the first century BC it is probable that Cicero's wealthy friend and agent, Atticus (whose mansion on the Quirinal is described by Cornelius Nepos) had a similar establishment in Athens, where he had considerable business interests. In Imperial times villa libraries of the Roman type must have become familiar in Greece. Aulus Gellius spent a year at Athens studying under the famous and wealthy sophist Herodes Atticus who was appointed by his pupil and friend Marcus Aurelius to preside over the University,[2] and he describes the villa named Cephisia with its cool colonnades and running streams and birdsong, and the conversations that he and his friend Servilianus had with Herodes, during which the master would send for books from his library to reinforce his teaching.[3] We can safely guess that Plutarch had a library of his own at his school at Chaeronea; he quotes his sources more conscientiously than most writers, and is often at pains to compare his different authorities. In his *Demosthenes* he notes that to write history you would be wise to live in a great and famous city where not only books and libraries are abundant, but where you can converse at first hand with travellers and men of experience. 'But I myself,' he says, 'dwell in a poor little town, and yet do remain there willingly lest it should become less.' And he adds that while he was in Italy he was too busy to learn Latin; 'so that even somewhat too late and now in my latter time, I began to take my Latin books in my hand ... a marvellous pleasant and sweet thing, but withal, it requireth a long and laboursome study.' There is no doubt that Plutarch had a well furnished library.

Of Greek libraries in the Eastern Mediterranean, the most important were those at Alexandria and Pergamum. Tradition, though the literary and architectural evidence is slender, has always regarded the library at Pergamum as the rival of the Alexandrian Library;[4] Pliny[5] (quoting Varro) and Vitruvius were

---

[1] Lucian *Adversus indoctum*.
[2] J. W. H. Walden, *op. cit.*, p. 93.
[3] Aulus Gellius 1. 2.
[4] *Origins*, p. 35, 88.
[5] *Hist. Nat.*, 13. 70.

partly responsible for this belief; Rome in the second century BC drew its knowledge of Greek culture from Macedonia and Asia Minor rather than from Alexandria. The library was probably founded, or at least developed, by Eumenes II (*ob.* 159 BC) and Attalus II (*ob.* 138 BC),[1] more than a century after the rise of the Alexandrian Library. All the members of the Attalid dynasty were notable patrons of letters, but the Pergamene literary circle, though it included some famous names, was hardly as distinguished as the circle that the Ptolemies gathered round them. The only known head of the school and library was Crates of Mallos, the Stoic philosopher who visited Rome in 168 BC and established an interest in Greek studies there. There was a Pergamene bibliography similar to that of Callimachus in Alexandria. Dionysius of Halicarnassus, searching for records of the orator Dinarchus, confesses that he got no help from either the Alexandrian or the Pergamene catalogues.[2] There is a possible reference to the Pergamene catalogues in the notice of the poet Alcman in the Suidas lexicon, which suggests that they survived into Byzantine times.

All the successors of Alexander established royal, or state libraries. The Alexandrian Library has been considered elsewhere[3]. In the Macedonian capital of Pella there was probably a palace library from the time when Aristotle acted as tutor to the young Alexander; and the literary circle established there during the long reign of Antigonus Gonatus (278–239 BC) is sure to have been provided with a library. When the last Macedonian king, Perseus, was captured at the battle of Pydna, 168 BC, the Roman general Aemilius Paulus seized the public treasury, but allowed his sons to take the royal library, and it was presumably brought back to Rome where it formed the centre and inspiration of the Scipionic Circle.[4] With it came the Greek historian Polybius, to act as tutor to the general's two sons.

The remaining division of Alexander's empire was centred on Antioch and was founded by Seleucus I in 300 BC and enlarged by Antiochus the Great (224–181 BC). It grew to be one of the richest and busiest cities of the Eastern Mediterranean; Josephus

[1] Strabo. 13. 4. 2.
[2] Dionysius *De Dein* 2.
[3] *Origins*, pp. 27–38.
[4] Plutarch *Aem. Paul.* 28.

called it the third city of the Empire. The poet Euphorion of Chalcis, after marrying a rich widow, was able to retire to Antioch, where Antiochus the Great (according to the Suidas lexicon) appointed him to the charge of the public library. In the first century BC the last of the Seleucid dynasty, Antiochus XIII, established a museum and library there. In later days it became not only a centre of extravagant gaiety and fashion, but a great university city. Libanius, the last of the great sophists, had his school there in the fourth century AD and S Jerome, John Chrysostom and Julian were associated with it.

Reference has already been made to evidences of libraries in Rhodes and Cos. Smyrna, which was rebuilt by two of Alexander's generals, was a well-planned city with straight streets, colonnades in two storeys, a shrine of Homer, and a library,[1] but nothing else is known of this.

In Imperial times, it seems likely that libraries sprang up in almost every town and city, though only in very few instances is there any record of the use that was made of them. Under the Antonines there were Imperial regulations providing for the appointment of teachers of philosophy, literature and medicine at all cities, small as well as large, their salaries to be borne by Imperial funds if local revenues were insufficient.[2] Education thus came to be accepted as in some measure an Imperial service, and where schools flourished libraries are likely to have followed. Certainly in the Eastern Mediterranean they seem to have been ubiquitous, and we can only list some of those whose existence is confirmed.

(Perhaps the most notable were the two imperial foundations in Athens, one made by Trajan and the other by Hadrian.) Trajan's library is known only from two inscriptions. The first is addressed to Athena Polias, the Emperor Caesar Augustus Nerva Trajan Germanicus, and the city of the Athenians by the 'priest of the wise Muses', T. Flavius Pantainos, who with his children Flavius Menandros and Flavia Secundilla had dedicated from his own means the colonnades, peristyle and library with its books and all the decorations of the building.[3] The inscription is dated by

---

[1] Strabo 14. 1. 37.
[2] J. W. Walden *op. cit.* pp. 86–90.
[3] *Hesperia* 1935. 4: pp. 330–2; 1936, 5: pp. 41–2.

Trajan's title Germanicus (and not Dacicus, which he assumed
AD 102), and it will therefore be *c.* AD 100. It is known that
there was an archon named Pantainos at about this time. Another
inscription found near by announces that no book must be taken
out of the library, and that the library will be open from the
first hour to the sixth. This is of particular interest, for no comparable regulations for classical libraries have survived. It is
unlikely that the practice of taking books out of a library was
ever directly authorized, but it probably existed, and it must
have been difficult to check in view of the habit of using colonnades for reading. One would have expected the library to be
open for more than six hours in the morning; gymnasia were
usually open from dawn to sunset.

Hadrian's library came thirty years later. He spent the winter
of AD 128 in Athens dedicating the magnificent new temple of
Olympian Zeus and Zeus Panhellenios, and taking to himself the
title of Olympius. Pausanias describes the luxurious furnishings
of this great group of temples and colonnades, built of Phrygian
marble and alabaster, with golden roofs and full of statues and
paintings, and with stores of books. Clark gives a description
and ground plan of the Stoa of Hadrian, which formed part of
these buildings; five rooms on the east of the colonnade are
thought to have been the library, and the resemblance to the
ground plan of the temple and library at Pergamum is noted.[1]

At Ephesus the chief town of the province of Asia, the residence
of the pro-consul and an important commercial and banking
centre, traces of the foundations of a library survive. It was built
by Tiberius Julius Aquila Polemaeanus, who left 25,000 denarii
for its upkeep.[2] There is a lively description of life in Ephesus in
S. Paul's time in *Acts* 19, where we learn of the public and
voluntary burning of the libraries of those who practised 'curious
arts' (i.e. sorcery and magic) to the value of 50,000 pieces of silver,
which must have represented considerable collections. The ruins
of the library of Ephesus suggest a building with pigeon-holed
walls, possibly with a gallery or upper storey.

[1] Paus. 1. 18. 9; Clark, *Care of Books*, 1901, p. 16; see also the article by M. A. Sisson in
Papers of the British School at Rome, 1929, XI, pp. 50–72.

[2] H. Stuart Jones, *Companion to Roman History*, p. 140; E. M. Clift, *Latin pseudepigrapha*,
1945, p. 38; Pinner, *The World of Books in Classical Antiquity*, 1948, illustrates its recon-
structed façade.

The younger Pliny tells us of a library at Prusa in Bithynia, where he was acting as Imperial legate on behalf of Trajan.[1] The library had been founded by Dion Chrysostom, and in due course he presented it to the city for public use. It so happened that his wife and child had been buried in the precincts of the library, and when later the statue and shrine of the deified Trajan were placed in the library, the delicate question arose as to whether it was seemly and decent for these to be in the same building as the deceased members of the founder's family. We are not told how this awkward situation was resolved, but it was just the kind of predicament to reveal Pliny's ingenuous, but human, pomposity.

Aulus Gellius refers to a library at Patrae (Patras) on the Corinthian Gulf in Achaea, where Augustus had planted a Roman colony;[2] this, rather curiously, possessed a copy of Livius Andronicus' translation of the *Odyssey*. Indications of libraries are also recorded at Soli in Cyprus and at Delphi (first century AD), at Dyrrachium (Durazzo), at Eleusis and at Philippi (second century AD), and at Corinth.[3]

In Palestine and Syria various libraries are to be noted, not excluding the semi-monastic library of the Essenes known as the Dead Sea Scrolls, stored in caves overlooking the Dead Sea and dated to the first century before or after Christ. The volumes were of parchment, written with carbon ink; a few were on papyrus, and one on copper sheeting. The scriptorium where they were made survives in the neighbouring monastic ruins. Josephus describes the Essenes as a brotherhood of a definitely monastic pattern, owning everything in common and living under strict rule, and he notes that they were wonderfully devoted to the works of ancient writers, preferring especially those that can help soul and body: that is, devotional and medical books.[4]

No library at Jerusalem is mentioned by Josephus in his description of the city prior to its destruction, but Julius Africanus records a library in the Aelia Capitolina, the non-Jewish colony founded by Hadrian AD 135.[5] Eusebius records his debt to a

[1] *Ep.* 10. 81.
[2] Aulus Gellius 18. 9. 5.
[3] E. H. Clift, *op. cit.*
[4] J. M. Allegro, *The Dead Sea Scrolls*, 1956; Daniel Rops, *Daily Life in Palestine at the Time of Christ*, 1962, pp. 278, 398–400.
[5] P. Oxy 412. The same passage also mentions a library at Nysa in Caria.

Christian library founded at Jerusalem by Bishop Alexander (*ob* AD 250). Eusebius was however mainly indebted to the great library founded at Caesarea by Origen and Pamphilus to support the teaching at what was in effect the first Christian university; probably the greatest of all the libraries in the Eastern Mediterranean, prior to the foundation of Constantinople.[1]

There are many other towns in this region where libraries can with fair probability be assumed to have existed. Tarsus, for example, in Cilicia, the centre of the linen industry: no mean city, and we may recall that S. Paul acquired there not only his skill in tent-making but his knowledge of Greek literature. He could quote Aratus, Menander and Epimenides, and S. Jerome in discussing the value of pagan texts remarked on this fact. There was a university, or at least a school of philosophy, at Tarsus in the first century BC, and as we have seen Strabo rated it as superior to Athens at that time. Gadara, overlooking the Sea of Galilee, would be another claimant. Menippus the Cynic was a native, and so was Meleager, who compiled the first edition of the Anthology, calling it the *Garland*; he speaks of Gadara as the Syrian Athens. Still another might be Nicomedia, the capital of Bithynia. Here indeed in the early fourth century AD Diocletian established his own capital in the divided empire, building palaces, theatres and baths to rival the magnificence of Rome and Antioch and Alexandria, and amongst his foundations there was an Imperial library. A letter to the Imperial Chamberlain from Theonas, Bishop of Alexandria comments on its administration, the tasks of arranging and cataloguing the volumes, and of copying, correcting and repairing them.[2] Nothing else is known of this library, but from these roots the long library tradition of Constantinople may in due time have sprung.

Other famous towns in the Eastern Mediterranean could be named. Whenever a city grew rich in commerce and trade and produced men of letters and philosophers, we can be certain that it possessed schools, and almost certain that it possessed a library.

[1] The school and library provided for secular as well as theological studies, including philosophy except for the atheists (i.e. the Epicureans). It was supported by a scriptorium with a staff of shorthand writers and women scribes, at the expense of Origen's friend Ambrosius. See J. Danielou, *Origen*, 1955.

[2] J. W. Thompson, *Ancient Libraries*, 1940; *Anti-Nicene Fathers* 6. pp. 158–61.

CHAPTER V

The Roman Public Libraries

THE evidence for the establishment of national libraries in
Rome, and of the municipal libraries that, by the second
century of our era, were springing up in most of the towns
of the Empire, is disappointingly meagre.[1] Their existence is
confirmed by literary or archaeological evidence, but little is
known of their administration or contents. They doubtless
supplied a need to an increasingly literate population, but their
literary significance is small, compared with the Alexandrian
and Byzantine libraries. No great scholars were closely connected
with them. They had no noticeable effect on Latin literature, nor
did they play any part, so far as is known, in handing down the
Latin classics to the medieval period. None produced any bibliography of Latin literature or carried out any editorial work
comparable to that of Callimachus and his colleagues at Alexandria. They were in fact by-passed by the chain of scholarship,
which in Italy was handed down in the main by individual
scholars and teachers until its links were gathered up by the
Church. In short, their record is undistinguished.

The first project for a national library in Rome came to
nothing. Suetonius tells us that Caesar planned the establishment
of as large a library as possible for Rome, and entrusted Marcus
Terentius Varro with its organization.[2] He could not have chosen
a better man, for there was nobody in Rome with a higher
reputation for scholarly learning and creative research. Unfortunately Caesar died, and Varro was outlawed by Antony
(43 BC) before the project could be realized, and his probably
large collection of books was plundered. When the civil war

---

[1] The best authority is E. H. Clift, *Latin Pseudepigrapha*, 1945; see also J. W. Clark,
The Care of Books, 1901, and the *Oxford Classical Dictionary*. Boyd's *Public Libraries and
Literary Culture in Ancient Rome*, 1915, is unreliable. For private collections in Rome, see
Origins, pp. 39–53.

[2] Suet. *Caesar* 44.

ended he was allowed to continue his private studies and editorial work, but the scheme for a library was abandoned.

The fourth century *Notitia* and the *Mirabilia Romae* credit the city of Rome with nearly thirty public libraries. Only seven or eight are definitely known to history; all were associated with temples. Three were founded during the reign of Augustus: the *Bibliotheca in Atrio Libertatis*, the *Porticus Octaviae*, and the Palatine Library; and others were established by Tiberius, Vespasian, Trajan, Hadrian and Severus Alexander.

The library *in Atrio Libertatis* had a distinguished founder in Gaius Asinius Pollio (76 BC–AD 5). He was both soldier and man of letters, and the close friend of Horace, Catullus and Vergil, whose fourth Eclogue was addressed to him. In 39 BC he was awarded a triumph for his victory over the Parthini of Illyria, and the spoils of his campaign were devoted to the library in the temple of Libertas. It was of this library that Pliny used the famous words which the Library Association has incorporated in its motto: *ingenia hominum rem publicam fecit.*[1] In this passage Pliny is speaking of the 'new fashion' of adorning libraries with the portraits and statues of those whose immortal spirits are in communion with us in such places. This 'new fashion' was new only in Rome; Alexandria and Pergamum had known it for two or three centuries. It is a natural and laudable custom which still survives today. Bishop Isidore followed it in the seventh century, and so did Otto III at the end of the tenth century. At Ashburnham House, where the Cottonian library was damaged by fire in 1731, the fourteen original cases were surmounted by busts of the twelve Caesars, with Cleopatra and Faustina, and their names survive in the familiar shelf-marks. In Bodley's library, the painted frieze installed by Thomas James in the Picture Gallery served much the same purpose.

In another passage[2] Pliny notes that the only living author represented by a portrait bust in Pollio's library was Marcus Varro, and this has caused speculations as to whether the library was planned to fulfil Varro's abandoned scheme; perhaps even Varro's collections were acquired for it. Pliny here describes it, with one of his frequent flights of imagination, as the first library

[1] Pliny *Hist. Nat.* 35. 2.
[2] *Hist. Nat.* 7. 30.

in the world to have been founded with the spoils of war; he had forgotten even so recent an example as the library that Lucullus founded at his villa with the spoils of his campaign against Mithridates, about which Plutarch remarked that the use to which Lucullus put his books was worthier than his acquisition of them.[1] Pollio's library was opened at some time between 39 BC and Varro's death in 27 BC; probably indeed before 33 BC, when the Octavian library was established. Ovid gives the date of opening as April 13th.[2]

The Octavian and Palatine libraries were established by Augustus himself. The *Porticus Octaviae*, named after Augustus' sister, stood in the Campus Martius, between the Capitoline Hill and the river. The original temple was the work of Quintus Metellus in the middle of the second century BC. He had fought at Pydna, and may well have been familiar with the temple and library at Pergamum, which is said to have inspired the original design;[3] this is conjecture, however, and no pre-Augustan library is recorded. The plan consisted of a court, 443 by 377 feet, surrounded by a double colonnade and containing two temples of Juno and Jupiter. Behind the temples stood a *schola* (debating hall), and behind this again a *curia* in which the Senate sometimes met. On either side of the *curia* were the Greek and Latin libraries, conveniently near the colonnades, which must have served the usual purpose of a reading room for users of the libraries. It was usual in Rome to keep the Greek and Latin collections in separate departments.

The precincts of the temple were filled with sculptures in marble and bronze, and it must have ranked high among the magnificent buildings of Rome. Ovid refers to it in the *Ars* when he advises the would-be lover in summer time to take a leisurely stroll in the Pompeian arcade, or where the twofold gifts of mother and son have given us halls rich with foreign marble:

> *Aut ubi muneribus nati sua munera mater*
> *Addidit, externo marmore dives opus.*[4]

Octavia dedicated the *Porticus* to the memory of her young

[1] Plutarch *Lucullus* 42.
[2] Ovid *Fasti* 4. 621.
[3] Clark, *Care of Books*, 1901, p. 13.
[4] Ovid *Ars* 1. 67.

child Marcellus. It was damaged in the great fire of AD 80, and later restored by Domitian, who sent scholars to Alexandria to secure fresh copies of the books destroyed. Suetonius in recounting this fact uses the plural, though he does not name the libraries concerned (*bibliothecas incendio absumptas*).[1] Elsewhere he does indeed use the plural in referring to the Porticus libraries, but he may have included also the Palatine library, which was damaged in Nero's fire AD 64.

The temple and library of Apollo on the Palatine hill was begun by Augustus 36 BC and dedicated eight years later. In size and plan it is believed to have been similar to the Octavian building, with separate Greek and Latin libraries, and a *curia* between them. The *curia* contained a great statue of Apollo in gilded bronze, with portraits on the walls in relief of great writers. Under the pedestal of the statue, Augustus buried a selection of the Sibylline books in two golden caskets; these were the only items worth preserving in a collection of 2,000 prophetic writings which were then in circulation; the rest were destroyed.[2] Tacitus mentions a meeting of the senate here.[3] It was thrice damaged by fire: once, as already noted, AD 64, again under Commodus AD 191, and finally destroyed in the fire of AD 363.

It was from these three Augustan libraries that Ovid's works were excluded. His bitter lament on the progress of his *Tristia* is worth study. It went first to the august presence of the *custos e sedibus illis praepositus* at the Palatine, who 'bade me quit that holy place', *sancto iussit abire loco*. Then the *Tristia* sought the Octavian library, but this also was forbidden; and at the temple of Libertas, 'the first to welcome learned books', *quae doctis patuerunt prima libellis*, it met with the same summary rejection.[4] It is sad that we should know more about the books excluded from these libraries than the books they contained. It seems probable that Augustus exercised a political control over their contents. His destruction of prophetic writings, noted above, suggests this. He is known also to have excluded the youthful works of Julius Caesar from the Palatine library.[5] The exclusion

[1] Suet. *Domitian* 20.
[2] Suet. *Augustus* 31.
[3] Tac. *Annals* 2. 37.
[4] Ovid *Trist.* 3. 1. 1–72.
[5] Suet. *Julius* 56. 7.

of Ovid's works, together with the exile of the poet, was presumably a political, rather than an ethical, measure, though the full story behind this unhappy affair is unknown. There were *duo crimina, carmen et error*;[1] it is plain that the *error* was the major fault, and it is probable that it had some reference to the Imperial family. The *Ars* had been published for seven years when sentence of banishment was pronounced, and its author was exiled to Tomis (Constantza), south of the Danube estuary. The *Tristia* were composed partly on the journey and partly at Tomis.

The Palace Library of Tiberius (*Bibliotheca Domus Tiberianae*), also on the Palatine Hill, is known only from casual references by Aulus Gellius and Fronto. Aulus Gellius introduces a genealogical discussion on the Cato family with the words 'When Sulpicius Apollinaris and I were sitting in the library of the Palace of Tiberius with some of our friends, it happened that a book was brought to us inscribed M. Cato Nepos . . .'[2] Fronto, writing to his royal pupil, Marcus Aurelius, comments on two of Cato's speeches, and imagines the Emperor despatching his boy to fetch them at once from the libraries of Apollo. 'This would be useless however, for the two volumes have followed me here. So you must get round the librarian of Tiberius' library; you will have to lubricate the wheels a little, and when I return to town, he and I will divide the spoils.'[3] This suggests that, though it was not normal practice to lend books for reading outside the library, the rules would be waived for an important personage at an appropriate price.

There is a possibility that Tiberius established a second library in the temple of Augustus which he erected in honour of his deified predecessor. Pliny mentions a bronze figure of Apollo, fifty feet high, *in bibliotheca templi Augusti*;[4] and Suetonius relates that Tiberius dreamt on his birthday that a great statue of Apollo, which had been brought from Syracuse for the library of the new temple, would never be dedicated by him.[5] These passages might refer either to the Palatine Library, or to a new library established by Tiberius.

---

1 Ovid *Trist*. 2. 207.
2 Aulus Gellius 13, 20.
3 Fronto, *Ad M. Caes*. 4. 5.
4 Pliny *Hist. Nat*. 34. 7. 43.
5 Suet. *Tiberius* 74.

Like the Palatine Library, the Palace Library of Tiberius was damaged by fire under Commodus AD 191, when Galen states that some copies of his books were lost,[1] and finally destroyed AD 363.

The Pax Library (*Bibliotheca Pacis*) was founded by Vespasian in the forum that bears his name. A writer in the *Historia Augusta* seeks the verification of a fact here.[2] Aulus Gellius has two references. Anxious to study logic, and searching for a work by L. Aelius Stilo (the first great scholar of Rome, and the teacher of Varro and Cicero), he found a copy at this library though it did not give him the information he sought.[3] Elsewhere he notes, in the course of a grammatical argument, that there was a volume of the letters of the learned grammarian Sinnius Capito deposited in the temple of Peace, and he proceeds to quote from them.[4] Josephus, describing the triumph awarded to Titus after the capture of Jerusalem, AD 70, says that, with the Empire now firmly established, Vespasian built the temple of Peace with remarkable speed, adorning it with paintings and statues from all over the world. There also he deposited the golden vessels from the Temple at Jerusalem, but the books of the Law and the crimson curtains of the Inner Sanctuary were for safety's sake preserved in the Palace.[5] The temple was destroyed by fire, AD 191, when practically all the contents were lost.[6]

Probably the most important of the imperial libraries was the Ulpian library, established by Trajan in his own forum. Here again the Greek and Latin libraries were separate, lying one on either side of Trajan's column, between the Basilica Ulpia and the temple of Trajan.[7] The measurements of each room are given as 60 by 45 feet, which (as with other ancient libraries where the dimensions are known) seems to offer very little accommodation for a library of any size. There are more references by contemporaries to its value however, than to that of any other of the Roman libraries.

[1] Galen *De comp. med.* 1. 1a.
[2] Pollio. *Tyr. Trig.* 31. 10.
[3] Aulus Gellius 16. 8.
[4] Aulus Gellius 5. 21. 9.
[5] Josephus *Bell. Jud.* 7. 5. 7.
[6] Dio Cassius 72. 24, Herodian of Syria 1. 14. 6.
[7] H. L. Pinner in *The World of Books in Classical Antiquity*, 1948, has useful plates depicting reconstructions of the interior and exterior of the Basilica Ulpia.

Aulus Gellius recounts how one day, when he was sitting in the library of Trajan's temple, searching for another reference, the edicts of the ancient praetors chanced to fall into his hands, and he was glad to read them and become familiar with them.[1] Aulus Gellius was a confirmed haunter of public libraries; his type is familiar today.

One of the anonymous sepulchral epigrams[2] in the Anthology may be taken as referring to one of the greater Roman libraries in the second century, probably the Ulpian, though possibly the Athenaeum. It relates to the physician and poet Marcellus, of Side in Pamphylia, whose books (including a lengthy work on pathology in forty-two books of heroic verse) were deposited in the library of Rome by Hadrian and Antoninus Pius, 'so that among future generations he might win fame for his eloquence'.

Several references occur in the *Historia Augusta*. In one passage[3] Junius Tiberianus is explaining to Vopiscus the importance of seeing that the illustrious deeds of Aurelian were recorded for posterity. 'We possess his written journal and you must use this as one of your sources; You will find everything by careful research in the linen books, for he had his daily activities recorded therein, and I will see that the Ulpian library makes these available for you.' Vopiscus then adds that he has followed these instructions, and his facts can be checked by reference to his sources, including the linen books. The *libri lintei* were possibly as fictitious as the rest of the gambit to this biography, or as the original linen books which, according to Livy, contained lists of magistrates. Again, in the chapter on Carus and Carinus, Vopiscus notes that a statue of Carus' son Numidian, was placed in the Ulpian library.[4]

Three other references in Vopiscus are perhaps of more substance. In his *Probus*[5] he gives his sources in more detail than usual: 'I have mainly used the books in the Ulpian Library (in my days in the Baths of Diocletian) and those in the Palace of Tiberius; and I have used the registers of the clerks in the Porphyry Portico, and the *Acta Senatus et Populi*.' The Porphyry Portico was in Trajan's forum, near the Ulpian library. This is our only

[1] Aulus Gellius 11. 17. 1.
[2] A.P. 7. 158.
[3] Vopiscus *Div. Aurel.* 1. 7. *ibid.* 8. 1; 24. 8.
[4] Vopiscus, *Carus* etc. 11. 3.
[5] *Probus*, 2. 1.

authority for the removal of the Ulpian library to the Baths of Diocletian, which, like all the great baths in Rome, was a sports and cultural centre as well as a bathing establishment. Without independent confirmation, not much confidence can be placed in Vopiscus' facts.

In his *Tacitus*,[1] Vopiscus, citing his authorities, says that there is in the Ulpian library, *in armario sexto librum elephantinum*, an ivory book in the sixth press in which is inscribed a decree of the senate, signed by Tacitus himself with his own hand; for decrees pertaining to emperors were for a long time entered in ivory books. The presses were evidently numbered serially, and were open to public access.

In the same biography we learn that the Emperor Tacitus, choosing to imagine that he was descended from the great historian whose name he bore, ordered that copies of all the historian's works should be placed *in omnibus bibliothecis*, and to guard against loss through the carelessness of readers, *ne lectorum incuria depiriret*, ten fresh copies were to be made every year by the government stationery office and deposited in the libraries. This suggests a high rate of loss or damage; papyrus was no doubt still being used for such publications. That the Emperor was not really a descendant of the historian is shown by the difference in the names of their *gentes*.

The last testimony of the existence of the Ulpian library comes in the middle of the fifth century from Sidonius Apollinaris, Bishop of Auvergne. At this period it must have been the only great library surviving in Rome, and presumably it had begun to acquire Christian as well as pagan works. Sidonius' father-in-law, Avitus, had succeeded Valentinian III, who was murdered by the mob just before the vandals sacked the city. He honoured his son-in-law by erecting his statue between the Greek and Latin libraries in Trajan's forum, AD 455. In one of his letters the good Bishop ingenuously wishes that Nerva Trajan could see his enduring statue placed among the authors in the two libraries, *cum meis . . . titulis*; this phrase must refer to the Bishop's honours and distinctions, not to his own books, though his odes at least must have found their way on to the shelves.[2] The event made a

[1] *Tacitus* 8. 1.
[2] Sid. Ap. *Ep.* 9. 16.

considerable impression on the Bishop. In one of the odes, addressed to Priscus Valerianus, Praetorian Prefect in Gaul, he writes, 'It avails me nothing that there is added to my laurels my statue in bronze, shining red in the Ulpian portico, or the cheers that still re-echo through the hollows of Rome (*concava Roma*), while people and senate alike applaud my statue'.[1]

If the Ulpian library survived till this time, however, its glory must have faded, and the applause of the populace must have been as hollow as Rome itself. Nearly a hundred years earlier the last of the great Roman historians and the greatest since Tacitus, Ammianus Marcellinus, recorded the disappearance of its libraries in words of gloom. Writing of the middle of the fourth century, he paints a tragic picture of his times. Villas once famous for scholarly pursuits are given over to sport and idleness. Philosophy and oratory are gone, driven out by the music hall and the theatre. Libraries are sealed forever like the tomb: *bibliothecis sepulchorum ritu in perpetuum clausis*. Later, after describing the trial and execution of Theodorus and his accomplices under Valens, AD 371–2, he says that, to allay the popular clamour, thousands of books and rolls (*innumeri codices et acervi voluminum multi*) were seized from various houses, and being pronounced illegal, were burnt under the eyes of the judges, though most were treatises on the liberal arts and on jurisprudence. Later again there followed a ruthless campaign against people accused of magic and other crimes. As a result, throughout the eastern provinces owners of books in their terror burnt their entire libraries; 'we all at that time were creeping about in Cimmerian darkness, *omnes ea tempestate velut in Cimmeriis tenebris reptabamus*, with the sword of Damocles hanging over our heads.'[2] The main centres of destruction seem to have been at Rome and Antioch.[3]

The world is still familiar with madness of this kind, but the darkness was not as black as Ammianus imagined. The Alexandrian libraries were no more, but new libraries were even then opening their doors in Constantinople. While Ammianus was writing, S. Jerome was quite possibly in Rome, gathering his own beloved collection of books and meeting his disciples for prayer

[1] *Carm.* 8. 7.
[2] Amm. Marc. 14. 6. 18; 29. 1. 41; 29. 2. 4.
[3] Gibbon *Decline and Fall*, 25.

and the study of Hebrew at Marcella's mansion on the Aventine; S. Ambrose was Bishop of Milan; S. Augustine was teaching rhetoric in Rome or in Milan, where in 386 his conversion took place. The *City of God*, one of the great works of Latin as well as of Christian, literature, did not appear until after Ammianus' death; it was in part written to restore man's faith in the world around him. A new world was beginning, at the very time that the old world lay dying.

To return to the imperial libraries. There are slight evidences of still other libraries in the city. Hadrian established at least one library in Rome, the Athenaeum, and possibly a second. The Athenaeum was primarily a public hall for lectures, but a passage in Sidonius Apollinaris suggests that it may have contained a library. He is writing to a friend about a neighbouring villa, and speaking of the innumerable books in its library he says, 'You might have supposed you were gazing at a schoolmaster's study or the presses of the Athenaeum or the piled-up shelves of a bookshop'.[1] The second library, possibly dating from Hadrian's time, is said to have been on the Capitoline Hill, and to have been destroyed in the fire AD 191.[2] In the third century a library was added to the Pantheon, the temple in the Campus Martius built by Agrippa and rebuilt by Hadrian. Julius Africanus in a fragment[3] refers to the 'beautiful library in the Pantheon which I myself designed for the Emperor'. This would be under Severus, c. AD 220. A library in the temple of Asclepius is mentioned in the *Memorabilia Romae*, in the passage stating that the city had twenty-eight libraries; nothing else is known of this.

There is abundant evidence, literary, archaeological and epigraphical, for the existence of municipal libraries in the provinces, especially in the second century. The passage in Aulus Gellius about the library at Tibur (Tivoli), eighteen miles from Rome in the Sabine hills, is familiar to many.[4] It was the hottest time of the year, and the writer was with a number of friends at a country villa there. They were drinking quantities of iced water, or rather

---

[1] Sid. Ap. *Ep*. 2. 9. 4. The phrase is *Athenaei cuneos*, which signifies 'theatre' or 'auditorium', but the other terms (*pluteos* and *armaria*) imply the presence of books, and without them the comparison would lose its point.
[2] Orosius 7. 16; E. H. Clift, *Latin pseudepigrapha*, 1945, p. 31.
[3] P. Oxy. 412.
[4] Aulus Gellius 19. 5.

melted snow, when they were interrupted by a physician who told them that iced water was good for grain and trees but unwholesome for humans; and to prove his point he fetched a volume of Aristotle from the local library, which was in the temple of Hercules and well supplied with books, and cried, 'At least you must credit this wisest of men and stop ruining your health'. Thereupon Aulus Gellius foreswore iced water for the rest of his days, while his friends made their peace with it in various ways. From this passage it might appear that the Tibur library was prepared to lend books for reading elsewhere; the incident might of course have taken place in the temple precincts, or it might indeed have been a piece of imaginary gossip. There is no reason to suppose that books were normally taken away from the library precincts. In another passage, Aulus Gellius mentions a work by Claudius, the Sullan annalist, which this library possessed.[1]

The library which the younger Pliny endowed, and with considerable ceremony opened, at Como, AD 97 is well known; it was intended for the sons of gentlemen in the neighbourhood.[2] Apuleius in the mid second century mentions his researches at Oea (Tripoli) *in bybliothecis publicis apud clarissimos scriptores*, and speaks of the public library in Carthage as a place of learning.[3] There are remains of just such a library at Timgad (Thamugadi) in Numidia, a settlement founded by Trajan, AD 100. An inscription records that it was erected by M. Julius Quintianus Flavius Rogatianus at a cost of 400,000 sesterces. This library occupied a complete *insula* to the north of the forum. It was nearly square in plan, 28 by 23 m., with an open peristyled courtyard in front and a semi-circular domed hall, 40 feet in diameter at the back, between rows of bookstores or carrels. The hall was filled with book-recesses and tiered galleries, on either side of an alcove containing a statue, possibly of Minerva. There is said to have been accommodation for 23,000 volumes.[4]

Inscriptions bear witness of libraries at Suessa Aurunca in

[1] Aulus Gellius 9. 14. 3.
[2] Pliny, *Ep.* 1. 8. 2.
[3] Apuleius *Apologia* 91; *Florida* 18.
[4] *Bulletin of the Board of Celtic Studies*, XVI, Pt. II, May, 1955; H. Stuart Jones, *Companion to Roman History*, p. 140; there are useful photographs in the French official guide to Timgad.

southern Latium (the Bibliotheca Matidiana), in the Etruscan city of Volsinii, and at Tortona in Liguria, the latter with the early date of 22 BC;[1] there are possible remains at various other places, such as Pompeii and at Noreia in Noricum. It is probable that by the second century AD most of the larger towns in the Western Empire were provided with libraries.[2]

Though direct testimony is lacking, circumstantial evidence leads us to expect libraries to have been associated with the more important of the schools and universities which spread through Western Europe in later Imperial times. These would include Carthage, where S. Augustine was educated; Ravenna, which became the seat of the Emperors of the West, and where Fortunatus, Bishop of Poitiers, was educated in the sixth century; Toulouse, which produced the late grammarian Virgilius Maro; Bordeaux, where Ausonius' uncle was a professor; Marseilles, where Tacitus was educated; and not impossibly the many other Gallic schools such as Autun, Lyons, Nîmes, Vienne and Narbonnc. Though no formal university existed at Rome, there were various Imperial chairs established from the time of Vespasian, and it is possible that institutions such as Hadrian's Athenaeum served as an academic library. The law and medical schools must surely have had their libraries. The three recognized law schools were at Rome, Constantinople and Berytus, and the medical school at Rome was established by Vespasian. The work of late scholars such as Flavius Caper, Nonius Marcellus and Macrobius, whatever its value, was evidently the fruit of research in learned libraries.

Nothing very significant is known about the organization of any of the Roman libraries. Closed presses (*armaria*) replaced the pigeon holes which were probably used for the rolls at Alexandria and Pergamum. The *armaria* may not have accommodated so many rolls as the pigeon holes, but it is unlikely that these libraries held very large collections, and they must have given a more finished appearance to the buildings. They were normally surmounted by portrait busts with inscriptions. The remains of at least one of these presses in the Ulpian library survive, consisting of a rectangular compartment with traces of folding doors

[1] E. H. Clift, *op. cit.*, pp. 36–38.
[2] For the possibility of libraries in Roman Britain, see *Origins*, pp. 54–70.

of bronze. It has been suggested that the great hall of the Vatican library (AD 1587) embodies the general principles of the design of one of the Roman libraries.[1]

Nothing is known of any catalogues of the Roman libraries. The Latin word for catalogue is *index*, which is also used for a book-title. A phrase in Quintilian suggests that library catalogues were not unfamiliar. Nobody (he says) is so ignorant of these Greek poets as not to be able to transfer a list of them from a library to his own books.[2] The word *index* is not common in this sense, and it implies a list rather than an organized catalogue. Thus Pliny, referring to a chronological list of his uncle's books, says *fungar indicis partibus*.[3] Nothing comparable to Callimachus' bibliography seems to have existed in Rome, and one suspects that Roman librarianship was not highly developed.

As already indicated there is no reason to believe that any of the libraries lent books for reading at home, despite the story of Aulus Gellius at Tibur. Fronto's advice to Marcus Aurelius, also quoted above, implies indeed that it was not usually permitted, except under pressure from important people, and we have seen that it was directly forbidden at Trajan's library in Athens.[4] It is however hard to think how it could be prevented. Books were kept either in small storerooms or in closed presses, and were not always studied where they were stored, so that observation would be difficult. There is no evidence of any barrier, and no dress offers such opportunities for concealment as a toga. It is not known whether any mark of ownership was applied to the rolls. Nor is anything certain known of times of opening, except that Trajan's library in Athens was open from the first hour to the sixth: a curiously limited period which is not likely to have been general.

Such records as have survived regarding the staff of the Roman libraries are trivial and insignificant. With the exception of Varro, whose project did not come to fruition, and Asinius Pollio, who probably did little beyond providing funds for his library, not a single man of real distinction in scholarship and letters was associated with any of the libraries. Suetonius gives the names of

[1] Clark, *op. cit.*, p. 49; see also pp. 31–40, where there is a valuable discussion of classical library fittings.
[2] Quint. Inst. 10.
[3] Pliny *Ep.* 3. 5. 2.
[4] p. 73 *supra*.

the first librarians of the Octavian and Palatine libraries.[1] Gaius Julius Hyginus was appointed by Augustus as director of the Palatine library. He was a freedman, either from Spain or Alexandria, and a pupil of Alexander Polyhistor. He was himself a schoolteacher, and a friend of Ovid. Columella, quoting his treatise on bees, implies that Virgil was indebted to him.[2] He wrote many works, including one on agriculture and a commentary on Virgil. Nothing however has survived, and it is impossible to judge his quality. He died very poor. He had a freedman Julius Modestus who was a grammarian, and is said to have 'followed in his footsteps', but whether this means he succeeded him at the library is not clear. A later successor was M. Pomponius Marcellus, another grammarian, who, as Sandys says, began life as a boxer and ended it as a pedant.[3]

Gaius Melissus, a protégé of Maecenas, was appointed by Augustus to the Octavian library. His claim to literary distinction rests on the compilation in his old age of some collections of quips and jokes; he also invented the *fabula trabeata*, a type of high-life comedy.

One or two other names are known. Martial addresses an epigram to Sextus at the Palatine library, begging room for his little books, close to where the works of Catullus, Pedo and Marsus lie.[4] A few names and titles appear in inscriptions.[5] *Procurator bibliothecarum* occurs in several; *a bibliotheca* is mentioned frequently, once with *magister* and once with *vilicus*, but often by itself. Ovid uses the title *custos praepositus* for the head of the Palatine library.[6] One inscription refers to *Hymenaeus medicus a bibliothecis*;[7] perhaps an officer at a medical library.

Neither Greek nor Latin writers had much interest in details of organization, and we are as ignorant about the routines and methods of teaching at universities and schools as we are about those of libraries. One has the impression however that neither Augustus nor his successors took the Roman libraries sufficiently seriously. If they had endowed one national library at Rome,

[1] Suet. *De grammaticis* 20, 21.
[2] Columella *De re rustica* 1. 1. 13.
[3] Sandys, *Hist. of Class. Schol.* vol. I, 1903, p. 187.
[4] Martial *Ep.* 5. 5.
[5] For details see C. E. Boyd, *Public Libraries and Literary Culture in Ancient Rome*, 1915.
[6] Ovid *Tristia* 3. 1. 67.
[7] *CIL.* 6. 8907.

appointing to it as able a group of research scholars as the Ptolemies found for their Alexandrian library, the history of Western scholarship might well have been different. If for example Augustus had placed Ovid at the head of the Palatine library, instead of driving him to the utmost extremity of the Empire, might he not have emulated his beloved hero Callimachus in his bibliographical work, and gathered round him a circle of poets and scholars of sufficient fame to found a tradition of librarianship and research which could have endured for four centuries or more till Rome became Christian? But speculation, however interesting, is idle. If there is one lesson that the history of classical libraries teaches us, it is that a great library must have at its head great scholars to carry out not only bibliographical research, but creative work. No library can be left to take care of itself. Unless it is fired and inspired by genius and ability, it dies.

CHAPTER VI

Classical Bibliography

THE details of book production in classical and post-classical times have been briefly described by many writers, and by none with more clarity and authority than Sir Frederic Kenyon in his *Books and Readers in Ancient Greece and Rome* (2nd edition 1951), and in his equally lucid article on 'Books' in the *Oxford Classical Dictionary*.[1] There is no need to repeat these details here, but something can be said to fill in the background to the picture that Kenyon depicts.

Note first that, as Kenyon himself says, 'the external form of books has at all times affected, and been affected by, their contents'. This is a bibliographical fact which is true in all periods of the history of scholarship; and it is one of the reasons why the scholar and critic as well as the historian of libraries needs to know something of book production. There has at all times been a constant interaction between the physical characteristics of the book, the arrangement and style of its text, and the organization and methods of the libraries in which it is stored. This is evident in all periods of literature, both before and after the discovery of movable type, and it would provide a very fruitful field for research.

The material used for writing (whether it be stone or wood, parchment, papyrus or paper, or some other substance such as linen or silk or slate or strips of palm leaf), and the form of assembly (whether it be roll or tablet or codex) have a profound effect on the actual work of the writer and on the handwriting of the scribe, as well as on its ease of storage and chances of survival. Contrariwise the needs of the writer and convenience of his readers affect the materials used by the scribe or printer. In the classical period, this interaction is shown clearly in the

[1] See also J. Černy, *Paper and Books in Ancient Egypt*, 1952, and E. G. Turner, *Athenian Books in the Fifth and Fourth Centuries B.C.*, 1952.

editing of classical texts into 'books' of appropriate length for one or more rolls at the Alexandrian library, and in the replacement of the roll by the codex to meet Christian needs in the second and third centuries.

There was no standard height or length for a papyrus roll, so long as rolls were in the main collected in small quantities by individual users. In such circumstances the size is of minor importance, provided that the text is legible and the papyrus is not too long for easy handling. Papyrus could be bought in rolls of up to twenty sheets (about fifteen feet) but the scribe would cut or lengthen the roll to suit his text. The normal length of a literary text in roll form would be from fifteen feet to thirty-five feet; a roll of thirty-five feet would take one 'book' of Thucydides, or perhaps two of Plato's *Republic*. When the first national collection on a really large scale was being organized at Alexandria, the problems of storage were faced for the first time. It is probable that the great majority of the volumes in the Alexandrian Library were edited and copied in the library's own scriptorium, and such evidence as there is suggests that a standard size of roll was adopted for convenient storage in bins or pigeon holes, and that texts were edited to conform to this uniform size. It is known that the editors introduced the arrangement of texts into the 'books' that are still familiar today; Zenodotus for example divided the *Iliad* and the *Odyssey* into twenty-four books each, probably two books to a roll; and other authors received similar treatment.

So also in Rome, the *Metamorphoses* and *Fasti* of Ovid, are divided into fifteen and six books respectively, and the division has no obvious logical or narrative basis. When the division appears artificial, it can be guessed that the length of the roll was the governing factor, and it is possible that the division in this case was made by Ovid himself. It is possible too that, with the foundation of the Augustan state libraries, a standard size of roll was evolving in Rome. When the division into 'books' survives the replacement of the roll by the codex it thus becomes a convenient anachronism. Division into 'books' has another advantages in that it facilitates reference to particular passages; a need which makes itself felt with the advent of textual and literary criticism and the publication of commentaries. References to particular passages in other texts are not common in the classical period, and in the absence of page or line numbers, passages could only be identified by the number of the book in which they occur.

The appearance of the roll, with its sheets of papyrus glued together into a long strip, is sufficiently familiar from the descriptions and illustrations given by Kenyon, Clark and other authorities; the finished article looks rather like a large photographic spool, on an average about eight or ten inches high. There is no evidence of any attempt at decoration or ornamentation till the Augustan age in Rome when, as is plain from many references in the Augustan poets and in Martial, publishers did what they could to beautify a rather unpromising and intractable object. The roll was at that time wound on a cylinder with projecting ornaments or knobs in ivory or colours (*umbilici, cornus*), and was finished with a coloured parchment cover, fastened with laces and identified with a title label (*sittybus*). The title might also appear at the end of the strip, like a colophon in a printed book; when a reader had finished a roll, the title would then show at the end, unless the roll was re-wound. It is difficult to suppose however that this was the reason for placing the title at the end, as Kenyon suggests.[1] The text was written in rather narrow columns[2] on the recto of the papyrus, where the fibres run horizontally. Opisthographs with writing continued on the verso are not common; this extension was probably made in the main for notes or school work not intended for publication, to economize on papyrus.[3]

The rolls in a small collection were stored in any convenient receptacle—cupboards, chests or buckets (*armaria, scrinia, capsae*) with the labels projecting. In large libraries such as Alexandria or Pergamon, pigeon-holed shelves on brackets were probably used, and as we have already mentioned, the scribes probably made their rolls a uniform size to fit the recesses. The closed *armarium* apparently developed in Imperial times and survived in monastic libraries till the Renaissance or later. The word *armarium* signifies a wardrobe or cupboard; it might be a separate piece of furniture, or it might be 'built in', i.e. simply a hole in

[1] Kenyon, *op. cit.*, p. 61. When a cylinder or spool was used, as in the Augustine period, the roll would have to be re-wound, unless a second spool were available as in a camera; and there is no evidence of this.

[2] *ibid.*, p. 55.

[3] *ibid.*, p. 63. See for example Martial *Ep.* 8. 62.

the wall, such as the hole which the younger Pliny describes as housing his bedside books (*Pariete eius in bibliothecae speciem armarium insertum est*);[1] these were the books he enjoyed not merely reading, but re-reading again and again. (If you remember Barrie's *Window in Thrums*, you may recall that Jimsie Duthie kept his small store of books in just such a hole in the wall; probably a common enough expedient in all ages). In whatever way rolls were stored, they cannot have added anything to the appearance of the room, as leather bound codex volumes can do. It should be remembered however that it was not till the eighteenth century that the aesthetic value of bound volumes as a wall decoration was really appreciated; before that, hardly any thought was given to their appearance on the shelves.

There are two points to stress about the make-up of books in roll form. First, in the classical period at least, the script seems almost deliberately designed to make its interpretation difficult. There was no separation of one word from another. There was scarcely any punctuation or paragraphing. In Greek texts there were rarely any accents or breathings. The παραγραφή (a dash closing a sentence) and the rough breathing were recognized by Aristotle, though they were not in common use in his day. Doubtless the easy interpretation of continuous and undifferentiated text is largely a matter of practice and knack. It is however to the credit of the Alexandrian Library that its research workers saw the need to remove the difficulties of reading such texts, in order to simplify the task of the student and to minimize the risk of ambiguity. This can indeed be regarded as one of the important achievements of the Alexandrian Library, and especially of Aristophanes of Byzantium, who introduced the three accents to mark correct pronunciation and various symbols for use in textual criticism. Accents were not however universally employed in all texts till much later. The rules of grammar were also standardized by the Alexandrian workers, and Dionysius Thrax who was a pupil of the last known librarian, Aristarchus of Sancothrace, published his τέχνη γραμμαπκή which defined both the rules and the accents and stops.

The second point to note is that from its very nature the papyrus roll suffered from grave disadvantages as a tool of scholarship.

---

[1] *Ep. 2. 17.*

It was clumsy to use, requiring both hands to manipulate it. It was extremely awkward to refer backwards and forwards in the text, as we constantly need to do in studying a difficult work; this might involve unwinding and re-winding twenty or thirty feet of papyrus. Moreover papyrus itself is a fragile and perishable material, particularly in any climate less dry than that of Egypt, and constant re-copying is thus necessary. In these circumstances a change to a more durable material and a more convenient form of book was bound to come sooner or later.

The evolution of the parchment codex is described briefly by Kenyon, and in more detail by C. H. Roberts.[1] It was as dramatic and far-reaching a change as the development of printing in the fifteenth century. Similarly the replacement of papyrus by parchment was an equally important change—quite as important as the later replacement of parchment by paper. The origins of the codex are obscure, but it seems fairly certain that it was a Roman discovery[2] which the Christians in Egypt developed in the second century of our era, possibly even in the first century. We can be reasonably sure that the idea was derived from the multi-leaved tablets which were in common use throughout the classical period.

The tablet in some form or other has always been a convenient medium for written records, especially for temporary records when durability is not required. Basically it is simply a piece of wood with a smooth surface on which writing can be scratched. Durability can indeed be given if clay is used instead of wood, and the words inscribed and fixed by baking. Clay tablets belong mainly to the Middle East, where sunheat is available. In other countries where timber is more plentiful, wood is easily fashioned for this purpose. References to inscribed wood are common in Northern literature; e.g. the carved message which Tristram left on the road in Iseult's path, or the runestaves which could be used for secret messages or magical purposes. Sooner or later it was discovered that the writing was more legible if the wooden surface was whitened. If on the other hand the wood was coated with wax, the writing could be erased with the blunt end of the

---

[1] C. H. Roberts, 'The Codex', *Proc. Br. Acad.*, 1954, pp. 169–204.

[2] There was no recognized Greek equivalent for the terms *membranae* (notebook) and *codex*. C. H. Roberts, *op. cit.*, p. 176.

stylus and the tablet used again. The earliest surviving waxed tablets come from Iraq, and are cased in ivory and multi-leaved. They date from the time of King Sargon, *c.* 715 BC, and are almost contemporary therefore with Homer, and about five centuries earlier than any other surviving waxed tablets. In this case the wax was a mixture of beeswax and sulphide of arsenic—a composition known to have been used from Assyrian inscriptions. In Roman times beeswax softened and coloured black with pitch was used. For notice-boards a harder coating of gypsum was preferred. Tablets in constant use needed re-waxing frequently; it is said that a schoolboy's tablet required re-waxing every month.

Waxed tablets were used by everyone throughout the classical period for rough notes, for letters and often for the first draft of literary work. Their use continued indeed through the medieval period; in monastic times they were used for notice-boards; Shakespeare has many references to them. Leigh Hunt[1] traces their evolution into pocket-books which were more convenient to carry about, but he says that Italian tablets could still be bought in the shops in his day. Slate tablets were still being used in some schools early in the present century. Both in the Middle East and in Greece and Rome it was customary where necessary to lace several tablets together by using leather thongs, cords or rings, and they could then be sealed if privacy was desired. The binding of tablets together in this way provides an obvious model for the codex form of book.

The only reference to writing in Homer is the passage in the *Iliad* (6. 168) describing how the King of Argos sent 'tokens of woe' engraved on a folding tablet ($\dot{\epsilon}\nu$ $\pi\dot{\iota}\nu\alpha\kappa\iota$ $\pi\tau\nu\kappa\tau\tilde{\omega}$) to the King of Lycia, recommending Bellerophon (in Professor Webster's words) as an 'expendable brigand'. The similarity of this story to another letter surviving from the Hittite period leads Professor Webster to suggest that they are the Western and Eastern ends of the same legend.[2] Pliny quotes the passage from the *Iliad* in his account of papyrus, and it is interesting to note that he translates $\pi\dot{\iota}\nu\alpha\xi$ by the word *codicilli*—small codex.

Several different terms were used by the Greeks and Romans

[1] Essay on pocket-books and keepsakes.
[2] *From Mycenae to Homer*, 1958, p. 25.

for the tablet, e.g. the word *codex* itself, and *codicilli*, *tabella*, *tabula*,[1] *pugillares*, *cera*, πίναξ, δέλτος (the original Greek tablet being shaped like the letter Δ). '*Prima cera*', '*secunda cera*' stood for the first or second pages, etc. *Pugillares libelli*, or *cerae* (literally, a fistful of tablets), were small handbooks of from two to eight leaves of ivory, metal or wood with a waxed surface, the leaves joined by rings and protected with a cover of parchment or wood. The diptycha was a larger and heavier tablet with two hinged panels of ivory, ebony or boxwood. The diploma was usually a two-leaved tablet of bronze,[2] given to soldiers on completion of their service as a certificate of the privileges they had earned.

When used for gifts or love-letters the covers might be decorated with ivory, gold or precious stones. Thus the love-letters which Cleopatra sent to Antony while he was dispensing justice on his tribunal to kings and tetrarchs were on tablets of onyx and crystal.[3] It is easy to see how such coverings evolved into the jewelled bindings of Byzantine and Carolingian times.

The common use of tablets provides another instance of the interaction between physical form and literary content. It is probable for example that the dimensions of a tablet may sometimes have governed the structure of a poem by Ovid or Catullus or Sappho. A medieval instance of this is quoted by Helen Waddell.[4] The verses of Baudri, Abbot of Bourgeuil (1046–1134) were fashioned to suit the elegant tablets of green wax, with space for just eight hexameters, presented to him by Ralph d'Escures, Abbot of S. Martin's at Séez, who died Archbishop of Canterbury in 1122. Again, the use of a stylus on wax had its influence on the development of the Latin cursive hand, just as the use of parchment had its effect on book hands, tempting scribes to emphasize their downstrokes and producing the uncial form of letter. The stylus on wax tends to produce an angular hand with disconnected strokes. Similarly the use of stone for inscriptions produced the familiar square Roman capitals. Still another instance of this interaction is the possible origin of the

---

[1] C. H. Roberts, *op. cit.*, p. 171. *Codex* and *tabula* were interchangeable.

[2] Brass tablets were used for State records intended to be permanent. Cf. The tablets recording the treaty of friendship between Rome, Sparta and the Jews, which the latter placed in their public record office; 1 Maccabees 8. 22; 14. 18.

[3] Plutarch, *Antony*, 58.

[4] *The Wandering Scholars*, 7th ed., 1934, p. 95.

Chinese vertical script frrom the narrow strips of bamboo or wood employed for writing during the Shang period.

The beginning of the parchment book, as contrasted with the folded tablet, can be traced with a good deal of plausibility to the first century AD in Rome, when folded leaves of parchment were being employed for notebooks. There is a reference in Suetonius[1] which implies that Caesar used this method for his despatches. Suetonius is listing Caesar's writings, and he adds 'There are also extant some of his despatches for the Senate. Apparently he was the first to arrange such documents in paged form and in the shape of a notebook (*quas primum videtur ad paginas et formam memorialis libelli convertisse*). Previously consuls and generals sent in their reports written straight across the sheet (*transversa charta*). Professor Černy[2] regards this simply as a change from transverse writing to the normal form of a literary text on a roll. It is difficult however to regard a paged *memorialis libellus* as anything but a codex notebook.

Martial's *Epigrams* are full of references implying that paged pamphlets of parchment were familiar in the first century AD. These sometimes took the form of keepsakes or gift books, but it seems likely that larger works were also published in this shape. An examination of the 'Christmas present' epigrams makes it plain that the works Martial had in mind were not all miniatures or epitomes. The *Cicero* for example was big enough to occupy a traveller's time on a long journey.[3] The *Ovid* is described as bulky (*massa tabella*).[4] The volumes could be held in one hand[5] —a simple feat with a codex, but impossible with a roll. The word *multiplex*[6] points strongly to the folding of parchment sheets into quires; the *Homer* is gathered in many-folded skins, and this epigram is entitled *Homerus in Pugillaribus Membranis* which must indicate a parchment handbook.

There was in Martial's time close contact between Rome and

---

[1] *Div. Jul.* 56.

[2] *Paper and Books in Ancient Egypt*, 1952, p. 22. Kenyon (*op. cit.*, p. 57, note) advances still another, and I think improbable, explanation of this rather obscure passage. The theory proposed above is supported by Lewis and Short, s.v. *libellus*. See also C. H. Roberts, *op. cit.*, p. 175.

[3] *Ep.* 14. 188. On these see C. H. Roberts, *op. cit.*, pp. 177–9.

[4] *Ep.* 14. 192.

[5] *Ep.* 14. 185.

[6] *Ep.* 14. 184. 192.

Alexandria, and it is possible that a codex edition of S. Mark's Gospel was brought from Rome to Egypt towards the end of the first century. The reason for this is that the end of this Gospel is probably missing, and it is far more likely for the last leaf of a codex to be lost, than the last piece of a roll.[1] It is the beginning of a roll that may suffer damage rather than the end; but either the first or last leaves of a codex are vulnerable, and may only too easily become detached and lost. The evidence suggests that the codex form of book was familiar not only to Martial's circle of friends in Rome, but to Christians everywhere, in the first century AD. It is almost certain for example that when S. Paul in 2 *Tim*. 4. 13 refers to his *membranae*, he was thinking of parchment notebooks in this form; possibly even of S. Mark's Gospel in this form.[2]

In Egypt the Christians quickly adopted the codex for standard or authorized editions of the scriptures or other works of importance. It had everything to recommend it. It gave greater security to important documents and records, especially if the text was on parchment. Quite as important was the fact that by this means a lengthy text could be made available for easy reference within one binding. The resulting volume was comparatively light and reasonably portable; it was simple to read aloud from, and reference backwards and forwards was easy; and if not too bulky, it could be held in one hand. On an average, a codex had six times the capacity of a roll. It was a revolutionary change, and in the main a Christian contribution.

The pagans were dilatory in adopting the new method, partly perhaps because their need of books was less specialized than in the case of the Christians, whose devotions and ritual and theology depended very closely on the written word.[3] A few pagan codices survive from the second century, but it was not till the third and fourth century that the codex was generally adopted for pagan literature.[4] By this time it had come into general use in Christian circles, and similarly parchment had replaced papyrus.

[1] Unless of course the roll has been read through without re-winding. For a further discussion of S Mark, see C. H. Roberts, *op. cit.*, p. 187.

[2] C. H. Roberts, *op. cit.*, p. 191.

[3] There is no reference to the codex form in either of the Plinys or in Lucian, and only one reference to a parchment notebook in Galen; all these writers were interested in the bibliographical aspect. See C. H. Roberts, *op. cit.*, p. 180.

[4] C. H. Roberts, *op. cit.*, p. 184.

There is no question about the superiority of parchment over papyrus for the codex book. The papyrus codex was a transitional form, probably confined to Egypt, and surviving examples are found mostly among the Chester Beatty scriptures. A single vertical fold of a papyrus sheet gave a quire of two leaves, and by combining these either a single large quire of, say, fifty leaves could be formed, or a succession of smaller quires of eight, ten or twelve each. Papyrus however will not stand folding more than once, and even a single fold weakens it. There need be no surprise therefore that parchment, which can be folded many times without damage to its fibres, superseded papyrus, and that the Latin *membranae* came to signify the codex form. In Rome the parchment books that Martial describes did not apparently establish themselves as serious rivals to the roll for a considerable time. The jurist Ulpian, who died AD 228, defines *liber* as including both *volumina* and *codices*; and we can assume that the change was occurring gradually in Rome at that time. Constantine the Great is said by Eusebius to have ordered fifty copies of the scriptures to be made on vellum for the Patriarchal library in his new city.[1] This enormous undertaking was probably carried out at Caesarea, and there is a possibility that the Codex Sinaiticus and the Codex Vaticanus were rejected copies from this order; they are full of errors which suggest copying by dictation and in haste.[2] Shortly afterwards, *c.* 350, S. Jerome is describing how papyrus volumes in the library at Caesarea which had been damaged were replaced by vellum copies.[3] And about the same date, Themistius describes the foundation of the new academic library at Constantinople, for which the texts were transferred from rolls to codices.[4]

By the fifth and sixth centuries Byzantine scriptoria were beginning to produce finely bound and illuminated manuscripts on vellum. The famous purple codices date from this period; they were portions of scripture written on purple vellum in gold or silver ink. About this same time Cassiodorus in his *Institutiones* was describing the codices in the Vivarium library in Southern

[1] Eusebius *Vita Constant.* 3. C. H. Roberts, *op. cit.*, p. 201.

[2] T. C. Skeat, 'The Use of Dictation in Ancient Book Production' (*Proc. of the British Academy*, XLII). But see C. H. Roberts, *loc. cit.*

[3] *Ep.* 14

[4] C. H. Roberts, *op. cit.*, p. 202.

Italy. He tells for example how he arranged for S. Jerome's Bible to be copied in a small hand on fifty-three gatherings of six folios each (i.e. 636 pages), so that the compactness of the writing might shorten the length of the copious text.[1]

In addition to the fact that parchment can be folded many times into quires without damage, its durability in a damp climate renders it infinitely superior to papyrus for book-production. Martial and the other Latin writers are full of references to the damage that rain and damp can do to papyrus; a shower will destroy it beyond recognition, and to try to store rolls in a damp room was fatal. It is apparent that rolls had to be constantly re-copied if they were to be kept in good condition in a wet climate.

Parchment could of course be employed in roll form, and where parchment was comparatively cheap (i.e. where cattle and goats were plentiful, as in Syria and Palestine) this method has been employed from very early times. Most of the Dead Sea Scrolls were of parchment, though a few were of papyrus, and one (evidently intended for special preservation) was on copper sheets riveted into an eight inch strip. This proved in fact less durable than parchment, for the copper had oxidized and could only be deciphered by cutting it into small pieces. The roll form has, however, advantages for certain special types of document, and all through the medieval period it continued in use for cartularies, legal documents, records of court proceedings, for accounts, for annals, pedigrees and genealogies and sometimes for music, carols or hymns. Where matter of this kind has to be preserved in safety without too frequent consultation, and especially where it takes a tabular form rather than a continuous text, the parchment roll is still an excellent method. In England for example the Chancery rolls have proved a very durable and compact form of record. It should be noted that there are two main types of medieval roll: (1) the Chancery type, where the membranes are sewn together end to end, and (2) the Exchequer type, in which a pile of membranes, often of different sizes, is sewn together at one end and then rolled. In either case the text will be in one large column running the length of the roll. Its convenience for any material that requires arrangement in a long column is evident. For example, there is a pedigree roll, c. 1640,

[1] I. XII. 3; Jones' ed., p. 99.

of the Shirley family, thirty feet long, in the Staunton Harold archives at Leicester. At Bristol the city annals were recorded in the seventeenth century on parchment strips wound on a reel. Similarly the account by the fifteenth century antiquarian John Rous of the Earls of Warwick is on parchment rolls in both its versions (the Lancastrian version in English and the Yorkist version in Latin).

Still another and perhaps rather unexpected use of the roll form was for actors' parts on the Elizabethan stage. Only one actor's part has survived, that of Orlando Furioso in Greene's play of that name. It consists of a long paper roll of strips pasted end to end, and written on one side only.[1]

We can now return to the papyrus roll, and to Greek and Latin literature in general, in order to discover whether some of those bibliographical features which seem to us an almost essential part of modern books had in any degree a place in contemporary texts of the classical period. In general we shall find that they have a very small part to play; it is perhaps mainly the vast quantity of modern books and the size of our modern collections that makes them seem necessary today. Nevertheless we may marvel at the amount of scholarly work which was carried out in classical times in the absence of most of our present bibliographical aids.

One serious difficulty was the lack of any method of quoting exact references; at least it may seem serious to us, though it probably did not trouble the scholars of the time unduly. As has already been mentioned, there was no page or line numbering, and the only form of text measurement was a completely artificial one known as the stichometric unit which was used to estimate the pay due to scribes and the completeness of their work. The στίχος was based on a hexameter line of sixteen syllables or thirty-six letters, and as the lines of prose in a papyrus roll were not much more than half of this, it served no other purpose at all. Under the Edict of Diocletian the scribe was awarded pay at the rate of twenty or twenty-five denarii per 100 στίχοι. Sometimes this unit was used to give an idea of the size of an author's output. Josephus for example described his work as consisting of twenty books and 60,000 στίχοι; and Diogenes Laertius stated

[1] W. W. Greg, *The Editorial Problem in Shakespeare*, 2nd ed., 1951, p. 46.

that Aristotle's works ran to 445,270 στίχοι.[1] Callimachus added a note to the entries in his bibliography to mark the number of στίχοι in each work, and some extant manuscripts give similar information, though only a few give marginal notes of the στίχοι in hundreds.

There are modern parallels to the stichometric system in the use of the em in printing as a measurement of lines and as the basis for reckoning the compositor's pay. Similarly at some medieval universities where professional scribes were employed, their work was checked by the division of the exemplar into *peciae* of strictly defined length. The *pecia* was a sheet of parchment derived from a single sheepskin, which could be folded into four folio pages or eight quarto pages, with two columns to the page,[2] sixty lines to each column, and thirty-two letters to each line.

This kind of measurement is of interest bibliographically, but it is of no use in citing references; and in the classical period the only method was to cite the number of the book in which the reference occurs. This limitation in fact persisted through the medieval period until paging in arabic figures became common. It is not always realized how much, not merely of mathematics and science but of our daily life, has depended on the introduction of arabic numerals, which came into use in Europe in the twelfth and thirteenth centuries.[3] Before Arabic paging became customary, medieval references usually cited the number of the book or chapter, with some key words to mark the passage. Thus Richard de Bury in *Philobiblon XIII* quotes Gratian: *Scribit tamen sic distinctione 37, Turbat acumen.* For the same reason indexes with paged references scarcely appear till Renaissance times. A very few writers in the classical period give contents lists; the elder Pliny did so, and so also did Polybius, though in his case the list has not survived.

Nor were the titles recognized in the way they are today. Most titles were plain statements of the subject, often prefixed by *De* or περί; very few were deliberately chosen for effect. If a

[1] O.C.D. *s.v.* stichometry.

[2] C. H. Talbot, in Wormald and Wright, *The English Library Before 1700*, 1958, pp. 67–8.

[3] The use of the abacus persisted into medieval times mainly because of the difficulties of calculation in Roman figures; and for the same reason Alcuin's pupil, Hrabanus Maurus, felt it necessary to teach his clerks to count up to a million on their fingers.

work carried a title, it was often hidden in the form of a colophon at the end of roll; and stored rolls bore an identifying label of some kind. Often however in the absence of a recognized title the first words of the text were used; thus *Arma virumque* stood for the Aeneid, and *Aenadam Genetrix* for Lucretius' *De rerum natura*.

Bibliographies as part of a historical or scientific work were rare. Most writers who relied on earlier material regarded their own compilation as superseding their sources, so that references to sources were deemed unnecessary. Vitruvius and the elder Pliny acknowledged their sources conscientiously, and Plutarch was at pains to compare the value of his various authorities. A few others, such as Arrian, Dionysius of Halicarnassus and Diodorus Siculus, quote some of their authorities; and a few biographers such as Diogenes Laertius give very rough bibliographies of their subjects. The fullest bibliographies were probably the Alexandrian and Pergamene πίνακες; and there were of course many Byzantine works of reference such as *Suidas*, though by modern standards the lists are vague, and they often break off with καί τ'ἄλλα, etc. One of the Oxyrhynchus fragments[1] is a piece of a roll giving a bibliography of Menander which is exceptionally systematic and complete. It lists the plays in alphabetical order, with notes of the date of production, a resumé of the plot and a critical appreciation.

Dates of publication were rarely given. They would indeed have had less significance than they do under modern conditions. Revised editions during the author's lifetime were also rare; Cornelius Nepos and Strabo issued revised editions of their works.

There was in general no recognition of literary property or copyright. In a very few cases the need for an authorized text was realized. The Athenians maintained an official text of Aeschylus, Sophocles andEuripides, and the Peripatetics attempted to preserve an authorized text of Aristotle, though with limited success. In spite of this it is remarkable how close we can get to what was probably the original version of most classical texts: in general, the average text contains no more uncertainties than are found in Shakespeare.

[1] *Oxy. Pap.* 10. 1235.

As there was no copyright law, there were no pirated editions in the strict sense of the term. In Roman Imperial days however there are slight signs of a gradual recognition of literary property. Suetonius,[1] in describing the development of grammar after Crates, tells us that Servius Clodius stole a book written by his father-in-law, Lucius Aelius, before it had been published; he was disowned, banished, fell ill with gout and died: perhaps a rather harsh retribution. A passage in Seneca[2] suggests that a certain Dorus purchased the rights of Cicero's works from his heirs and from those of Atticus. There is a curious example of the rights of literary property in early Irish history. The departure of S. Columba for Iona was occasioned by a dispute as to the copyright of a psalter belonging to Finnian. S. Columba had secretly made a transcript of this manuscript, and Finnian appealed for redress to King Diarmaid. The king gave his ruling that a copy belongs to the original as a calf to the mother cow. S. Columba was not unnaturally incensed at this judgment and raising his clan he attacked and vanquished the king. Unfortunately an Irish synod excommunicated and banished him from the country on account of his aggressive instincts. The saint sailed northwards till he was out of sight of Ireland, carrying the disputed copy with him. But his exile has been doubted, as he returned freely to Ireland at a later date.

From copyright it is a natural step to censorship. Such censorship as existed in classical times was a question of expediency—usually political expediency.[3] Writers who offend the ruling power must expect interdiction, but the penalty sometimes fell on their persons rather than on their books. The story which Diogenes Laertius tells of the trial of Protagoras and the burning of his books in the agora in 411 BC is generally regarded as an invention. When Alexander died, Aristotle deemed it wise to hand over his school to Theophrastus and retire to Chalcis, but his writings suffered no harm. The only writer at the Alexandrian court who was so rash as to express disapproval of the marriage of Ptolemy Philadelphus with his sister Arsinoë (who had already been married to his half-brother) was the poet Sotades of Maronea.

[1] Suet. *De Gram.* 3.
[2] Seneca *De Beneficiis* 7. 61.
[3] There is no parallel in classical history to the moral censorship and deliberate indoctrination which Plato proposed for the 'guardians' in *The Republic*.

His fate was swift: prison, an escape, re-capture, thrusting alive into a leaden coffin and dropping into the Mediterranean. Ovid's banishment from Rome was due as much perhaps to political expediency as to any lapse of good taste in the *Ars*; but the *Ars* remained in circulation although it was rejected by the new Augustan public libraries. The Senate ordered the burning of the works of two Augustan orators, Titus Labienus and Cassius Severus, both masters of bitter invective; the former refused to survive his books and committed suicide, but the latter was exiled.[1] In later days Caligula restored their books to circulation. Suetonius recounts similar action by various emperors. Tiberius suppressed the works of a contemporary historian. Caligula, not to be outdone, contemplated the suppression of Homer, Virgil and Livy. Domitian had two books burned in the forum and executed several writers who offended him; one of these was the orator Hermogenes of Tarsus, and in his case his publisher also suffered the same fate. The poet C. Lutorius Priscus, emboldened by the success of a poem on the death of Germanicus, wrote another on the death of Tiberius' son, Drusus, who was ill at the time. Unfortunately for the poet, Drusus recovered. But the poem had been given a premature recitation, and the Senate condemned its author to death.

With Diocletian the long history of burnings and counter-burnings of religious works first began on a considerable scale. The campaign of persecution which began in AD 303 included the destruction of Christian writings, of Manichaean writings in Africa, of the works of the Egyptian alchemists and the so-called 'ancient' books ascribed to Pythagoras, Solomon or Hermes— really, as Gibbon says, the pious frauds of more recent adepts. This indeed is the first authentic event in the history of alchemy; some of the banned works on this subject are still extant, and date back to the first or second century BC.

Although the normal view of censorship in Imperial Rome was essentially pragmatical, the justly famous passage in Tacitus' *Agricola* 2 on the activities of Domitian and on the dangers and results of literary censorship is a remarkable foreshadowing of the

---

[1] Montaigne refers to Labienus' fate in his essay on the *Affection of Fathers*, regarding it as the earliest instance of such action, and confusing this orator with the more famous owner of the same name who was Caesar's legate in Gaul.

modern view of the question. He was perhaps the first to understand that the banning of an undesirable book was the surest way of establishing its reputation.

The routine of book production in a library and scriptorium of the classical period is largely hidden from us. There are tantalizing glimpses in the letters of Cicero, but they tell us very little. Tyrannio was Cicero's librarian, and Cicero was lost in admiration of the way in which he re-organized his library and arranged his books. 'Since Tyrannio has put my books in order, it seems as though my home has acquired a new life; nothing is more delightful than those bookcases of yours now that my title labels display the books.'[1] *Pegmata* (wooden fitments) is the word here used for bookcases; there is no clue as to their appearance, but they were presumably some arrangement of pigeon-holes. Tyrannio employed one or two craftsmen for routine tasks; they were supplied by Atticus and were probably therefore skilled workers. They were described as *librarioli* or *glutinatores*,[2] and their duties included fastening together the sheets of papyrus, making title-labels ('*quos vos Graeci, ut opinor, σιλλύβους appellatis*') with special strips of parchment (*membranulam*), attaching these to the rolls, making the parchment covers for the rolls, and general repair work. 'Your men' (he tells Atticus) 'have made my library beautiful by making up the books and title labels.'[3]

But there is no direct evidence as to how the copying was done. Many of the volumes in Cicero's own collection, and in that of his brother Quintus, would have been bought either in the Roman bookshops or in Greece through his agent Atticus; one letter implies that Cicero was saving up his money to acquire Atticus' own collection to comfort his old age.[4] Such copying as was needed was doubtless done by Tyrannio and his assistants. But how was the copying organized in the larger libraries? A wealthy publisher and business man such as Atticus employed in his household a large and highly educated staff of readers and copyists (*pueri litteratissimi, anagnostae optimi et plurimi librarii*[5]),

---

[1] *Att.* 4. 8. The phrase *mens addita* as applied to Cicero's home suggests the metaphysical principle of logical order, and so some system of classification for his library.
[2] *Att.* 4. 4b.
[3] *Att.* 4. 5.
[4] *Att.* 1. 10. 4.
[5] Cornelius Nepos *Att.* 13.

and even all his footmen (*pedisequus*) were skilled at both tasks. The publishers and booksellers in the Argiletum would have been similarly equipped, though doubtless on a less luxurious scale. The great libraries of the ancient world however, such as Alexandria, Pergamon and Caesarea, which undertook editorial work and book-production on a considerable scale, must have had very large staffs of copyists. T. C. Skeat[1] examines the question how the copyists worked in such circumstances, whether taking down their material from dictation or transcribing individually from exemplars. Probably both methods were used, but it seems likely that individual transcription was the normal method, both in classical and medieval times. There are a very few cases where internal evidence suggests dictation, one being the Codex Sinaiticus. As suggested above both this and the Codex Vaticanus may conceivably have been rejected copies from the order for fifty vellum Bibles which Constantine gave to the library at Caesarea: a vast undertaking for any scriptorium, and one that was possibly carried out in a hurry. The wealth of evidence which has been collected on the classical and medieval habit of reading aloud while transcribing supports the view that individual transcription was much commoner than dictation.[2]

Chairs and tables were not common articles of furniture in the classical world, and copying was often done by placing the papyrus on the knee, which to us would seem an unnecessarily awkward method.

Evidence about library catalogues is limited almost entirely to the work of Callimachus at Alexandria. This was in effect a national bibliography of Greek literature, and it evidently survived as a standard reference work into Byzantine days. The only clue as to the form of entry lies in two extracts quoted by Athenaeus,[3] who refers for example to 'a book by Chaerephon catalogued by Callimachus under his heading of Miscellaneous (ἐν τῷ τῶν παντοδαπῶν πίνακι):

> Writers on banquets. Chaerephon. Dedicated to Shell [i.e. a parasite].

[1] T. C. Skeat, 'The Use of Dictation in Ancient Book Production', *Proc. British Academy*, XLII.

[2] J. Balogh, *Philologus*, 1926, 82; H. J. Chaytor, *From Script to Print*, 1945.

[3] Athenaeus, 244a, 585b.

Since you have bidden me. 375 lines'.

The last details are the incipit of the work and the stichometric entry. The other reference is to a work by Gnathaena, *Etiquette for Banquets*, which is placed in his Table III, Law. The most significant omission from these entries is the number of rolls occupied by the work. Both of course refer to short pieces which would not extend to more than a single roll. It is possible that where more than one roll was involved the number was given. It is noteworthy that an inscription from Rhodes which represents part of a library catalogue includes this information, and it does seem an essential item in a catalogue entry.[1] The entry in the Suidas lexicon identifies Callimachus' bibliography as *Tables of Eminent Writers with Bibliographies* in 120 volumes. There is no clue as to whether these were rolls or whether they had been transferred to codices, or whether indeed the work actually survived to the tenth century AD when Suidas was compiled.

Nor is there much evidence as to the arrangement of the entries in Callimachus, except that from various references in Suidas, Athenaeus and Diogenes Laertius it can be deduced that they were in seven main classes, viz. Dramatic poets, Epic and non-dramatic poets, Law, Philosophy, History, Oratory, Miscellaneous. Suidas gives the first volume as being a register of dramatic poets chronologically arranged. On the other hand the extract quoted above suggests a subject arrangement ('Writers on banquets') within the main class. S. H. Steinberg[2] states that the Alexandrian library was catalogued by the Incipits. There is no foundation at all for this theory, and in the quoted extracts the title and author heading precedes the incipit. Some combination of chronological and subject arrangement is indeed probable.

That the rival Pergamene library also sponsored a bibliography is confirmed by a brief reference to it in Dionysius of Halicarnassus.[3] It is also possible that the Suidas notice of the early Spartan poet Alcman refers to it.

There is no evidence of any similar catalogue at the other great library of the ancient East at Caesarea,[4] nor at any of the Roman

[1] See p. 63 *supra*.
[2] *Five Hundred Years of Printing*, 1955, p. 105.
[3] Dion. Hall. *De Dein.* I. 11.
[4] Eusebius included a partial catalogue in his lost *Life of Pamphilus*; see *Hist. Eccles.* 6. 32. 3.

libraries. The Latin word for πίναξ is *index*, though this also stands for a book-title. Quintilian in referring to the Greek elegiac poets states that it would be easy to draw up a list of them in a library, but this gives no clue to the arrangement of the Roman state libraries.

The need for an elaborate system of classification did not arise till the multiplication of printed books and development of scientific research turned knowledge into a tangled skein which no student could hope to unravel without such aids. The seven headings of Callimachus may well have been adequate at Alexandria, though there may of course have been subdivisions.[1] We can deduce from Vitruvius' story[2] of how Aristophanes of Byzantium produced a number of rolls from certain presses to prove his allegation of theft against the contestants in the poetry competition at Alexandria, that there was some sort of finding list available for this purpose, even though Aristophanes is said to have relied on his memory for this feat; it looks at least as though the rolls were produced without delay while the judges were deliberating. A reference in the *Historia Augusta*[3] implies that the presses in the Ulpian library at Rome were numbered serially (*in armario sexto librum elephantinum*) which may indicate some kind of classified arrangement. The only certainty about the Roman libraries however is that the Greek and Latin departments were separated.

The description Cassiodorus gives of his Vivarium library in the sixth century[4] suggests that he was feeling his way towards a system of symbols marked in red at the beginning of each volume to help students in identifying the many patristic commentaries. This is probably the first recorded instance of the use of classification symbols in Western libraries. Chinese libraries however had found the need for a classification system two or three centuries before the time of Cassiodorus. In AD 281 the opening of the tomb of a Chinese nobleman who had died six centuries

[1] They are indeed the same type of broad heading used in many medieval monastic libraries. See p. 151.

[2] Vitruvius, *De Arch.* 7 (Preface).

[3] *Script. Hist. Aug.*; Tacitus, 8. 1.

[4] See p. 129. This very elementary set of symbols may be compared to the elaborate system of about 400 symbols used by Bp. Grosseteste in compiling the subject index to his great concordance of patristic literature. See R. W. Hunt in D. A. Callus *ed. Robert Grosseteste Scholar and Bishop*, 1955, p. 123, and Bodleian Library Record IV, 241.

earlier produced a find of over 100,000 bamboo tablets; an important discovery, for they were inscribed with original texts which had escaped the tampering of later scribes and editors. The sorting and cataloguing of these tablets led to a classification system that is said to have been used in Chinese libraries ever since.[1]

Classical libraries escaped one problem that confronts the modern librarian—that of handling periodicals and serials. The only known periodical in the classical period was the Roman official gazette (*Acta*) instituted by Julius Caesar in 59 BC,[2] and continued for a considerable time under the Empire. It had no fixed title; indeed, knowing contemporary editorial habits we could not expect this. It was variously described as *acta populi, acta publica, acta diurna urbis, diurna actorum scriptura, diurna populi Romani, libri actorum*. Some authorities have distinguished two or three separate gazettes, one being the *Acta Senatus* (i.e. 'Hansard'), which may have been separate from the *Acta diurna*, but this is uncertain. Nothing is known of its format. Its contents included (a) the proceedings of the senate, edited by a senator appointed by the Emperor, (b) a law report transcribed by shorthand writers (*actuarii*), (c) imperial enactments, and (d) items of general news. Copies were available in bookshops, and some were sent to the provinces and to troops overseas; others were deposited in libraries. Both Tacitus and Suetonius relied on the *Acta* as a source of minor information. The only other historian who cites it is Vopiscus.[3]

The absence of newspapers and literary periodicals meant that writers had to seek other means of advertising their work. The common method both in Athens and Rome was the public recital. Pliny[4] discusses in detail the practice of giving recitals, not only of speeches, but of histories, tragedies and lyric poetry prior to publication; and he claims that this helps him in revising and polishing his text. He analyses his own practice as follows: (1) private revision, (2) reading aloud to two or three friends, (3) giving it to others to annotate, (4) discussing their criticisms, (5) a public recitation before a large audience. Elsewhere we find

[1] L. Carrington Goodrich, *Short History of the Chinese People*, 1948, p. 72n.
[2] Suet. *Div. Jul.* 20.
[3] Suet. *August.*, 36; Tac. *Annal.* 3.3; 5. 4; 12. 24; 16. 22; Vopiscus, *Probus*, 2. 1.
[4] *Ep.* 7. 9.

Pliny and Tacitus exchanging speeches for mutual comment.[1] In another letter[2] he writes that, as Tacitus' histories will be immortal, he would appreciate a place in them himself; with this object therefore he sends an item of news from the law courts in which Pliny himself figures, for in his opinion it was worth more attention than it was given in the *Publica Acta*. These letters are indeed revealing; more so perhaps than Pliny intended.

Some writers must have relied largely on their booksellers to advertise their books; Martial describes the bookshops in the Argiletum with their pillars plastered with advertisements (*scriptis postibus hinc et inde totis*), and the rolls stacked in pigeon-holes.[3] There is ample evidence that both Athens and Rome were well supplied with bookshops. A fragment of Eupolis[4] (*c.* 430 BC) refers to bookshops, and Socrates speaks of bookstalls in the market.[5] There is a story of how Zeno first met his teacher Crates, the Cynic philosopher, in an Athenian bookshop, where he had picked up a copy of Xenophon's *Memorabilia* and was browsing in it.[6]

The names of several Roman booksellers are known: the Sosii brothers, who published for Horace: Atticus, who published for Cicero; Tryphon, who issued Quintilian's books; and Secundus and Atrectus, who were among Martial's publishers. Strabo[7] complains of inferior booksellers in Rome who issued books that had not been properly corrected. The existence of a second-hand market is implied by Cicero,[8] and confirmed by Lucian.[9] There is evidence also for the spread of bookshops in the provinces. Pliny[10] noted with surprise that there were booksellers in Lugdunum (Lyons), and was delighted to learn that his own books were on sale there. Martial refers to bookshops at Vienne in Gaul,[11] and Aulus Gellius to similar shops at Brundisium.[12]

[1] *Ep.* 7. 20.
[2] *Ep.* 7. 33.
[3] *Ep.* I. 117.
[4] Eupolis fr. 304.
[5] Plato *Ap.* 26d.
[6] Diogenes Laertius 7. 2.
[7] Strabo XIII. I. 54.
[8] Cicero *Q. Fr.* 3. 4. 5.
[9] Lucian, *Adversus Indoctum*.
[10] *Ep.* 9. 11.
[11] *Ep.* 7. 88.
[12] 9. 4. I.

It remains to add some notes on the writer's raw material and tools in the classical period. Of all the various materials which have been used for written records in the history of Western civilization, the only kinds to achieve real importance from a bibliographical point of view have been papyrus, parchment and paper. Stone, lead and bronze were in common use for inscriptions intended to be permanent, and their study belongs to epigraphy rather than bibliography. Bronze and other metals were used for inscribed coins, and their study belongs to numismatics. Copper sheeting was used for one of the Dead Sea Scrolls, though it has proved more perishable than parchment. As has already been noted, wood, either whitened or waxed, was in common use for tablets, and for more permanent record in tablet form (e.g. for the *diplomata* granted at Rome to exservicemen), bronze plates were used. Ostraca (potsherds) were used, mainly in Greece and Egypt, for voting tablets, tax receipts and school notes. Linen was apparently used for archive purposes in Rome; the *libri lintei* according to Livy were registers of magistrates kept in the temple of Moneta. In Imperial times the *libri lintei* were amongst the archives stored in the Ulpian library.[1] Still other materials were in common use in the East: clay by the Babylonians, strips of palm leaf in Ceylon and India, and in China bamboo strips and silk, which were replaced about AD 150 by rag paper.[2]

Papyrus

The main authorities on papyrus are Theophrastus and Pliny. Theophrastus[3] describes the plant and its manifold uses, for fuel, carpentry, boatmaking, sails, mats, ropes and food as well as for writing material. The Egyptians, he says, chewed it uncooked, boiled or roasted, and elsewhere[4] they were indeed described as παπυροφάγοι. The stem is πάπυρος, the pith βίβλος. Pliny gives an account[5] of the manufacture of papyrus in all its various grades, and the relevant passages are printed by Kenyon.[6] The best grades

---

[1] Vop. *Aur.* 1. 7.
[2] T. H. Tsien, *Written on Bamboo and Silk*, 1962.
[3] *Hist. pl.* 4. 8. 2. Cf. the varied uses of bamboo described by T. H. Tsien, *op. cit.*, p. 103.
[4] Schol. Aesch. *Supp.* 761.
[5] *H.N.* 13. 11, 12.
[6] *Books and Readers in Ancient Greece and Rome*, 1951, pp. 121–5.

were *Augusta, Livia and Hieratica*: the cheapest, *Emporetica*, was used only for wrapping purposes, including the covers of rolls (though parchment was used to cover better quality volumes). The younger Pliny[1] speaks of the difficulty of writing on rough absorbent papyrus which produces blots; this might well be the 'Emporetica' grade. There are several references to the unhappy effects of rain or damp on papyrus,[2] and Vitruvius advises that the study and the library of a villa should face east, both for the sake of the morning light and to avoid decay through damp.[3]

The modern standard work on the manufacture of papyrus is N. Lewis, *L'Industrie du Papyrus*, Paris, 1934, and there is useful information in Rostovtzeff's *Social and Economic History of the Hellenistic World*, 3 v., 1941.

Parchment

Parchment was evidently a common writing material in the cattle-raising districts of Asia Minor and Palestine where skins were plentiful. Herodotus[4] says that the Ionians from a very early period called their books διφθέρας because they used skeepskin or goatskin in place of papyrus, which was scarce, and he adds that many of the barbarians (i.e. Persians) even now use parchment for writing. Diodorus Siculus states[5] that the Persian royal archives were on parchment in the time of Cyrus the Younger. There is little to support Varro's story (quoted by Pliny[6]) of the discovery of parchment at Pergamum as a substitute for the papyrus which the Ptolemies were unwilling to export for the use of the rival library; parchment must have been known there for a long time, and the Pergamene library may well have reverted to its use if there were difficulties in the way of importing papyrus; the story however lacks confirmation. The term *charta Pergamena* for vellum is not found earlier than Diocletian (AD 301), the classical term being *membrana*. The durability and flexibility of parchment was not apparently noticed by classical writers: Quintilian recommends it[7] especially for those with weak eye-

[1] *Ep.* 8. 15.
[2] e.g. Martial 3. 100.
[3] *De Arch.* 6. 4. 1.
[4] 5. 58.
[5] 2. 32.
[6] *H.N.* 13. 70.
[7] 10. 3. 31. See C. H. Roberts, *op. cit.*, p. 175.

sight, though wax is better for writing, as it is easy to correct mistakes. Martial also implies that reading wax tablets is a strain on the eyes.[1] Parchment seems to have become the accepted medium in the East earlier than in the West. S. Augustine, early in the fifth century, found it necessary to account for his use of parchment for a letter, owing to the lack of papyrus and the absence of his tablets;[2] it is curious that any apology was needed at this date. Sidonius Apollinaris was still in the fifth century AD writing his odes on papyrus, though vellum codices were familiar in the villa libraries of Gaul in his day.[3]

Writing Instruments

A series of epigrams in the Anthology[4] specifies the various tools needed by the writer. These include: (1) the leaden disc ($\mu\acute{o}\lambda\iota\beta os$) for ruling lines; (2) the sponge ($\sigma\pi\acute{o}\gamma\gamma os$, 'flower of the sea') for erasing on papyrus. Erasing on parchment was done with a scraping knife;[5] (3) pumice ($\kappa\acute{\iota}\sigma\eta\rho\iota s$) for smoothing papyrus and for sharpening reed pens; (4) the pen ($\kappa\acute{a}\lambda\alpha\mu os$) made from reed stems. The quill pen (*penna*) came into use in the sixth century AD, and Isidore distinguishes between the two kinds; (5) the penknife ($\gamma\lambda\acute{\upsilon}\phi\alpha\nu ov$ or $\sigma\mu\acute{\iota}\lambda\eta$); and ink ($\mu\acute{\epsilon}\lambda\alpha\nu$). To these must be added the stilus for writing on wax, with its reverse end flattened for erasing. In another epigram[6] Palladas describes how Nature, honouring the laws of friendship, invented instruments whereby parted friends can converse: pen, paper, ink, handwriting, symbols of the soul that sorrows far away. Palladas was an impoverished dominie in Alexandria, *c.* AD 400; in another epigram[7] he cries that he is giving up teaching and selling the tools of the muses ('$\acute{o}\rho\gamma\alpha\nu\alpha$ $Mov\sigma\acute{a}\omega\nu$), the books that brought him only lamentation and woe.

Ink

Pliny[8] distinguishes between (1) *atramentum* (carbon ink

[1] *Ep.* 14. 5.
[2] Kenyon *op. cit.*, p. 118; Migne, *P.L.* XXXIII, 80.
[3] Sidonius *Carmen* 9. 9. 11.
[4] *A.P.* 6. 62–68, 295.
[5] *Jeremiah* 36. 23. Martial (*Ep.* 14. 7) refers to parchment specially prepared for erasing.
[6] *A.P.* 9. 401.
[7] *A.P.* 9. 171.
[8] *H.N.* 35. 25.

resulting from the combustion of resin or pitch or pine, mixed with gum or glue, and sometimes adulterated with soot; (2) *indicum*, which can stand for both Indian ink and indigo; and (3) *sepia*, obtained from cuttle-fish. Atramentum could be preserved, he adds, from mice (which apparently found it edible) by the addition of wormwood.

The ink commonly used on papyrus was a mixture of three parts of lamp-black or carbon and one part of size; a stable compound chemically, but sensitive to damp and easily sponged out while wet.[1] For parchment a solution of oak galls and iron, not always stable chemically, was employed.[2] Ink made from oak galls has however been identified on the papyrus fragments at Herculaneum, though there are no literary references to its use before Philo of Byzantium in the second century BC. It is generally supposed to be difficult to write on parchment with atramentum, but the ink used on the Dead Sea scrolls of parchment is of a carbon composition, and has proved durable, with very little fading. Inkwells in the nearby scriptorium contained traces of carbon ink.[3] Coloured inks came into use in post-classical times, and *rubrica* came to signify a title or heading painted in red. The purple ink used for imperial signatures was *encaustum*.[4]

The Making of books

Our information about the appearance of the finished papyrus roll and its ornamentation comes from the Augustan poets and from Martial; and one has the impression that they are describing what we should call de luxe editions, rather than the popular everyday format. Tibullus[5] pictures his ideal volume as a roll of snow-white papyrus of fine quality, its surface polished smooth with pumice (which suggests that good papyrus was stronger than might be imagined), and bound with golden vellum; the title will be engraved on the top edge of the papyrus, and the knobs (*cornua*) will be painted in colour. Extant papyrus is

[1] Sidonius (*Ep.* 9. 16. 15) complains that in the frosty winters of Gaul it tended to congeal on his pen.
[2] E. H. Minns in *O.C.D.*, s.v. Palaeography.
[3] J. M. Allegro, *The Dead Sea Scrolls*, (Pelican, 1956).
[4] For further discussion of inks see W. H. Langwell, *The Conservation of Books and Documents*, 1957. On Chinese ('Indian') ink see T. H. Tsien, *Written on Bamboo and Silk*, 1962, pp. 164 ff.
[5] 3. 1. 7.

yellowish. It was doubtless whiter when new, but probably not snow-white. The verso was sometimes dressed with oil of cedar or juniper to give it a golden tint. The title could be written in red, and the vellum cover was often purple.[1] Martial complains[2] of the uses to which unsold copies were put: cooks found them handy for wrapping fish and groceries, and schoolboys used the verso for their exercises. If a wealthy patron can be secured however, the reputation of the book is made; it can be turned out in a fine edition, anointed with cedar oil, tricked out with decorated endpapers[3] and painted bosses, bound in fine crimson (*purpura*) and with its title in glowing scarlet.[4] Ornate volumes such as this are distinguished from everyday bindings (*cotidiana*); one of Martial's fine books had been sent to Domitian's secretary, Parthenius, and he appeals for its return unopened: *libros non legit ille sed libellos*, he reads official documents, not books.[5]

This study of the background of classical bibliography is intended merely to supplement and illustrate the important and valuable work of Kenyon and the other authorities in this field. Bibliography has still scarcely achieved the status of an exact science, though that it has pretensions towards this will be evident from a study of the work of some of its modern practitioners. No such claims could have geen made for it in classical times; indeed it did not then exist as an organized body of knowledge at all, and it is only from scattered and casual allusions that we can guess something of the way in which their books were put together and collected and used. If there had been more contemporary interest in bibliography, doubtless our knowledge of classical literature would have been vastly greater; a good deal of our ignorance is due to practices that we should now regard as slovenly from the bibliographical point of view. The classical writers had an all-embracing interest in the end they were pursuing, and a very slight interest in the means that led to it. The expansion and specialization of knowledge in modern times and the mass-production of books, has led us to value the means more highly than the ancients did; sometimes more highly than the

[1] Ovid *Tristia* I. I. 5; 3. I. 13.
[2] *Ep.* 3. 2; 4. 86; 13. I.
[3] *Et frontis gemino decens honore.* Both ends of the roll were decorated.
[4] *Et cocco rubeat superbus index.*
[5] *Ep.* II. I. *Libellus* in this sense stands for a pamphlet, official report or similar work.

end in front of us. The passage of time has in fact seen to it that, in spite of their unawareness of the importance of bibliographical method, we have in fact lost very little that really matters of the work of classical writers. Thanks largely to the scholars and editors of the Alexandrian and Byzantine libraries, the cream has on the whole survived, and by and large the things that have been lost are those of less value and significance; so that on balance we may perhaps feel grateful, remembering that however interesting the means may be, it is the end that counts.

CHAPTER VII

Cassiodorus Senator

IN the eighties of the fifth century, three men were born whose
influence on our life and culture for the next thousand years
and more has been profound. All three came of Italian aristocratic families, and two of them provided the strongest links that
bound medieval Christianity with the heritage of pagan Rome.
One was Boethius, whose *De consolatione*, even though it is basically a reversion to paganism, had a continuous influence on
Western thought down to the Renaissance and beyond. The
second was S. Benedict, who transferred his monastic community
from Subiaco to Monte Cassino somewhere about AD 520. Here
after prolonged study of monastic traditions he published the
original edition of the famous Rule, *c.* 526. It spread throughout
Christendom with quite remarkable rapidity, being known and
quoted within a very few years of this date in Constantinople,
Africa and Gaul, as well as in Italy. The third was Cassiodorus,
the founder of the Vivarium.

Cassiodorus Senator—this was a personal name, not a title—
was born *c.* 487 at Squillace in Southern Italy, where his family
had been distinguished landowners and statesmen for at least three
generations. He held all the offices of state from Quaestor to
Praetorian Prefect, and served the Ostrogoth emperor Theodoric
as his chief adviser, aiming to preserve peace in Italy, and to build
a new Italian nation from a blend of Latin and Goth. On the other
hand Boethius, with the support of his father-in-law Symmachus,
and of scholars such as Priscian in Constantinople, was working
not merely for the revival of the true Roman traditions, but for
the reconciliation of East and West, Roman and Greek. The two
aims were thus in conflict.

Cassiodorus's magnum opus was his *Gothic History*, now surviving only in the epitome made by Jordanes. He began this great
work to please the Emperor Theodoric, who died in 526, and by

533 he was being recognized as an authority on the subject. In 535 he made his unsuccessful attempt, in co-operation with Pope Agapetus, to found a Christian university in Rome, on the pattern of the university that had flourished for so long a period in Alexandria, or of that which the Jews had established at Nisibis. The project got no farther than the establishment of a library, which according to one account was destroyed in the capture of Rome in 546, but according to another survived to the end of the century; in the latter event, the library destroyed in 546 might possibly have been the Ulpian library. This was a critical period for academic foundations in the West. Universities were beginning to give way to monasteries as centres of education, just as in a later age at the coming of the friars monastic schools gave place to the new universities. In the sixth century, Monte Cassino and Vivarium succeeded, where the Roman university failed.

During the next few years, c. 538, Cassiodorus gave up his official position as Praetorian Prefect, and turned increasingly to religion. He published his long and detailed *Commentary on the Psalms*, which was at once an encyclopaedia of all knowledge and a demolition of all the heresies from which orthodoxy had suffered; his elaborate treatise on the soul, the *De Anima*; and his collection of state papers and official correspondence known as the *Variae* which reveal his attempts to give to Gothic barbarity the dignity of Roman dress.

In 540, when Ravenna was captured by Belisarius, he went with the defeated general Vitiges to Constantinople. There he seems to have remained for fourteen years, and to have attained a position of influence. He revised his *Gothic History*, modified it to suit the new situation and continued it up to 551, when the Italian exiles in Constantinople were still hoping for a restoration of Romano-Gothic Italy. This hope was proved vain by the complete extermination of the Ostrogoths under Narses in 555–562. Cassiodorus returned to Squillace about 554, at the age of sixty-seven, and devoted the rest of his life to the conversion of his ancestral home into a monastic establishment where he could realize the ideals he had first set before him thirty years earlier in planning a Christian university in Rome.

The relation between Monte Cassino and the Vivarium is obscure. There is nothing to suggest that S. Benedict knew

Cassiodorus; he died *c.* 553–5, probably before the Vivarium was founded. There is internal evidence, however, that Cassiodorus was familiar with S. Benedict's *Rule*; it was indeed widely circulated in Christian circles, and he could hardly escape some knowledge of it. Indeed it would be surprising if he had not himself visited Monte Cassino on his journeys between Ravenna and Squillace. It must be remembered that the *Rule* was not designed merely for the community at Monte Cassino, but was intended to be of universal application within the Church, and to codify and regulate the practice and discipline in religious houses everywhere. S. Benedict did not himself found an order, so much as a code of laws which became the foundation stone of all later Benedictine tradition, and indirectly also of most of the other great orders. The fact that this tradition carries his own name, and that his *Rule* implicitly if not explicitly enjoins the tasks of copying, reading and study as part of the daily labours of the monks, may cause us to forget the contribution of Cassiodorus to the intellectual vitality of the tradition. The original *Rule* was not intended primarily for a community of scholars. The community following the *Rule* was, however, intended to be self-contained, and there was to be everything necessary for the well-being of the community within their enclosure, including 'water, mill, garden, bakery and diverse arts' (c. 66) to avoid the need for monks to go wandering outside, this being bad for their souls. The *artes diversae* probably comprised all the crafts connected with the maintenance and decoration of the buildings as well as the work of the scribes. The copying of books is not directly mentioned, any more than the other customary tasks which were generally accepted; but it is implied by the injunctions regarding daily reading and instruction in sacred learning. Dom John Chapman suggests that every monk would probably copy a book for his own use; some would copy books for the use of others; and a few would be expert calligraphers to write in fine uncials for the Church. Others again would teach the younger monks, and some might teach the *rustici* or their children.

The emphasis in Cassiodorus is different and the interest in the written book much more explicit. E. K. Rand has pointed out that it was Cassiodorus who made both sound learning and the copying of books a definite part of monastic discipline; and it was he who, above all others, saved the ancient Latin authors and the Fathers of the Church for the Middle Ages. It was he, moreover, who provided for the earlier monastic institutions the bibliographical guide that they needed for the organization of their libraries and scriptoria, in the shape of his *Institutiones* and *De Orthographia*, which describe in detail the practical work and the purpose of the community at Vivarium.[1]

Squillace lies on the south-eastern coast of the toe of Italy. Its ancient name was Scylaceum (the *nauifragum Scylaceum* of the Aeneid). There is a charming account of the district in George Gissing's *By the Ionian Sea* (Chapman and Hall, 1901). He describes Cassiodorus as 'the delightful pedant, the liberal statesman and patriot, who stands upon the far limit of his old Roman world and bids a sad farewell to its glories', and adds that one winter in Devon he had with him 'the two folio volumes of his works, and patiently read the better part of them; it was more fruitful than a study of all the modern historians who have written about his time. I saw the man; caught many a glimpse of his mind and heart, and names which had been to me but symbols in a period of obscure history became things living and recognizable'.

The village of Squillace is perched on a hill some miles inland, and a painting of it serves as a frontispiece to Gissing's book. There is a railway station on the coast, but Gissing decided to approach it by road from Catanzaro. On his left was the long flat-topped mountain, 'steep, dark and furrowed with innumerable torrent beds', the Mons Moscius of old time which sheltered Cassiodorus's monastery. Along the valley ran the yellow torrent of Pellena which Cassiodorus himself described—'a fishing stream which you should not regard as dangerous because of the size of its waves, or contemptible because of their smallness'.

---

[1] The standard edition of the *Institutiones* is by Professor Mynors (Oxford, 1937). There is a translation by L. W. Jones, *Introduction to divine and human readings* (Columbia University Press, 1946). Both have important introductions and the Index auctorum in Mynors gives a useful idea of the scope of the Vivarium library. See also van de Vyver, *Cassiodore et son oeuvre*, in *Speculum*, 1931, VI, pp. 244–92, and *Les Institutiones de Cassiodore et sa fondation à Vivarium*, in *Revue bénédictine*, 1941, LXIII, pp. 59–88; and E. K. Rand, *The New Cassiodorus* in *Speculum*, 1938, XIII, pp. 433–47; also Professor Momigliano, *Cassiodorus and Italian culture of his Time*, in *Proc. of the British Academy*, XLI (Italian Lecture, 1955). The latter has a very full bibliography. George Gissing's *By the Ionian Sea*, 1901, should not, of course, be overlooked. For S. Benedict, see especially Dom John Chapman, *S. Benedict and the 6th Century*, 1929.

Cassiodorus used its water to irrigate his gardens and drive his mills, to furnish his fishponds and to fill the bathing pools that he provided for the sick and infirm. 'But these matters,' adds Cassiodorus apologetically, 'are pleasures of the present, not a future hope of the faithful. The former are transitory; the latter will abide without end. But placed as we are, let us be brought rather to those desires which make us reign with Christ.' Some of the MSS contain a coloured drawing of the monastery, with its two churches of S. Martin and S. Januarius, and its ponds filled with fish.

Gissing found the valley heaped with blocks of granite, for here the limestone of the Apennines gives way to the granite mass of Aspromonte in the toe of Italy. The vegetation was scanty —little but thin orchards of olive. Has it changed so greatly, he asks, or did its beauty lie in the eyes of Cassiodorus, for whom it always represented home? Squillace itself Gissing found to be a small place, an 'unpaved street of squalid hovels', ankle deep in flood water. Its 'albergo Nazionale' was a one-storey cabin with a row of four or five windows, a filthy kitchen and a dining-room which also served as a bedroom. Here he was confronted by a dish of *peperoni* and a stew of pork and potatoes, which latter defeated him (it smelt abominably and was as tough as leather) and an undrinkable wine. The village impressed Gissing as the most ugly and repulsive collection of houses he had ever seen; the people had a dull, heavy aspect, and it was full of lean, black pigs and gaunt, low-spirited dogs. Scylaceum must indeed have been a different sort of place from the Squillace of today.

The monastery itself lay under Mons Moscius (now called Coscia di Staletti), and not far from the sea coast. All the land about here had belonged to the family of Cassiodorus for many generations. It was famous for its horses, and Theodoric had obtained his cavalry mounts there. The monastery was in two parts, consisting of coenobites and anchorites. At the foot of the mountain was the headquarters, where Cassiodorus and his *carissimi fratres* lived in community. Far above this was another retreat, Castelliense, designed for those monks who, preferring a severer discipline, chose to become anchorites and to enjoy the *'montis Castelli secreta suavia'*, the solitary sweetness of Mount Castellum. Today, high on the mountain, stands the church of

S. Maria de Vetere, whose name may point to the site of Castelliense.

For manual work in farm and garden Cassiodorus depended on a third class of monks, more cold-blooded, as he describes them, quoting the *Georgics*:

Frigidus obstiterit circum praecordia sanguis

or as Gissing less kindly calls them, the hopelessly stupid. Cassiodorus comforts these pleasantly with a verse from the Psalms: 'Thou shalt eat the labour of thy hand: happy shalt thou be, and it shall be well with thee,' and with another verse from the *Georgics*, 'Let my delight be the country and the running streams amid the dells'. For these weaker brethren he carefully added to the library appropriate textbooks: Gargilius Martialis *De hortis*, Columella *De re rustica* and Aemilianus on agriculture in twelve books.

The coenobitic part of the Vivarium was not without its comforts. Bathing pools were built for the sick. (Heathendom, says Gissing, had been cleaner, but we must not repine.) For them too and for pilgrims special food was provided—young pigeons, delicate fish, fruit and honey. A new kind of automatic lamp was invented which burned brightly without human attendance, the oil presumably being supplied by gravity. Sundials and clepsydras were provided to mark the hours by day and night. These served 'to summon the soldiers of Christ, warned by most definite signs . . . to the carrying out of their divine tasks as if by sounding trumpets'.

Gissing also explored a grotto by the seashore, said to have been one of the caverns used by Cassiodorus as a fish preserve. The fish ponds were used to trap both sea and river fish, and were constructed so that the fish swam into them unwittingly, not realizing that they were captive, thus providing a constant supply of food for the brothers. He looked also up the valley at the Fontana di Cassiodoro, still so called, and wondered by what strange chance the name had survived. That a vague memory still lingers in the locality was made plain when Gissing mentioned the name to a railwayman, who burst into a roar of laughter. 'Cassiodorus! Ha, ha! Cassiodorus! Ha, ha, ha!' On his being pressed to explain his mirth, it transpired that it was solely due to delight at hearing a familiar name. There was simply a hazy idea that he was a man of times gone by. But how did Gissing know anything of him? From books, Gissing replied, including books written by the great man himself over a thousand years ago. This was too much for the incredulous railwayman. 'Did I mean to say that books written more than a thousand years ago still existed?' The idea, he implied, was past all reason; and so perhaps it is, like many another true idea.

This then is the situation of the monastery, scriptorium and theological school into which Cassiodorus turned his ancestral home, and where he spent the last years of his long life; and it was here he wrote the works that specially concern us: the *Institutiones divinarum et saecularium litterarum* and the *De orthographia*, which together with the *Etymologiae* of Bishop Isidore of Seville remained the standard bibliographical encyclopaedias for centuries.

The *Institutiones* is designed as a handbook and guide for the monks at Vivarium. The second part deals with the familiar *artes liberales* of the Romans: grammar, rhetoric, dialectic, arithmetic, music and geometry. The first part is concerned, however, with theology, and with the daily routine of the monks, and gives detailed instructions on the care of manuscripts, their revision and correction, and the production of copies. In the treatise *De Orthographia* Cassiodorus continued his teaching on the accurate copying of manuscripts. The *Institutiones* is in effect a bibliographical survey of the literature of the time, and it must have been used as such by countless succeeding monastic librarians. It is evidently based directly on the Vivarium library, and is thus an eloquent witness of the size and scope of that great library— certainly the richest collection that Christianity had yet produced in the West. For each subject of knowledge discussed, Cassiodorus explains and comments on the books he has provided in the Vivarium library. Some passages refer to the actual location of the books: 'for example *in armario supradicto octavo*, in the eighth press aforementioned I have left a commentary in Greek by John Chrysostom . . .'—exactly, for example, as the *Historia Augusta* in an earlier century located a book 'in bibliotheca Ulpia in armario sexto'. There seem to have been at least ten presses in all at Vivarium; the Greek MSS were all in the eighth press. There is no safe clue as to the size of the Vivarium library or its arrangement, except that the books were kept in presses, and that the eighth press was devoted to works in Greek such as the commentary quoted above. The *Codex Amiatinus*, which was written at Jarrow, shows in its frontispiece the prophet Ezra seated before a press containing the nine volumes of Cassiodorus's revision of S. Jerome's version of the Scriptures, and it has been suggested not only that this was the type of press used at Vivarium, but that in the original *codex grandior*, the figure of Cassiodorus himself appeared, this being changed to Ezra at Jarrow. The illustration is given the place of honour as frontispiece in Clark's *The care of books*, 1901, and is reproduced also by Diringer in *The illuminated book*, 1958.

The most fruitful estimate of the size of the library would be one based on the *Index auctorum* in Mynors' edition of the *Institutiones*. This suggests a collection of perhaps 300 works, some of which would, no doubt, be duplicated. It is worth noticing that Dom John Chapman estimated that if the community at Monte Cassino totalled 150 monks, a stock of three or four thousand books would have been required from the beginning, to provide sufficient reading material for the hours of study required by the *Rule*, which amounted approximately to 1,250 a year. It is, however, unlikely that any library of the period had as many separate codices as this.

Many of the books in the Vivarium were produced in the scriptorium under Cassiodorus' supervision, and elaborate instructions are given on the duties and responsibilities of the copyist. Of all manual tasks, Cassiodorus says, that of the copyist attracts me most. The scribe not only instructs his own mind but spreads the divine precepts far and wide: 'Every word of the Lord written by the scribe is a wound inflicted on Satan.' Cassiodorus is never at a loss for an etymological argument to drive home his teaching. Scribes are called *librarii*, he says, because they minister to the just scales (*libra*) of the Lord. Elsewhere he derives the word 'book' (*liber*) from the adjective meaning 'free', because before the invention of papyrus, books were made from bark removed and 'freed' from the tree. Cassiodorus notes carefully the textbooks in his library which, together with his own *De orthographia*, will guide the copyist in his grammar, spelling and accentuation; 'I have collected', he says, 'as many of these works as possible.' In addition he has trained a team of skilled book-binders, so that the outward appearance of his books may be beautiful and worthy of their sacred contents. Cassiodorus would have been familiar with the elaborate work of the copyists and binders in Constantinople, including no doubt, the famous biblical codices in gold or silver ink on purple vellum of which many still survive. There is no hint here of the puritanism which beset the iconoclasts a century later, nor of the need for economy which in an earlier century made it necessary for the Imperial Library at Nicomedia to use coloured vellum and gold leaf only with the express permission of the Emperor.[1] On this point Cassiodorus quotes the parable of the guest who had no wedding garment, and was bound hand and foot and cast into the outer darkness; the books in his library must be worthily clad. The Vivarium library contained a codex of sample bindings, so that the binders might choose in each case the style they preferred.

It has sometimes been suggested (e.g. by Abbot Butler in *Benedictine Monachism*) that the first members of S. Benedict's community were little more than farm workers and peasants, who at best were semi-literate. There is in fact nothing to support this; and it is plain that the monks at both Monte Cassino and Vivarium were educated men, drawn from middle-class or aristocratic families. The manual labour which, outside service hours, filled their lives, consisted of copying, binding and illuminating as well as perhaps carpentry and stonework. The agricultural and domestic work at both places must have been carried out by slaves and serfs. There were no rural schools in sixth-century Italy, and the serfs would have mostly been illiterate; they were accepted into a 'third order' by Cassiodorus, but were not admitted to the full religious life. As in later days, many of the first religious houses were founded by wealthy landowners on their own estates (the houses established by S. Gregory the Great and Paulinus of Nola as well as Cassiodorus and S. Benedict are examples), and it was natural for the menial work to be carried out at first by the staff of the estate. The monks themselves, however, were forbidden to work on the

[1] Thompson, *Ancient libraries*, 1940; Ante-Nicene Fathers 6, 158–161.

farms, except during harvest and other emergencies. At Vivarium there was certainly an inner circle of highly-educated men who were responsible for the literary output of the monastery: Epiphanius, who translated various theological commentaries and compiled a *Historia ecclesiastica tripartita* which continued Rufinus's edition of Eusebius; Mutianus, who translated S. John Chrysostom's commentaries on the Epistle to the Hebrews and a treatise on music; and Bellator, the almoner at Vivarium, who translated works by Origen and S. Clement of Alexandria and compiled many Biblical commentaries. Still another Vivarium publication was the great translation of Josephus's *Jewish Antiquities* in twenty-two books, which S. Jerome himself said that he could not translate on account of its size.

Special provision was, however, made for less accomplished monks who found reading and study difficult. Abridged versions of certain textbooks were compiled; for example, a work on rhetoric by Fortunatianus in three books was compressed into a short volume 'in order to overcome the reader's natural aversion to a complicated treatise and to concentrate on the essentials'. The works of Cicero and Quintilian on rhetoric were bound together, so that both were conveniently at hand for the student of that subject: a practice more convenient to the reader than to the librarian. Similarly translations of Aristotle by Cicero, Victorinus and Boethius were collected in a single codex. Gaps in the collection are sometimes noted; for example, it had not so far been possible to acquire a copy of Martianus Capella, but Cassiodorus hopes that his own *Institutiones* may serve as a humble substitute. One has the impression that the ordinary monk for whom the *Institutiones* was compiled, though fully literate, was not widely educated. Greek was unfamiliar to him, and he did not take easily to difficult or scholarly works. It was doubtless with such readers in mind that Cassiodorus followed the example of S. Jerome in arranging the Scriptures by *cola* and *commata*, that is, in sense lines to make them more easily understood by those who found punctuation difficult. S. Jerome states that he copied the method from MSS of Cicero and Demosthenes, but actually it already existed in the poetical works of the Old Testament such as the Psalms and Proverbs.

Although pagan learning was well represented on the shelves

of the Vivarium, especially in the technical field of the liberal arts, the greater part of the collection must have been theological. The inclusion of pagan texts is justified by the familiar (and quite proper) argument that they are not the least important means of teaching us how to understand the Scriptures. It was perhaps the size of the theological collection which led Cassiodorus to introduce a system of classification symbols in this subject: the earliest, I think, of which we have any detailed knowledge. To enable the student to identify more easily the many patristic commentaries, these are marked in red ink at the beginning of each codex with appropriate symbols. For example, commentaries on the Octateuch are marked OCT; on Kings, REG; on the Psalms, PSL; on Solomon, SAL; on the prophets, PROP; on the Hagiographa AGI; on the Gospels, EU; on the Epistles, AP; on the Acts and the Apocalypse, AAA. There is no direct reference to a catalogue of the library, but in this passage (I.26) the use of the word *indices* ('I have set down relevant symbols as indices for the codices . . .') may suggest a shelf list thus marked.[1]

Cassiodorus died at a great age, *c.* 583. The fate of the Vivarium and its library is a matter of guesswork. The last that is certainly heard of it is in 598, when the Bishop of Taormina was empowered by the Pope to defend the monks against an encroaching usurper. From that date onwards, Southern Italy became increasingly Greek in character and in fact. Greek influences came chiefly from Syria and Egypt, whence Greek monks fled after the destruction of Antioch and Alexandria, first to Sicily and then to Calabria. After the extermination of the Ostrogoths in 555–62, the country lay devastated and in ruins, and in 568 the Lombards invaded most of Italy without opposition. They did not, however, reach the toe of Italy, which remained under Byzantine control. Cassiodorus was a Roman, using the Roman liturgy and Latin texts, which must gradually have lost their importance in Squillace. In 732 the Greek rite was prescribed as obligatory in Calabria. From the ninth century Calabria suffered from continual raids by the Saracens, and in 1060 it was plundered by the Normans. In the thirteenth century a monastery dedicated to S. Gregory Thaumaturgos was established at Squillace.

The monastery of Bobbio, near Pavia, was founded in 612,

---

[1] Cassiodorus' symbols may be compared to those used by Bp. Grosseteste. See p. 110.

thirty years after Cassiodorus' death. It has been suggested without any good evidence that the pre-Columban books in the Bobbio library may have been brought from Vivarium, this being the only likely source for them in Italy other than the Papal library (destroyed in the time of Pope Agapetus), and the private collections of the Abbot Eugippius and the family of the Anicii, to which the nun Proba (whom Cassiodorus claimed as a relative) belonged. The descriptions given by Cassiodorus of his books are not sufficiently exact, however, to enable any of them to be identified with the books at Bobbio, and the theory of their transfer is not accepted today. All that we can say is that the *Institutiones* may well have served the librarians at Bobbio and elsewhere as a bibliographical guide.

There is some support also for the belief that certain of the Vivarium texts served as archetypes for copies made in the Carolingian period. Amongst these was, of course, the Codex Amiatinus, already mentioned. This was written at Jarrow under Abbot Ceolfrid (642–716). Bede tells of the many improvements which Ceolfrid made to the twin monasteries of Jarrow and Wearmouth, or rather (as he says) to the single monastery of S. Peter and S. Paul in its two separate places. Amongst these was the development of the library which Abbot Benedict had founded; under Ceolfrid's zealous care it was doubled in extent. The accessions included the three Pandects of a new translation which he had brought from Rome, that is, S. Jerome's Vulgate. Two of these were given to the two monasteries. The third was intended as a gift for the Pope, and in his old age Ceolfrid, having resigned his abbacy, set out for Rome with this gift, but his journey was never completed. He died soon after reaching the Lingones (Langres) on September 25, 716, and was buried there in the church of the three twin martyrs. The anonymous life of Ceolfrid states that some of his companions travelled on to Rome and delivered his gifts, including the Codex, to the Pope. There is, of course, no trace of the two copies at Jarrow, but the one delivered in Rome was the Codex Amiatinus. This came somehow into the possession of the Abbey of San Salvatore on Mount Amiator in Tuscany; and when this house was suppressed, its books were transferred to the Laurentian Library, where comparatively recently it was found that this great manuscript was not only English, but that it bore Ceolfrid's partly-erased name. It is more than likely that this Codex, which was one of the main sources of the revision of the Vulgate in 1590, was copied directly from the *codex grandior* which was edited by Cassiodorus from S. Jerome's Vulgate.[1]

Whatever the fate of the books themselves, the *Institutiones* survived as a bibliographical encyclopaedia throughout the Middle Ages. In particular, Book II on Secular Letters became a standard school textbook, along with Martianus Capella, Boethius, Priscian and Donatus, and many of the Vivarium publications appear frequently in medieval catalogues. It may be fairly said that the libraries of the Benedictine houses owed even more to Cassiodorus than to the precepts of their own founder saint.

[1] On the miniature of Ezra in the Codex Amiatinus, see R. L. S. Bruce-Mitford in *Evangeliorum Quattuor Codex Lindisfarnensis*, Vol. II, 1960, and *Times Literary Suppl.*, January 13, 1961. Both the Codex Grandior and at least two volumes of the *Novem Codices* of Cassiodorus (a Vulgate Bible in nine volumes) were in Northumbria at the end of the seventh century. It has been suggested that the portrait of S. Matthew in the Lindisfarne Gospels was derived directly from the Ezra miniature in the Codex Amiatinus. Mr. Bruce-Mitford concludes however that they are independent of each other, though based on a common archetype. The archetype is held to have been the frontispiece of the *Novem Codices*, where it represented both Ezra and Cassiodorus as well. The titles of the volumes in the armarium in this miniature have been identified by Dr David Wright by means of ultra-violet light, and have proved to be in the order of S. Augustine, which was followed by the *Novem Codices*. The Gospel Book (the seventh volume of the *Novem Codices*) is believed to have provided the portraits of the Evangelists in the Lindisfarne Gospels, while the text came from a Gospel Book from Naples.

A coloured reproduction of the Ezra miniature, together with a coloured reconstruction of the press at the Vivarium in use by a scribe appears in the *National Geographic Magazine*, December 1962.

CHAPTER VIII

The Religious Life and Learning

I. THE SOLITARY LIFE AND THE RISE OF LITERACY

THE corporate libraries and scriptoria of Western Europe owe their original inspiration to Cassiodorus and S. Benedict, but the spirit of individualism which is the mark of the ascetic life has roots that are wider and deeper than this. East as well as West contributed to the development of our monastic system, and its intellectual vigour sprang from the re-shaping of the ideals of Eastern asceticism by the organized Western Church, working within the framework of the Roman civil state. The intellectual achievements of the Eastern ascetics were considerable, and their transmission to Western Europe, particularly to Southern Gaul, served to modify the centralizing influences of the highly organized and urbanized Roman system. In this transmission the written word played the major part, and the contribution of individual books and corporate libraries to the shaping of the monastic system is thus beyond doubt.

In the fourth and fifth centuries, though imperial authority was tending to break up, the classical literature and traditions of Rome were still a living force in Gaul, and probably in the other Western provinces too. Here as elsewhere Roman civilization was an urban civilization, and the machinery of church government was being built in the pattern of Roman civil administration, with episcopal sees located in the centres of provincial government. The Gallic culture of the day, with the new religion happily embedded in a classical framework, is plainly visible in the pages of Sidonius Apollinaris and Ausonius; it is typified in the villa libraries described by Sidonius, with their classical and Christian sections side by side, much as the earlier imperial libraries of Rome had their Greek and Latin sections side by side.

The Benedictine Rule itself had eastern sources. The earliest were the rule of Pachomius at Canopus in Egypt, which had been translated by S. Jerome, and the *Longer* and *Shorter Rules* of S. Basil. Both regarded the corporate life as a higher ideal than that of the anchorites, because it encouraged the service of humanity, rather than pre-occupation with self; S. Basil's remark, 'If you always live alone, whose feet will you wash?' focuses the point neatly. Primarily, however, S. Benedict's source was John Cassian of Marseilles.

Cassian's birthplace is uncertain; possibly the Dobrudja, possibly Kurdistan. He was however well educated, and familiar with the Greek language. He entered a monastic community at Bethlehem *c.* 380, and about five years later went with his cell-mate, Germanus, to Egypt, where the ascetic movement had been flourishing for almost two centuries. There he met Evagrius, the Greek Origenist whose writings (condemned by Justinian and till recently believed lost) formed the most important statement of the intellectual basis of the ascetic theory. When the Origenists were expelled from Egypt in 399, Cassian went to Constantinople, where he was ordained deacon under John Chrysostom. After the fall of John Chrysostom in 404, he travelled to Rome, where he lived till the city was sacked by Alaric in 410. He then went to Marseilles, where he founded his twin monasteries, one for women and one for men, dedicated to S. Victor, and where he published his *Institutes* and *Conferences*. In these works he tried to adapt and temper the theory of Origenist asceticism to the conditions of Gaul. He did not however draw up a detailed code of practical rules, but contented himself with a series of instructions for beginners in the coenobitic life. Throughout his life, he regarded the corporate life of the monastery as a half-way house or training ground for the ultimate perfection of the solitary life. In this he differed from both S. Basil and S. Benedict. He never himself reached this ultimate perfection, regarding himself as only partly trained for the topmost rungs of the ladder. Always however he stresses the individualist approach, rather than that of corporate worship; the familiar versicle 'O God make speed to save us' began with Cassian as 'O God make speed to save *me*'.

The ascetic theory, with its concentration on the relationship of God and self and its indifference to the world around one, had its effect on the daily routine at Marseilles. There was no place in the scheme for creative intellectual activities. Work was simply a method of keeping idle hands occupied; no purpose behind the work was needed. Apart from ordinary domestic duties, repetitive tasks which did not distract the mind from the art of contemplation were preferred. Writing and reading are mentioned as manual tasks of this kind, but they served no higher aim. The monastic schools, libraries and scriptoria of later days could never have been built on this foundation.

S. Benedict and Cassiodorus knew and revered the work of Cassian and made explicit provision for the study of his *Institutes* and *Conferences*. The Benedictine Rule gave a detailed practical framework for Cassian's teaching, and added to it the idea of *stabilitas* and a carefully drafted constitution which would provide for the ordered continuance of the tradition through the generations. The idea of the solitary life as the ultimate goal was virtually rejected, and the emphasis on stability meant that observance of the Rule must be lifelong; life is too short for any monk to advance so far that he can dispense with the discipline and obedience of the corporate life. Moreover, both S. Benedict and Cassiodorus found a place in their scheme for the creative intellectual work which was to develop in the coming centuries as one of the glories of Western monasticism. Cassian's influence proved enduring, but only within the Benedictine framework; though for a time it served to give direction and guidance to the ascetic movement, especially in southern and central Gaul. S. Honoratus, Bishop of Arles, founded his famous community on the island of Lérins, off the coast at Cannes, *c.* 410 with the encouragement of Cassian, and this apparently included a number of hermitages to which senior monks could retire. However the strength of the ascetic movement in the West lay in the more remote and less urbanized districts further north, particularly in Brittany and in Ireland, where from the sixth century onwards it became a vigorous force for a long period, colouring the whole Celtic Church with its individualist approach to religion.

What was the source of the ascetic tradition in Ireland? Mrs Chadwick in her *Age of the Saints in the Early Celtic Church* (1961) answers this question as fully as the evidence allows; and the lack of contemporary written evidence means that some guesswork is inevitable. The intellectual achievements of the Egyptian and Syrian ascetics, of which Mrs Chadwick gives a detailed summary,[1] were outstanding, and they must have been the main source. In Ireland—a country with no urban life whatever, and lying outside the confines of the Empire—the standard of scholarship and culture was just as remarkable. There are no Irish library catalogues for the fifth or sixth centuries, but there is considerable circumstantial evidence for a direct or indirect connection between early Irish culture and that of Egypt and Syria. The most likely channels for such contact would be Aquitaine and Galicia, which are known to have had close relations with Ireland; and Mrs Chadwick concludes that it can only have been through the transmission of the written word in books that knowledge of the Eastern anchoritic discipline can have reached Ireland.

There is no evidence that Cassian's *Institutes* or *Conferences* reached Ireland before the seventh or eighth centuries.[2] A more likely immediate source is the strongly individualist tradition established by S. Martin, a native of Pannonia on the Danube, who after service in the army established his convent, consisting of a group of cells or caves, at Ligugé. He became Bishop of Tours *c.* 371, and died 397, leaving behind him a vigorous tradition of legends and miracles illustrating the ascetic life. In the following century, an eastern ascetic named Abraham escaped from captivity on the Euphrates and established a community of eremites at S. Cierges, and there are accounts of many hermits in central Gaul in the works of Gregory of Tours.

S. Patrick, who is believed to have received his training at Auxerre under S. Germanus and possibly also at Lérins, may well have been familiar with the work of Cassian and S. Honoratus, and must certainly have known the legends of S. Martin; indeed there is a possibility that he brought a copy of the *Corpus Martinianum* of Sulpicius Severus to Ireland. That S. Martin was well known in Britain is suggested by the dedication of at least two fifth-century churches to him at Canterbury and Whithorn; S. Ninian met S. Martin at Tours on his return from his pilgrimage to Rome, and the church at Candida Casa was built in his honour. In Ireland however S. Patrick introduced the Roman organization of territorial episcopacy, selecting Armagh for his

---

[1] *op. cit.*, pp. 37–60.
[2] Owen Chadwick, *John Cassian*, 1950, p. 201.

own see; there is no suggestion that he consciously set on foot an ascetic movement, though he may possibly have introduced the Celtic dating of Easter from Roman Britain.[1] The episcopal organization was overset in the sixth century, by the rapid spread of independent monastic communities, each dominating the surrounding district and tending to replace the episcopal sees, and many establishing schools and scriptoria, which gained them fame and literary pre-eminence. The most notable was perhaps the monastic school at Lismore on the River Blackwater in Munster, which became a centre of Latin studies in the seventh and eighth centuries and is known to have had close relations with Aquitaine and Galicia. The monastic and ascetic influence seems to have originated in the South, particularly in Munster, early in the fifth century; S. Patrick's influence took root in the North about the same period. The missionary spirit, as well as the ascetic, was strong in the Irish church, and in the sixth and seventh centuries its influence spread to Iona, Scotland and Northumbria, while S. Columban carried it to the Continent, founding his chain of monasteries in Burgundy and Switzerland, and at Bobbio in Italy.

If the wanderlust was distinctively Irish, the asceticism which claimed to justify it, whether native or not, must have been inspired or strengthened not merely by the tales of S. Martin and the hermits of Gaul, but more directly by Eastern models. There are so many correspondences between Celtic and Coptic art, and further study will doubtless produce more. Two in particular relate significantly to the practices of Irish scriptoria. The satchels in which Irish books were often kept bear a striking resemblance to the satchels still in use at the Abyssinian library which Robert Curzon describes and illustrates in his *Visits to Monasteries in the Levant*, ch. VIII; and there are indeed oriental motifs in the decoration on the satchel of the Book of Armagh. Moreover the normal Irish method of making up books in quinions (quires of five conjugate leaves) may well have had Coptic origins; there are similarities too in the intensely black carbon ink and the ink horns (made from the end of a cow's horn) used in both Irish and Coptic book production. If such relationships are valid, a direct connection between the Irish and Coptic

[1] *Medieval Studies presented to Aubrey Gwynn*, S.J., 1961, p. 14.

cultures is implied, rather than an indirect link through Southern Gaul.[1]

The arrival of S. Augustine in Canterbury and the death of S. Columba in Iona coincided in 597. S. Augustine was explicitly charged by Gregory the Great not only to convert the English but to secure Catholic unity in Britain. 'But as for all the bishops of Britain, we commit them to your care, that the unlearned may be taught, the weak strengthened by persuasion, and the perverse corrected by authority.' The Celtic perversity proved obstinate, and the inevitable clash between orthodoxy and individualism was not resolved till the Synod of Whitby, 663, when Colman, worsted by S.Wilfred's oratory but unrepentant, withdrew first to Iona and then to an island off the coast of County Mayo. Southern Ireland had already conformed; there had been direct contact with Rome earlier in the century. Northern Ireland remained obdurate till 697, and Iona till about 716. Conformity was however a gradual process, for there were many liturgical and administrative issues besides the date of Easter and the tonsure. Racial as well as religious independence was at stake.

The conflict had one significant result in Ireland. Under its stimulus the oral traditions of the Age of the Saints in the sixth century were during the seventh and eighth centuries committed to writing in the form of *vitae*, *acta*, penitentials and rules, in order to formulate the case for the defence. The new written traditions originated largely in the scriptoria of Tallaght and Finglas, the two monasteries on the banks of the Liffey, named the 'Two Eyes of Ireland'—eyes here replacing the ears of the oral tradition. In much the same way the oral traditions of the provincial and local kings, tracing their descent from Adam and Eve and their early migration from Spain, were committed to writing under the threat of danger, first during the Norman invasion in the eleventh and twelfth centuries, and secondly in the sixteenth and seventeenth centuries when the Gaelic social order finally collapsed.

If the ascetic movement answered a native and instinctive need in the Celtic Church, this would go far to explain its enduring vigour, and the enthusiasm which through the centuries led so

---

[1] W. G. Wheeler, *Libraries in Ireland before 1855*. (Thesis submitted for Diploma in Librarianship, University of London, 1957.)

many hermits to dwell in their caves or island sanctuaries, or to undergo that special form of ascetic discipline known as *peregrinatio*, which sent Irish scholars wandering over the Continent, to the distraction of orthodox teachers such as Alcuin and of Theodulf, Bishop of Orleans, who trounced them in bitter, though elegant, satire for their levity, their lack of dependability, and their quarrelsome habits.[1] This common feature of Irish asceticism was not a pilgrimage in the ordinary sense, but a withdrawal from one's home, a tearing up of one's roots, to live, not in a settled island or cave, but a peripatetic existence roaming over the face of the earth. This is what Adamnan had in mind, as Mrs Chadwick remarks, when he related how S. Columban left Ireland and *pro Christo peregrinari volens enavigavit*. This doubtless is what drove S. Columban across Western Europe, S. Brendan and his kind to the Shetlands, the Faroes, Iceland and perhaps even America, and that great scholar, John Scotus Erigena, to the palace of Charles the Bald.

The ascetic withdrawal, whether realized in an island sanctuary or in travelling abroad, was something more fundamental than any of the issues that were debated at Whitby. It is indeed one expression of that spirit of independence and impatience of external authority that distinguishes the northern races. S. Cuthbert in his dying words charged his monks to have no communion with the schismatics 'who err from the unity of the Catholic faith, either by keeping Easter at an improper time, or by their perverse life'. But he himself had judged it right to spend his last years in the island solitude of Farne, in 'his humble residence on a rock, where the waves of the ocean shut him out from all the world'. The traditions of Lérins, where such retirement was provided for, would have been well known in Northumbria. Benedict Biscop had taken his vows and received his training at Lérins, and when Wearmouth was founded he placed it under the Benedictine rule, based on the practice of seventeen monasteries he had visited in his travels. The 'large and noble library'[2] came from Rome, and he introduced the 'Roman mode of chanting, singing, and ministering in the church'. Bede, who

[1] Helen Waddell, *The Wandering Scholars*, 7th ed., 1934, p. 45.
[2] Estimated to amount to about two hundred volumes (Knowles, *Saints and Scholars*, 1962, p. 14.)

tells us this, was steadfast in his loyalty to the Roman order, but his heart was with the Celtic scholars, and there was a continual coming and going between Wearmouth and Ireland.

For our purpose, the importance of the ascetic approach to religion in the Celtic Church is that under the challenge of Roman orthodoxy it stimulated the formulation of oral traditions in writing; under the influence probably of scholars from Aquitaine it encouraged some measure at least of Latin studies, especially at monastic schools such as Lismore which had close contacts with Gaul in the sixth and seventh centuries; it gave birth to the discipline of *peregrinatio* which sent Irish scholars travelling to continental centres of learning; and not least it brought to life a literature rich in poetry which (as Mrs Chadwick says) 'speaks to us today with an urgency and a beauty against which there is no appeal'. And she adds that the most remarkable aspect of this Western asceticism is that, in addition to the formulation of rules and penitentials, it should also have produced 'a literature in which the individual personality develops and becomes articulate. Of all the early peoples in our islands these scholars and ascetics were the first to speak in the first person to us today, and the contact seems immediate. Is it because this is scholars' poetry— and all scholars, children of the Classics, speak the same language? —I mean, speak in the same kind of way? They understand one another'.[1]

The individual approach to religion continued as a force in its own right and as a stimulus to literacy and literature throughout the middle ages. The anchoritic life regained something of its earlier popularity between the twelfth and sixteenth centuries,[2] but the individual view found a different and a wider expression in an awakening of interest in personal religion among layfolk and in the spread of the cult of mysticism. Aelfric's lives of the saints, his translations from the Bible and homilies were composed early in the eleventh century quite definitely for laymen. The first real signs however of the new emphasis on individual and personal religion appear in the prayers, meditations and letters of S. Anselm, Lanfranc's pupil and successor at Canterbury, in whose

---

[1] N. K. Chadwick, *The Age of the Saints in the Early Celtic Church*, 1961, p. 161.

[2] Even Lanfranc, while still at Bec, was with difficulty dissuaded from a plan to become a solitary; this must have occurred at some personal crisis in his life, but no details of this survive.

hands medieval Latin became a new and living language, and in the teaching of S. Francis and S. Bonaventura.[1] Ascetic practice received fresh impetus by the foundation of the Cistercians, the Carthusians and the Carmelites. There were ten Carthusian houses in England, and most were late foundations, dating from the late fourteenth or early fifteenth century. They came at a time when there was, in lay as well as religious circles, a quite significant awakening of personal religion, marked not only by the growing number of anchorites and mystics, but by the extraordinary popularity of their writings. It is plain that this coincided with a new interest in reading amongst laymen, and especially amongst women of the more leisured classes.

As early as the thirteenth century, Matthew Paris' lives of S. Alban and other saints were written in Anglo-Norman verse for layfolk, and his own notes on a fly-leaf of one of these books suggest that they were of special interest to the aristocratic ladies whom he numbered in his circle of friends; but he deemed it advisable to illustrate them, copiously and skilfully with his own coloured drawings for the benefit of those who found reading difficult. The note implies that these ladies passed his books round amongst their friends from hand to hand.[2] By Chaucer's time the situation was changing, and a demand was arising for devotional works amongst the newly emerging middle classes. The famous mystics of the fourteenth and fifteenth centuries were the direct spiritual heirs of the mysticism of the early church—of S. Gregory of Nyssa, S. Basil, S. Macarius, Evagrius and the fathers of the desert, and of the pseudo-Dionysius. On the Continent the revived interest in mysticism is revealed in S. Bernard's *Sermons on the Canticle*, the work of the Victorines, Hugh and Richard (especially in Richard's *Benjamin Major* and *Benjamin Minor*), S. Bonaventura's *Itinerarium mentis ad deum*, the *Dialogue* of S. Catherine of Siena and in the teaching of the Dominican friars in the Rhineland.[3] But it was the writings of the English mystics and anchorites that circulated amongst English laymen and began to appear in the manors and merchants' houses

[1] The antithesis between learning law and organization on the one hand, and personal religion on the other, is well depicted in Prof. Knowles' short essay on S Francis (*Saints and Scholars*, 1962, pp. 86–98).

[2] Richard Vaughan, *Matthew Paris*, 1958, p. 170.

[3] For further study see David Knowles, *The English mystical tradition*, 1961.

of the fifteenth century. One of the most widely known was the Yorkshire hermit, Richard Rolle. Over 400 copies of his works are still extant (there are for instance fifty-four in the Bodleian, forty-nine in the British Museum and forty-four in the Cambridge University Library); and inventories and wills attest his popularity among laymen, especially in the north.[1] There are said to have been so many attempts by the Lollards to claim his authority by tampering with his writings that the nuns of the Cistercian house of S. Mary, Hampole, which was near his hermitage, kept the authorized versions of his books securely in 'chained bonds' in their library. Equally well known was Nicholas Love, the prior of the Carthusian house of Mount Grace at Ingleby in Yorkshire, and the author of the *Mirror of the Blessed life of Jesus* (c. 1410), which was a translation of the *Meditationes vitae Christi*, licensed by the Archbishop for reading by the devout laity and to the confutation of heretics or Lollards. It was probably the most popular book of the century, and it is written in admirable English: indeed R. W. Chambers claimed that Love did more than any other writer to provide a model for future writers of English prose.[2] Over 100 copies have survived, twice as many as of *Piers Plowman* or the *Confessio Amantis*, for example, and twenty more than the *Canterbury Tales*.[3] The *Scala Perfectionis* of Walter Hilton, the Augustinian canon (d. 1496) has maintained its popularity to the present day. Dame Juliana's 'Sin is behovely, but all shall be well and all shall be well, and all manner of thing shall be well' must have comforted many men and women of fifteenth-century England; and though only one complete copy has survived, the story of Margery Kempe's pilgrimages and religious experiences, dictated to two clerks in her old age, may well have found a place on many lay bookshelves. There were others of course: the *Cloud of Unknowing*, the *Mirror of Simple Souls*, and not least the *Imitatio Christi*, which, though it was the work of a Dutch Augustinian canon, quickly became a favourite in English houses. A great deal of the copying of these and similar works was carried out by the Brigittine nuns at Syon and by the Carthusians at the London Charterhouse, Sheen and Mount Grace. The

---

[1] Knowles, *op. cit.*, p. 65.
[2] H. S. Bennett, *Chaucer and the Fifteenth Century*, 1947, pp. 180, 216.
[3] H. S. Bennett, *The Library*, 1946, I, 168.

demand continued well into the sixteenth century, and many printed editions, particularly of Richard Rolle, were put out by the early printers. They must have been commonly represented in the small lay collections of the day, along with other devotional works, courtesy books, books of deportment, and herbals of especial interest to the women members of the household.

All these works placed a new emphasis on the importance of the individual on personal religion and the direct approach between creature and Creator—a very significant factor which, though it did not in any way cause the religious upheavals of the sixteenth century, at least made them both possible and more intelligible. It represents a deep-rooted instinct of which in a later century the Jesuits were to make profitable use, for their teaching constantly emphasized the individual approach to the problems of religion. It is certain that the popular interest in such works was a potent force in encouraging the spread of literacy in middle-class households in the fifteenth century, especially among women. Doubtless the influence worked in the other direction also. 'The emergence of a large literate class outside the ranks of the clerks and religious orders made it possible for the first time for a master to instruct his disciple, and for the mystic to describe his own experiences, in the simplicity, not yet formalized or conventionalized, of the vernacular language.'[1]

In the more aristocratic houses there was perhaps a tendency to prefer the Anglo-French romances and tales of chivalry, the *Romaunt of the Rose*, the *Morte d'Arthur* and its many sources, and the *Historia Brittonum*. The restricted popularity of these is confirmed by the fact that in the fifteenth century there were only two printed editions of the *Morte d'Arthur* compared with fifteen of the *Golden Legend*; Canon Maynard Smith notes that among ordinary people the saints were much more popular than the knights.[2] This is true, but in the humbler ranks of society the spirit of individuality found a different method of expression. Whenever a sense of frustration exists, individualism takes on a rebellious attitude. The embers were stirred first by the friars and then by Wyclif. In the countryside the pastoral work of the friars helped to encourage the anti-clericalism of the day, and in

[1] Knowles, *The English Mystical Tradition*, 1961, p. 47.
[2] *Pre-Reformation England*, 1938, p. 417.

the academic field schoolmen such as William of Ockham, separating faith and reason by an impassable gulf, provided food for sceptical thought to Wyclif and Luther. The ground was prepared, and the Lollard tracts and translations, circulating underground, bore their fruit. Literacy amongst the peasantry was limited in Wyclif's day, but such as it was, it must have been encouraged by the spread of the tracts; one of the earliest lay adherents to Lollardry, William Smith of Leicester, is known to have deliberately taught himself to read and write, after which he kept a Lollard school and wrote several books.[1] Lollardry found its converts chiefly among the craftsmen of the newly emerging industrial population for whom literacy would in any case be a desirable achievement. The same forces operate whenever underground propaganda is at work in a semi-literate population, as for example with Tom Paine and his *Rights of Man*, and still more noticeably with the spread of Wesleyanism in the eighteenth century. Wesley indeed understood clearly the value of literacy to his cause, and he was himself a pioneer in the popularization of reading, preaching its necessity to the spiritual life, circulating books and pamphlets in great quantities, and producing simplified versions of the masters expressly for this purpose.[2]

In all ages devotional manuals and works of religious propaganda have been powerful agents in the promotion of literacy. In the fifteenth century the evidence for this is strong, though circumstantial.[3] In the sixteenth and seventeenth centuries, with the spread of the printed book, the evidence is detailed and direct. It is significant that almost half the titles in STC (1475–1640) were in some sort religious in content and purpose, and, apart from the Bible and the Book of Common Prayer, popular works of devotion, such as *The Crumbs of Comfort* and the sermons of William Perkins, had very large circulations indeed.[4] The majority of these works were naturally the products of the reformed religion, but pre-Reformation writers were well represented. There were for example at least eight printed editions of

[1] K. B. McFarlane, *John Wycliffe and the Beginnings of English Nonconformity*, 1952.
[2] e.g. *Pilgrim's Progress* in a pocket edition at 4d. (1743), *Paradise Lost*, Young's *Night Thoughts*, etc. His *Collection of Moral and Sacred Poems* (1744) had a similar aim.
[3] *Infra*, p. 201.
[4] See Louis B. Wright, 'The Significance of Religious Writings in the English Renaissance', *Journal of the History of Ideas*, 1940, I, pp. 59–68, and the same author's *Middle-class Culture in Elizabethan England*, 1935. See p. 208 *infra*.

the *Scala Perfectionis* between 1474 and 1679, and it is noteworthy that this work figures in Sir William More's collection at Losely House in 1556. The *Imitatio* appeared in at least twenty-four editions in the period 1567–1639. This compares with about ten editions in the period 1563–1684 of Foxe's *Acts and Monuments*, which, judging from its survival in so many instances to the present century, must have been one of the commonest books apart from the Bible on the shelves of the smaller English homes during the slow emergence of a literate population. There is truth in the impression that England acquired the habit of reading first and foremost from the possession of a number of religious works, including of course the Bible. A few of these certainly were works of propaganda, but the majority from the fourteenth century onwards were manuals of devotion and personal religion, many boasting a heritage stretching back to the fathers of the Egyptian desert and the Christian Platonists.

2. THE CORPORATE LIFE AND SCHOLARSHIP

The ascetic life has its own importance in the history of religion. The fact that its practice stimulated in seventh- and eighth-century Ireland the formulation of oral traditions in writing and the birth of a rich native literature, and that in fifteenth-century England it gave an impetus to the spread of popular literacy, is an accidental side-issue which is nevertheless significant for our present purpose. Intense, personal feeling lies behind most creative writing, as it does behind most religious devotion, and it is natural for the two to walk hand in hand. Literacy is but the popular response, often of course at a humble level, to the common need to share in the creative work and devotion of the few who can transmit their experiences and feelings to the written page.

The ordered and disciplined life of the religious houses, based directly or indirectly on the Rule of S. Benedict and the ideals of Cassiodorus, led to a different goal. Both of course served primarily for the worship of God, but they travelled by different roads. The stability of the Benedictine corporate tradition, with its scriptoria and libraries governed by impersonal and inelastic rules, was the source from which medieval scholarship and academic studies took their root. We can trace the slow growth of the organized libraries which were needed to support these studies.

Many of the anchorites, not only in Egypt and Syria, but in the early Celtic Church and in medieval Europe, were scholarly and well educated; as often however with solitary workers devoting themselves unsparingly to a single aim, there are few if any clues as to their personal background. It may be possible to guess the sources of their teaching, but we know nothing of how they obtained access to them, or what sort of libraries they used or collected. Richard Rolle had a sound, if rather limited, knowledge of theology, and the books he needed were in some way or other at his command. The author of *The Cloud of Unknowing* and Walter Hilton were more widely read in theology than Rolle, and in their special field were undoubtedly learned men; the latter though for a time at least living as a solitary, may have had the use of the library at the priory of Thurgarton.[1]

By comparison the Benedictine library tradition is well documented, partly perhaps because the settled tradition was there, to be passed down through the generations, and partly because corporate possessions (including books) demand the preparation of inventories from time to time, and because corporate societies not only accumulate archives but find it necessary to record their annals. The main vehicle of the tradition was the Rule itself, which, through all its variations and revisions encouraged the habit of disciplined study, and provided a framework within which the tradition could be handed on. Within this framework the continuity of the tradition, with its roots in the classical age, was never completely broken. One powerful factor in the maintenance of the tradition was the adoption of Latin as the international language both of scholarship and of the Church, and the stabilization of the language for so many centuries was largely due to the teaching of grammar and rhetoric in the schools of the Church. Another factor was the comparative stability of the texts in which the tradition was enshrined. The textbooks of the fourth century grammarian Donatus, the *De consolatione philosophiae* of Boethius, and the encyclopaedias of Isidore of Seville and Rabanus Maurus, maintained their standing and vigour all through the medieval period. The direct links with

[1] Knowles, *The English Mystical Tradition*, 1961, pp. 55, 71, 101-2.

the classical period were secured in the main by Donatus, S. Augustine (who provided the chief link with Neo-Platonism, and whose masterpieces rank as high in Latin as they do in Christian literature) and Boethius (the last Roman, as Gibbon said, whom Cato or Cicero would have recognized as a compatriot). Boethius' constant aim was to interpret the whole range of Greek philosophy to Latin readers who no longer were familiar with Greek, and though he achieved this only in part, no Roman writer since Cicero had laboured so successfully at this task. The *De consolatione* was written while Boethius languished in his prison cell, but he looks back with regret to the comforts of his library at home; and he mentions that its walls were adorned with tiles of ivory and glass.[1] This is the last glimpse we have of a Roman villa library. Boethius died in 524; Sidonius Apollinaris, with his pictures of villa libraries in Southern Gaul, died about the same year that Boethius was born (480).

Isidore, the Visigoth Bishop of Seville (570–636) produced in his *Origines* a vast collection of facts and fancies summing up the whole of knowledge, and this remained a standard reference work for many centuries. This work included not only a history of Roman libraries and book production, based possibly on a lost work by Suetonius, but an elaborate description of his own library, which may well in some degree have set the pattern for later monastic libraries. His library was arranged in fourteen *armaria*, with portraits over each press. Seven presses were occupied by theology, two by poetry, and one each by history, moral theology, law and medicine, with one unspecified as to subject. If the contents of the shelves can be guessed from the portraits and from the sources he uses, these would include Galen and Hippocrates in translated editions, Boethius' translations from the Greek, Lucretius, Sallust, Vitruvius, Orosius, Eusebius (through S. Jerome), Lactantius, Solinus, and the *Prata* of Suetonius; not however Pliny's *Natural History*, nor any works in Greek. It was evidently a comprehensive collection for his day, but Isidore did not apparently give his monks free access to it. Their secular reading was to be confined to the grammarians, and he supports this restriction by an ingenious and ingenuous manipulation of Psalm 71; a faulty rendering of the ending of

[1] Boethius *De Cons.* I. 5. 20.

verse 15, combined with the beginning of verse 16, gives him the curious line *quia non cognovi litteraturam, introibo in potentias Domini*. Sandys observes that he would have been better advised to take as his precept the prayer of Cassiodorus: *praesta, Domine, legentibus profectum*.[1] The ninth century encyclopaedia known as the *De Universo*[2] by Rabanus Maurus of Fulda was based largely on Isidore. Rabanus was a pupil of Alcuin, and in a sense his successor in the educational tradition. The *De Universo* contains a chapter on libraries and bibliography, with a series of definitions largely drawn from Isidore. His sympathies were however wider than those of Isidore, and he encouraged the study of dialectics, which were to become so marked a feature of medieval logic. His librarian at Fulda was Gerbock, whom he appropriately styles *clavipotens frater*.

Through all these early centuries the stability of the library tradition is remarkable. There is a striking correspondence in the contents of libraries between the fifth and eleventh centuries, so far as these are known to us: in the libraries of Sidonius Apollinaris for example in the fifth century, of Boethius in the sixth century, of Isidore in the seventh century, of Bede and Alcuin in the eight century, of Rabanus Maurus and Servatus Lupus in the ninth century, of Gerbert, who became Pope Silvester II at the end of the tenth century, and the catalogue of the Bobbio library in the same century. In all these the same texts turn up again and again: Virgil, Horace, Statius, Plautus, Terence, Varro, the two Plinys, Ovid, Juvenal, Seneca, Lucretius, Persius, Martial, Sallust and Suetonius, in addition to the recognized Christian and patristic works in Latin. The correspondence is more than a coincidence; it is the result of a definite tradition, which changed little till the coming of the medieval universities.

Detailed evidence of the Benedictine library tradition is scanty however before the Norman period. Even Bede tells us little except that 'large and noble libraries' existed at Wearmouth and Hexham. He describes the erudition of Hadrian, Theodore, Albinus and Aldhelm, but he had no personal knowledge of the libraries that supported the Greek as well as Latin studies which they are said to have carried out.

[1] Sandys, *Hist. Class. Schol.*, I. 444.
[2] Migne PL CXI.

The great library of the cathedral school at York followed in the eighth century, in the tradition established by Benedict Biscop at Wearmouth. Alcuin tells us sufficient about it to convince us of its pre-eminence; neither England nor France could show a nobler collection till the twelfth century or later. We do not know how big it was, or how it was arranged and shelved, but it was rich in classical texts as well as theology and patristics, and it included an active scriptorium. Here the converging streams of Celtic and Roman culture bore fruit in the earliest outburst of Christian humanism. Under the influence of Irish scholarship the flight from the classics initiated by S. Jerome and S. Augustine and Gregory the Great was reversed, and temporarily at least they came into their own again. Alcuin viewed them not merely as the source of all knowledge and science, not indeed as the work of man nor the work of devils, but as the work of God; and if pagan hands can carry out God's work in this way, why should not Christian hands adorn it even more nobly? In Professor Knowles' words, 'Alcuin, indeed, precisely reverses Jerome. Jerome had turned to the monastic life as a flight from profane letters; Alcuin exhorts his monks to abandon the spade for the pen: *"Fodere quam vites melius fit scribere libros"*.'[1]

English and Irish scholarship, in one of the great missionary waves of history, spread outwards to the Continent, and with it went English and Irish libraries and books. S. Columban had gone to found Luxeuil and Bobbio and S. Gall, and at each great collections of classical and patristic manuscripts were amassed. S. Boniface had gone from Wessex and founded Fulda and Reichenau in Germany. Charles the Great called Alcuin to his palace school to re-organize French education and to lead the movement that blossomed into the Carolingian renaissance. Many books came with Alcuin from York to Tours; many others came from Italy; and unknown numbers were copied in Carolingian scriptoria, at Corbie, Fleury and elsewhere, providing us today with early (often the earliest) sources for our classical texts. In Italy itself the revival came later, especially in the eleventh century at Monte Cassino in the time of Desiderius, when the riches of that great Library were being deliberately gathered together.

[1] Wormald and Wright, *The English Library before 1700*, 1958, p. 142.

The Benedictine library tradition springs directly from the Regula Monachorum itself and from the work and writings of Cassiodorus, both of which for the first time give an intellectual purpose to the occupations prescribed for the monks. The references in the Rule are in chapters 48 and 49, in the section dealing with manual labour. Idleness (in the now familiar phrase) is the enemy of the soul; therefore the brethren should at certain times occupy themselves with manual labour, and again at certain hours with holy reading. Between Easter and October (that is in the summer timetable) reading was to be from the fourth hour till near the sixth hour. From October till Lent, reading was to be till the second hour, and during Lent till the third hour. At the beginning of Lent, each was to receive a book from the library and read it straight through; this was presumably a special Lenten exercise additional to the normal daily reading.

Later revisions of the Rule become more explicit about the programme of study. The *Constitutions* of Lanfranc,[1] which were themselves based on the practice of Bernard of Cluny, and were intended as a directive not only for Christ Church, Canterbury but for all the Benedictine houses in Norman England, give more detail about the annual exchange of books on the first Monday in Lent, when the volumes selected by the *custos librorum* for reading by the Brethren were placed together in the chapter house and distributed, and a list of the borrowings was drawn up.

Lanfranc's *custos librorum* was called the *armarius* by Bernard of Cluny. In practice however the duties were usually entrusted to the Cantor or the Precentor, who was also responsible for the service books, and for the archives of the house, its registers and necrology and its official seal. Lanfranc, in specifying the duties of the Cantor, says 'He takes care of all the books of the house and has them in his keeping, if his interests and learning are such as to fit him for this responsibility'.[2] As a result the Precentor developed into the annalist or chronicler; William of Malmesbury and Symeon of Durham are examples. In later times, particularly at St Albans, a separate officer appears, the Superintendent of the Scriptorium.

---

[1] Knowles, *The Monastic Constitutions of Lanfranc*, 1951, p. 19, 150; *Monastic Orders in England*, 1940, p. 522. See also *Origins*, p. 84.
[2] Knowles, *Monastic Constitutions of Lanfranc*, p. 82.

The Premonstratensian statutes entrust the librarian with the additional duty of borrowing books required by the monks from outside sources, with the approval of the Abbot or Prior. Both the Cistercian and the Premonstratensian statutes charge the librarian with the duty of opening and locking the presses. The Carthusians allowed two books to each brother, with a special injunction that they should be kept clean.[1]

The monastic horarium, as described by Lanfranc,[2] allows about five periods in each day, both in the summer and winter timetables, for study, talk or other tasks in the cloister. The main period for study would be in the afternoon, but there would be reading aloud in the refectory and during tasks in the cloisters. The only reference in Lanfranc to any strictly manual labour directs the Cantor to arrange for such reading during tasks, either by himself or by one of the children.[3] By this period all the more laborious work had been passed over to the servants of the house, and more time was available not merely for copying but for serious study and teaching.

The detailed organization of the monastic scriptorium and library, so far as this is known, is well documented.[4] In pre-Conquest days the arrangements were probably primitive and unsystematic, though this did not prevent the production of fine copying and illumination. From the first however, the library, the scriptorium and the school were closely associated; under any rule which imposes the duty of daily study, they form (next to the Church) the heart of every monastic establishment. In the earlier post-Conquest houses, while study would normally be carried out in the cloisters, the collection of books would be kept in various places according to their use. The service books would be in or near the Church; the books needed for reading in the refectory would be housed near that room; books needed for individual study would be in or near the cloisters; and the school books required by the novices would form another collection elsewhere. Thus at Durham, the main library was on the

---

[1] J. W. Clark, *Care of Books*, 1902, p. 63.

[2] Knowles, *Monastic Constitutions of Lanfranc*, p. XXXV.

[3] *ibid.*, 82 *n.*

[4] Francis Wormald and C. E. Wright, ed. *The English Library before 1700*, 1958; see also John Taylor, 'The monastic scriptorium', in *The Library*, 1890, II, 237, 282, and J. W. Thompson, *Medieval libraries*, 1957.

north side of the cloister, which was screened off into carrells 'finely wainscotted and fitted with desks', with the presses standing against the wall of the Church. Another collection was in the Spendiment or Treasury, in the undercroft of the Dormitory; of this, one part was *in communi armariolo* and generally accessible and another consisting of more valuable works was kept in an inner room. Books used for reading in the refectory were kept at the south end of the west walk of the cloister, within the doorway leading to the infirmary. Another collection was in a chest in the west cloister near the door of the Treasury, where the novices had their school. Still another collection, probably of service books, was in the chapel of the Prior. At a later date the books in the Spendiment and the cloister were moved to a new library over the Parlour in the East cloister, between the Chapter House and the South Transept; this may have taken place in the time of Prior Wessington (1416-46) who restored and enlarged many of the monastic buildings, including the Parlour.[1]

The Premonstratensian house of Titchfield in Hampshire provides an example of one of the smaller monastic libraries. This house, founded in the thirteenth century, contained early in the fifteenth century 326 volumes, many of course being composite. They were arranged in four presses in the cloisters, two on the east wall, one on the south and one on the north. Each press had eight shelves (*gradus*) marked with a letter and number. Each volume was marked on the first leaf, or on the *tabula* (cover) with its letter and number, and this press mark appears also in the catalogue; the numbers are only used where a subject runs to more than one shelf. The four presses are arranged as follows: (1) Bibles; (2) Bibles, Isidore, Theology, the Fathers; (3) Lives of saints, Sermons, civil law, canon law; (4) Medicine, grammar, logic, philosophy, English law, French works, miscellaneous.[2]

Many monastic catalogues are little more than inventories, sometimes added to chartularies or written into other books. Thus the earliest fragmentary catalogue at Durham was written on the first folio of a Bible which was one of the gifts of the

[1] H. D. Hughes, *A History of Durham Cathedral Library*, 1925, pp. 1-11.

[2] J. W. Clark, *Care of Books*, 1902, pp. 77-79; F. Madan, *Books in Manuscript*, 1893, p. 78.

Norman bishop, William de S. Carilef, who also built a great part of the cathedral. There were however, two other systematic catalogues besides the one at Tichfield, which reveal the arrangement of an organized library, at Lanthony and Dover Priory. The Lanthony catalogue (now in the British Museum) dates from the mid-fourteenth century, and shows that the books were kept in five presses, three devoted to Bibles and the Fathers, the fourth to law, philosophy, grammar and mathematics, and the fifth to large volumes. The first four presses contained a number of shelves (*gradus*), but there was only one shelf for the large books in the fifth. The catalogue gives no press mark, but it sometimes comments on the conditions or binding of the book.[1] The rather earlier catalogue at Dover Priory was compiled in 1389 by John Whytefield (probably the precentor), and is even more systematic. It is in three parts. Part I lists the titles, the folio chosen for quoting the opening words to identify the volumes, the number of leaves and the number of separate treatises in the volume, this being primarily for the precentor's use. Part II is a shelf list; each item in composite works is listed with the number and side of the leaf where it begins, and with the *incipit*. Part III is an author list in alphabetical order of the whole collection. This is a quite remarkable document and indeed unique amongst medieval catalogues in the care that has been given to its compilation and the completeness of the information it gives.[2] Its only rival amongst the English libraries is the catalogue of the Brigittines at Syon, compiled a century and a half later; this includes the donor's name in the information it gives about each book.[3]

The open cloisters cannot have encouraged concentrated study. This must have become a little easier with the provision of carrells, which began to appear in the thirteenth century. They are first recorded in the Augustinian chapters in 1232,[4] and at Westminster Abbey between 1258 and 1283; by the end of the century they were becoming fairly general in the larger houses.

---

[1] Wormald and Wright, *op. cit.*, pp. 25, 30. For English medieval catalogues in general, see N. R. Ker, *Medieval Libraries of Great Britain*, 1941, p. XIX.

[2] M. R. James, *The Ancient Libraries of Canterbury and Dover*, 1903.

[3] M. Bateson, *Catalogue of the Library of Syon Monastery, Isleworth*, 1898.

[4] H. E. Salter, *Chapters of the Augustinian Canons*, 1922, p. 26; J. R. H. Moorman, *Church Life in England in the Thirteenth Century*, 1945, pp. 328–41.

Even these can have offered little comfort, but the provision of either separate studies or special library rooms did not become general till the fifteenth century. At the Oxford Greyfriars only the minster, the lector and the doctors of divinity were provided with studies; the friars had to be content with a *studium* or combined desk and bookcase. At Durham, the Dormitory, which was built 1398–1404, was fitted with small wooden cubicles for each monk and novice for sleep and study,[1] but this was a comparatively late development. At St Albans, a group of studies between the dorter and the guesthouse chapel was built by Abbot Michael (*d.* 1349), so that students could be free of the distractions of the cloister. His successor Thomas de la Mare, added more studies and also glazed the cloisters and provided them with seats.[2] St Albans, always in the forefront of monastic scholarship, perhaps led the way in this kind of provision. The Carthusians, being a quasi-eremitical order, had always had individual cells; as has been noted, their English houses were mostly late foundations.

The special library room was probably called into existence by the need to re-organize the growing accumulations of books dispersed in various places in the larger houses, and for the most part they are a late development. They were however foreshadowed in a model plan known as the plan of S. Gall and dating from the early ninth century. This plan provided for a *bibliotheca* built over the scriptorium on the north side of the choir.[3] For most houses, however, one or more *armaria* in the cloister sufficed for the main collection, though at some Cistercian houses (notably Meaux and Kirkstall in the twelfth century) the *armaria* were collected into a *commune almarium claustri* or storeroom opening into the cloister and carved out of the sacristy or the ante-room of the chapter house.[4] In the early fifteenth century there occurred a great outburst of new library buildings or rooms at cathedrals, at the universities (Duke Humphrey's Library as well as several college libraries belong to this period) and at the larger religious houses, including the friaries such as the London Greyfriars. The provision of such a library at a monastery was

[1] H. D. Hughes, *op. cit.*, p. 8.
[2] Knowles, *The Religious Orders in England*, vol. II, 1955, pp. 40, 45.
[3] Knowles, *The Religious Orders in England*, vol. II, 1955, pp. 351–3.
[4] Wormald and Wright, *op. cit.*, p. 20.

often something of a problem, for it had to be near the church and cloister, and the buildings in this area were usually already complete. A common solution was to choose the same site as the Cistercian storeroom, but to place it on the first floor, where a more spacious room could be provided; the new library would then be over the sacristy, which lay between the transept and the chapter house. Durham, Gloucester and Winchester are examples of this. At Christ Church, Canterbury, the library was placed over the prior's chapel, and at Worcester it extended over the cloister itself and the south aisle of the nave. The library at St Albans was built in 1452-3 by Abbot Whethamstede, but its position is uncertain. This may well have been the best equipped of all English Benedictine libraries; this is suggested not only by the scholarly traditions of St Albans, but by the range of John Whethamstede's own works, especially the encyclopaedia known as the *Granarium de Viris Illustribus* which suggests the use of a rich collection of contemporary and recent works.[1] Though the library room is in the main a fifteenth-century development, there may have been occasional instances in earlier periods. A fragmentary catalogue of the Cluniac Priory at Bermondsey at the beginning of the fourteenth century ascribes volumes to shelves (*gradus*) XIV to XXIV, which may have been in a special room.[2]

Very little survives regarding the daily routine of these libraries and the method of using them. The Customs of the Augustinian Canons at Barnwell, which probably represent general Augustinian practice, are more explicit on this point than most. The precentor acts as *armarius* and is in general charge of the library. It is his duty to be familiar with all the volumes in the collection and to care for their safety; they should be inspected regularly for damage from insects or decay. The library is to be exhibited in Chapter at the beginning of Lent each year, when prayers are to be said for the donors and scribes at a special service. He is responsible for handing to the brethren the volumes they wish to study, and for entering on his register the names of borrowers against the titles lent. The borrower may not pass on his book to anyone else without permission; and a deposit may be required

---

[1] Knowles, *The Religious Orders in England*, vol. II, 1955, pp. 267-9.
[2] N. Denholm-Young, *Collected Papers on Medieval Subjects*, 1946, p. 168.

(possibly for loans outside the convent), the deposit being entered on the register. The permission of the Prelate is needed for the loan of very valuable works. Books needed for daily use in singing or reading are to be kept in a special place with easy access, and are not to be taken out of the cloisters or church into cells or odd corners (a favourite device which has worried librarians in every age). The books are to be dusted frequently and kept in repair, and the librarian is responsible for their binding. No corrections or changes are to be made in the books by the brethren without the librarian's consent. The *armarium* is to be lined with wood, to avoid staining the books with damp, and is to be fitted with vertical partitions and horizontal shelves to keep the volumes apart from each other, *ne nimia compressio ipsis libris noceat, vel querenti moram inuectat*; the writer of these instructions obviously understood all these familiar troubles. This is believed to be the only contemporary description of a medieval *armarium*. The books would usually have been kept flat on the shelves; and it was consequently the more important to avoid piling one book on another.[1]

Other duties of the librarian are revealed by the surviving manuscripts. It would have been his task to enter in each book an *ex libris* inscription as a mark of ownership, and sometimes also an *ex dono* inscription for gifts.[2] When pressmarks were used, these would have been added by the librarian, often at the top right-hand corner of the first page of the text; and any inventories or catalogues would have been compiled by him.

For obvious reasons, more is known about the contents of the monastic libraries than their organization, though even here our knowledge is limited enough.[3] Accessions to the libraries came partly from donations, partly from the monastic scriptorium, partly from exchanges with other houses and partly by purchase, for the accounts sometimes show that money was set aside for this purpose. Major accretions would often be due to the interest of a distinguished scholar in the work of the library; examples range from Benedict Biscop, who brought great numbers of books from Rome to Wearmouth, to Matthew Paris and John

[1] J. W. Clark, *The Care of Books*, 1902, p. 61.
[2] N. R. Ker, *op. cit.*, p. XVI, XVII.
[3] See especially N. R. Ker, *op. cit.*, and Wormald and Wright, *op. cit.*, ch. II, IV, V and VII.

Whethamstede at St Albans, and William Sellyng at Canterbury.

The contents of most libraries followed a fairly stereotyped general pattern, with of course many variations. They would include, besides service books, various Bibles, often glossed, Gratian's Decretum, Peter the Lombard's *Sentences*, and S. Benedict's *Rule*. There would be some patristics, Eastern perhaps as well as Western, probably including some works of Jerome, Augustine, Ambrose, Cassian, Cassiodorus, Boethius, Isidore, Hugh of S. Victor and often the complete works of Gregory the Great. There would be copies of Josephus, Eusebius, Bede and Grosseteste, and various lives of the saints. There would be a section on logic, including some Aristotle. There would be important sections on canon law, civil law and in the later period some statute law. There would be grammarians such as Donatus and Priscian, and some scientific and medical writers such as Euclid, Bartholomaeus Anglicus, Hippocrates and Galen. Finally, there would be some classical texts, and the contribution of the monastic libraries to the preservation of these texts has been stressed again and again.[1] It has been noted that a steady and substantial increase took place between the ninth and twelfth centuries in the classical authors appearing in library catalogues.[2] Works by authors such as Virgil, Terence, Ovid, Horace, Persius and Juvenal were multiplied many times over; Ovid for example appeared only three times in ninth-century catalogues, but this rose to twenty-four times in the eleventh century and seventy-seven in the twelfth century, by which time his works had become a common school textbook, with a popularity second only to Virgil. The climax of classical learning in the monasteries came in the period 1150–1200; after this, the discontinuance of the practice of accepting child oblates (the recruitment of children who had to be educated, and to learn their Latin, in the monastery) resulted in the decline of the monastic schools. Interest in classical studies consequently waned, and scarcely any new texts were copied, or old ones replaced.

The changes that were occurring at this time were however more complex than this. The classical renaissance of the twelfth century, which was marked by the rise of scholars such as John

[1] Knowles, *The Preservation of the Classics*, in Wormald and Wright, *op. cit.*; Bolgar, *The Classical Heritage*, 1954.
[2] Bolgar, *ibid.*, pp. 189, 413.

of Salisbury, and of civil servants such as Peter of Blois, resulted in a natural increase in the violence of the anti-humanist attacks of more conservative divines. Some of Cicero and Seneca was so close to Christian moral teaching that it could be accepted without great difficulty. But classical studies did not stop with these authors. Distaste for the erotic poetry of Ovid, and the fears and suspicion aroused by the study of dialectic and philosophy, led to a widespread condemnation of such pursuits. To some extent this could be met by the allegorical explanation of classical myths, much as the Bible was interpreted allegorically. The reaction against the classics however, was not entirely due to religious antipathy or questions of morality. The new profession of the law was the first of the professions to be laicized, and the first to demand academic training outside monastic walls; and it was in part this new profession that tempted young men away from both religion and classical studies.

'Law, either civil or canon, had become the *scientia lucrativa*. It is the lawyers to whom the key of the well is given, said the Chancellor of the University of Paris in 1238; a young man goes to theology for two years and gives it up for law, and is made an archdeacon, and though the devout questioned whether an archdeacon could be saved, a good many were prepared to risk it.'[1] By Roger Bacon's time civil law had become more important than canon law for ecclesiastical dignitaries. And though law has always demanded an expensive training, it offered then as now the chance of high honours and high profits. Unfortunately literature suffered more than theology from this new rival; students were tempted to go straight from Donatus and Cato to law, leaving out literature altogether.[2]

From another quarter the attack on classical studies was equally overwhelming. The new pre-occupation with the re-discovered Aristotle, the new studies of logic and metaphysics and natural science and medicine, fostered by the disciplines of the new universities, especially Paris, and by the law and medical schools of Bologna and Salerno, filled men's minds for two or three centuries to the exclusion of everything else. Not till the fourteenth century gave us Petrarch and Boccaccio in Italy was the spirit

[1] Helen Waddell, *The Wandering Scholars*, 7th ed., 1934, pp. 131–2.
[2] *ibid.*, p. 132.

of literary criticism re-awakened; and soon afterwards Poggio and Niccoli were resurrecting their texts of Quintilian and Lucretius and Vitruvius from monastic libraries that were not merely neglected but dormant. Petrarch kindled for the coming world of the renaissance a new ideal for the scholarly library, in which the purity and the quality of the text outweighs decoration and ornament, and the two major crimes are the piling up of unread volumes and the compression of great masterpieces into epitomes and *tabulae* and florilegia and indexes. Both these unhappy faults were the besetting sins of the later monastic libraries.

In the transition from monastic to academic education which took place in the thirteenth century, no lights were extinguished. They were merely transferred to a new place and re-trimmed. The new continental universities arose, in Italy, from the medical and law schools of Salerno and Bologna, and in France from cathedral schools such as those at Paris, Chartres and Orleans, and the medical school at Montpellier, which had been training recruits for the emerging professions of law and civil administration and medicine. In Norman England the secular cathedrals had grammar schools attached to them, and the schoolmaster (later called the Chancellor) acted in some cases as the Cathedral librarian; this was for example the case at S. Paul's in 1111.[1] They did not however in England acquire academic status as they did in Paris and Bologna.

The academic duties of teaching at the new universities were largely taken over by the new mendicant orders, whose arrival coincided with their establishment; and the duties of book collecting and copying became part of the academic machinery. New text books were needed and new methods of book production had to be evolved to suit the exigencies of academic study. Books were produced rapidly by the academic *stationarii* with less ornament, lighter binding, finer parchment, larger gatherings of folios, and the whole book of a smaller size. Exemplars were available at the bookshops which could be divided into *peciae* and copied by the students.[2] The new universities however were

[1] A. F. Leach, *The Schools of Medieval England*, 1916, p. 110.
[2] C. H. Talbot *in* Wormald and Wright, *op. cit.*, pp. 66–84, Dr Talbot also cites the double-column page as a new feature, but this had been common in English MSS for some time, and it is doubtful whether it saves much space.

still religious corporations, different in purpose from the monastic houses but quite as impersonal. In one sense the monasteries accepted the challenge and adjusted themselves to the new institutions, which not only offered training for the lay professions but also provided an opportunity for monastic higher education to be centralized. Both Benedictines and Cistercians opened 'nurseries' or training schools at Oxford; even the Gilbertines had nurseries at Cambridge and Stamford. Doubtless the chance of an Oxford education enriched the life of the more scholarly brethren in the later centuries, but nothing outstanding or brilliant emerged as a result.

It was not to be expected that the libraries of an impersonal corporation, whether monastic or academic, should produce any creative work of genius. Their purpose could only be to serve as the modest handmaid of scholarship. What in fact did they contribute to English medieval culture, apart from their first duty of the preservation of their books?

Their greatest contribution to learning was without doubt the series of chronicles which issued from their scriptoria.[1] The value of these as source material for the historian is beyond doubt, especially when they record contemporary events, as seen through the eyes of an intelligent observer familiar with affairs of state. Many great names stand out: Simeon of Durham, Eadmer of Canterbury, Henry of Huntingdon, Ordericus Vitalis of St Evroult, Florence of Worcester (who used for part of his material a lost version of the Anglo-Saxon Chronicle). Most important of all perhaps (apart from Bede himself) were William of Malmesbury (d. 1143), the librarian of the Wiltshire abbey which had maintained its interest in learning for four centuries, and where the library had been re-founded by Abbot Godfrey in William's youth, and Matthew Paris, the second in the line of superintendents of the scriptorium at St Albans. Of both it might be said, as Sir Frank Stenton said of Bede, that 'in an age when little was attempted beyond the registration of fact, these had reached the conception of history'. Professor Galbraith notes that 'in general, original composition was the last refuge of the historian, destitute as he approached his own time of any "better man" from whom

---

[1] On these see especially V. H. Galbraith, *Historical Research in Medieval England*, 1951, and Knowles, *The Monastic Orders in England*, 1940.

to copy'. Matthew Paris filled in this gap with more critical judgment than most. He was the close friend of Henry III and well placed to observe the contemporary scene at home and abroad. He may have written carelessly at times, and he had the common English prejudices, disliking foreigners and external authority of any kind, whether its source were Rome or West-minster. But he had a true sense of history, and he was both a good storyteller and a capable artist.[1] Professor Galbraith observes that the debt we owe to the Benedictine chroniclers, and especially to those of St Albans, for preserving the records of three centuries is enormous. The contribution of St Albans is particularly note-worthy, and indeed outweighs all the rest put together.[2] There is more than a spark of creative genius in the part that Matthew Paris played in the St Albans historical tradition.

It may be not inappropriate to mention here another twelfth-century writer who probably had a Benedictine background. The historiography and scholarship of the *Historia Regum Britanniae* may well be spurious, but Geoffrey of Monmouth was another thoroughly able storyteller, and if his work belongs to the field of imaginative literature, yet its effect on antiquarian thought both in England and on the Continent, remained astonishingly powerful for five centuries or more. The author of a 'best-seller' with so long a life cannot lightly be ignored, and indeed he still continues to engage the attention of scholars.[3]

The development of scholasticism was largely the work of the mendicant orders at Oxford and Paris, but as an academic discipline it penetrated so deeply into English intellectual life in the three centuries prior to the Reformation that its effects cannot be discounted. Early in the fifteenth century Poggio, searching English libraries for lost classical texts, found little to interest him either in bookshops or monastic collections, which showed him nothing but modern works of the schoolmen and the Fathers. Inexplicably his exploration omitted some likely places such as Canterbury, St Albans, Peterborough and Lanthony, where he might have found one or two texts of interest. He did not visit Oxford, but he would have found nothing there at that

[1] See Richard Vaughan, *Matthew Paris*, 1958.
[2] V. H. Galbraith, *op. cit.*, p. 31.
[3] e.g. Sir Thomas Kendrick, *British Antiquity*, 1950; R. S. Loomis, *ed. Arthurian Literature in the Middle Ages*, 1959.

date.[1] Nevertheless he was right in thinking that this was the main fare offered by English libraries. England may have been slow in assimilating the humanist revival, but it is easy to underestimate the contribution of the schoolmen. The sheer logical discipline of their studies through three or four centuries provided a solid foundation on which the art of thought and logical judgment could be based. The undergraduate beginning his studies at Oxford or Cambridge at the age of fifteen, and working through long years at the exercises and disputations required for his MA, BD and DD could scarcely complete his course till he was well into his thirties. If during this hard training he acquired the art of precise, logical thought and a sufficient command of language in which to embody it, this qualified him admirably for the responsibilities which won high rewards in the civil service. The irrelevance of his academic studies to the goal in sight counted for little. The by-products of his course gave him a trustworthy memory, a ready mastery of argument and fluent debating ability, and this above all was what the future civil servant or statesman required. Pearsall Smith in a telling passage[2] notes how many of the abstract terms of ancient or medieval philosophy have drifted down into the popular consciousness. Our commonest notions and most obvious distinctions were often, he says, by no means as simple and self-evident as they seem. They were the result of severe intellectual struggles through hundreds of years; and some of our most trivial words are tools 'fashioned long ago by philosophers, theologians and lawyers, and sharpened on the whetstone of each other's brains'.[3] The hard discipline of the schoolmen, however pointless it may seem at times, played its part in preparing the ground for later advances.

Humanism came to England too late to make any noticeable impact on the monastic libraries. The 'potential Maecenases' of the fifteenth century[3] drew their inspiration neither from monastic nor academic circles, and their manuscript collections from Italy aroused little interest in England. Humphrey Duke of Gloucester and John Tiptoft Earl of Worcester were noblemen. The ecclesiastical collectors, William Grey Bishop of Ely, Robert

[1] R. Weiss, *Humanism in England in the 15th Century*, 1957, p. 15.
[2] L. Pearsall Smith, *The English Language*, 1912, p. 187.
[3] R. R. Bolgar, *op. cit.*, p. 311.

Flemming Dean of Lincoln, John Gunthorpe Dean of Wells, and John Free (perhaps the most scholarly of this small band of enthusiasts) had no monastic background. Only William Selling[1] was a regular. He was a monk of Christ Church, Canterbury and a member of the new foundation of All Souls, Oxford. He studied in Italy, possibly from 1464-7 and again in 1486, and was made prior of Canterbury in 1472. He built the new library over the prior's chapel to house the Latin and Greek manuscripts he had brought from Italy; most of these were destroyed in the fire which occured when Cromwell's agents were carrying out their visitation. This apart, the few humanist collections to reach England in this century went eventually to Oxford; William Grey's to Balliol, Flemming's to Lincoln College, Duke Humphrey's of course and possibly John Tiptoft's also, to the University. In the early sixteenth century, the only monastic library to receive substantial accessions of this type was the great collection at Syon. Professor Knowles has noted that the chaplains and religious directors to the Brigittine nuns at Syon were scholars of distinction, many having been fellows of colleges at Oxford or Cambridge, and they left their books to the library at their death. The largest of these bequests was the collection of ninety-four volumes left by Richard Reynolds, who had been a fellow of Corpus Christi College, Cambridge, and was the friend of Erasmus, More and Reginald Pole. Cardinal Pole spoke of him as the only English monk who had a thorough knowledge of the three principal languages (Latin, Greek and Hebrew) and he was regarded as the ablest of the religious at that time. He died with the Carthusian martyrs in 1535.[2]

The few other traces of humanism in English monastic circles have been isolated by Professor Knowles.[3] There are for example the letters of Robert Joseph, a monk of Evesham, about 160 of which survive; all are in fluent and idiomatic classical Latin, and reveal an abundant knowledge of classical authors. There was the blind and deaf poet John Audelay, the Augustinian canon of Haughmond in Shropshire. There was the friar John Siferwas, the artist of the Sherborne Missal and the Lovel Lectionary, whose

[1] For Selling see Knowles, *The Religious Orders in England*, vol. III, 1959, pp. 87-90, and R. Weiss, *op. cit.*, pp. 153-9.
[2] Knowles, *The Religious Orders in England*, vol. III, 1959, pp. 212-21.
[3] *ibid.*, pp. 103-7.

work as a painter of birds is especially noteworthy. But these were exceptions. By and large humanism was foreign to the spirit of English monasticism. Nor did it ever take firm root in the pre-Reformation universities, in spite of the endeavours of Erasmus, More, Colet and Linacre and the foundation of Corpus Christi College, Oxford by Bishop Foxe in 1514.[1] Erasmus' influence was behind Colet in his foundation of S Paul's School in 1509, and this has been taken as the date for the introduction of human-ism into English education. He failed however to awaken much interest in Greek at Cambridge when he was there (1511–14), though Greek lectureships were established at Oxford and Cambridge not long afterwards. Nevertheless both Universities were still essentially medieval in outlook; and the term 'new learning' gradually acquired a theological rather than a humanistic significance.

It has been said that, for the schoolmen the cardinal sin was bad logic; for the humanists of the fifteenth century the cardinal sin was bad grammar. If both are indeed sins, then perhaps they are venial rather than mortal. We owe a debt to both. Neither Ciceronian nor scholastic Latin was hospitable to Aristotle, and the attempt to use it for the finer points of logic had peculiar results.[2] In Hallam's words,[3] 'it was as impossible to write meta-physics in good Latin, as the modern naturalists have found it to describe plants and animals'. Boethius (it was said) was the first to teach us to speak like barbarians; 'barbarous' was of course the humanist's word not merely for dog Latin, but for medieval Latin in general. But there are practically no Latin works by the fifteenth and sixteenth century humanists which are now read for pleasure and enjoyment, save possibly More's *Utopia*; the rest are moribund. On the other hand we owe to the humanists an escape from the tangled web of formal logic and rhetoric, and our ability to write worthily in English prose.[4]

The conflict between humanism and scholasticism was only

[1] On Erasmus see Knowles, *The Religious Orders in England*, vol. III, 1959, pp. 141–56. On the relations of More, Erasmus and Colet, Frederic Seebohm's *The Oxford Reformers* 2nd ed., 1869, is still of value.

[2] Terms for example such as Duns Scotus' *quidditas* and *haecceitas* which please neither eye nor ear.

[3] *Introduction to the Literature of Europe*, 1837, I, p. 18.

[4] On this general topic see especially Bolgar, *op. cit.*, and C. S. Lewis, *English Literature in the Sixteenth Century*, 1954 (Introduction).

beginning to gather weight in pre-Reformation England. The conflict between the Latin language and the vernacular on the other hand was a vigorous feature of English life in the fifteenth century. In this the religious, and indeed the Church in general, were wholeheartedly on the side of the Latinists. Latin was to remain the language of scholarship at least till the time of Newton. Its advantages were obvious. It was an international language; it was comparatively stable; and it was capable to a high degree of clarity, brevity and precision of meaning. This is not the whole picture however. The most powerful reason for the retention of the Latin tongue was that it was part of the mystique of scholarship. This was true of most branches of learning: law, medicine, science and particularly theology. As with the magic runes of Anglo-Saxon days, its virtue lay in its inscrutability; it was intelligible only to the elect; to the many who were semi-literate, it was (as we say) Greek, or double Dutch. Hence it was especially those Lollard tracts in the vernacular which were seized and destroyed. Hence also the fate of Reginald Pecock, Bishop of Chichester, who was so imprudent as to argue with the Lollards in their own language; and he could indeed write admirable English prose. There may have been unorthodoxy in his argument, but the language was sufficient to cause his downfall. The principle in this and other spheres has always been that only the professional is entitled to indulge in professional argument, and then only amongst other initiates. Amateur trespassers are warned off the field and may even be liable to prosecution; it is indeed one aspect of what we know today as the 'closed shop'. This attitude is not always so unreasonable as it sounds; it has its pros as well as its cons, as any medical man or scientist today will confirm. Every closed society guards jealously its own technical language (or jargon) which is more or less deliberately made unintelligible to outsiders.

The growing use of the vernacular and the appearance of so many translations into English in the fifteenth century owed little or nothing therefore to either monasteries or universities. One of our earliest translators, John de Trevisa (1326–1412) was indeed a fellow of Exeter and Queen's College, Oxford, but he was expelled, later becoming chaplain to Lord Berkeley. His translations, including the *Polychronicon* and Bartholomaeus Anglicus, were made for the use of his master, Lord Berkeley. The most notable monastic contribution to vernacular writing in the fifteenth century was perhaps the poetry of John Lydgate, who was professed at the Benedictine abbey of Bury, and possibly educated at Gloucester Hall, the Benedictine nursery at Oxford. His early reputation and popularity may seem difficult to explain at this distance; in part the reason may be in the new and substantial demand for vernacular works at that time. There were a few other isolated examples of monastic writing in English. The earliest was the work of the Gilbertine canon Robert Mannyng, the long octosyllabic poem *Handlyng Synne*, freely translated in 1303 from the *Manuel de Pechiez* of William of Wadington, 'in simple speech for love of simple men'. There were at least three Augustinian canons in the early fifteenth century who wrote in English: Osbern Bokenham of Stoke Clare, who translated into verse the *Lives of Holy Women*; John Mirk, prior of Lillishall, the author of the *Liber Festivalis* and the *Instruction for Parish Priests*, both in English, both very popular works; and the learned John Capgrave of Lynn, the author of the long poem in rhyme royal, the *Life of St. Katherine*, and the prose *Life of St. Gilbert of Sempringham*, in addition to many scholarly works in Latin.

The development of English prose owes much more to the parish pulpits and to the devotional works of the English mystics than to monastic or academic institutions. The vernacular preaching of parish priests, and from the thirteenth century of the friars, had kept our native language alive since Anglo-Saxon days. Both Chaucerian and Tudor English reflect the form in which the language had been crystallized in the pulpit, and the matter of the sermons and homilies, the stories and allegories which were the recognized fare of the medieval preacher.[1] Vernacular preaching to the laity had been normal practice for long enough; it had the blessing of such leaders as Odo of Battle, Abbot Samson and Bishop Grosseteste; the Bishop's allegorical romance, the *Chasteau d'amour*, was written in French and translated into English in the fourteenth century, and was widely read in both versions; it was intended definitely for lay use. The

[1] G. R. Owst, *Literature and the Pulpit in Medieval England*, 1933, and *Preaching in Medieval England*, 1926.

religious plays performed in churches and churchyards became during the thirteenth century gradually secularized, and were increasingly produced in the vernacular.[1]

The influence of the works of the English mystics has already been mentioned. All wrote in English. Richard Rolle used the Northumbrian dialect, and the *Pricke of Conscience* was explicitly intended for those who have no Latin. Nicholas Love's translation of the *Meditationes vitae Christi* has been described as 'the most beautiful prose of the century'.[2] Walter Hilton's *Scala Perfectionis* was originally in English, being shortly translated into Latin by a Carmelite friar, Thomas Fyslawe. Dame Juliana of course wrote in English, and Margery Kempe dictated her book in English. These, along with the translators of the *Golden Legend* and the *Imitation*, were the prime architects of the English prose that meets us a little later in the pages of Sir Thomas More.

The monastic and academic corporations of pre-Reformation England, working under their stable and impersonal discipline, produced the scholarly works of theology, philosophy and history, and transcribed the classical texts which they had in their keeping. These were the foundation stones on which were built the great libraries which post-Reformation scholarship in later centuries demanded. On the other hand, the vitality of English renaissance literature sprang by and large from the free, individual writers, unfettered and unhampered by any discipline save self-discipline, the ascetics and mystics of the fifteenth century with their long tradition of individualism going back to the Celtic saints and the Eastern hermits, the parish priests and friars with the spontaneity of vernacular homilies and manuals for the unlettered layman, and the rebels such as Wyclif and the Lollards, who shook themselves free of the guiding reins of tradition and set out on their own unorthodox path. This is the freedom which, whether it lead to truth or error, may kindle the creative fire of genius in the writer, and in the reader the desire for literacy and education.

---

[1] J. R. H. Moorman, *Church Life in the Thirteenth Century*, 1945, p. 143.
[2] H. S. Bennett, *Chaucer and the Fifteenth Century*, 1947, p. 180.

CHAPTER IX

S. Robert of Lincoln and the Oxford Greyfriars

IN the long period that separates the climax of the Benedictine Age in the twelfth century from the Tudor Reformation in the sixteenth, the history of English libraries must take special account of the influence of Robert Grosseteste, Bishop of Lincoln, who was born *c.* 1168 and died 1259.[1] His story illustrates very clearly the changes that were taking place in religion and education (and consequently in libraries) at this time. The great days of the monastic schools were drawing to a close; the new universities were rising in their place, and the coming of the friars had introduced not only a new missionary zeal into the Church, but quite new scholarly disciplines concerned with the necessary, but almost impossible, task of reconciling the teaching of Aristotle (whose works were now being studied for the first time in Western Europe) with the orthodox doctrines of the Church. New textbooks on new subjects were suddenly in great demand. They had to be light and portable and easy to copy; and new methods of book production emerged, with a great new army of professional scribes (in Paris, said Roger Bacon, their number was legion) to replace the workers in the monastic scriptorium.

The transition from monastic to academic teaching coincided with the ending of the monastic system of admitting child oblates—the recruitment of children who had to be educated in the monastic schools. The climax of classical learning in the monastic libraries came in the last half of the twelfth century; after that, interest in classical studies dropped as a direct result of the decline in child recruits, and the copying of texts almost came to a standstill. This was the time of the first and minor renaissance when the new universities in Italy and at Paris were springing to life. In the troubles of Henry II and the king of France, the

[1] The main authorities are F. S. Stevenson, *Robert Grosseteste*, 1899; S. Harrison Thomson, *The Writings of Robert Grosseteste*, 1940; D. A. Callus, *ed.* Robert Grosseteste, Scholar and Bishop, 1955.

English students in Paris migrated to Oxford, and a later migration from Oxford brought Cambridge into being.

The two great mendicant orders founded by S. Dominic and S. Francis in the early years of the thirteenth century reached Oxford in 1221 and 1224 respectively, and they soon spread through England. They drew their inspiration from two very different sources. S. Thomas Aquinas the Dominican was primarily the scholar, logician and champion of reason. S. Bonaventura the Franciscan, who was his friend, and fellow-student in Paris, lent towards Augustinian neo-Platonism and mystical theology and was the champion of faith and the contemplative life.[1] On the one side, reason and truth: on the other, faith and love and a certain independence of spirit. The Dominican Order was founded on the ideal of teaching and preaching, and for S. Thomas the contemplative life meant a life of disciplined study. The Franciscans on the other hand were primarily engaged in pastoral and missionary work, though they soon found that this needed a background of academic training. This was indeed their first break with their founder's ideal of absolute poverty, which forbade any brother to own anything but his habit and girdle and hose. Imitating the Dominicans, they became inevitably a learned order. 'Paris, Paris,' cried Brother Giles, 'Thou hast destroyed Assisi'; and he might well have said the same of Oxford.[2] For the next century or so, all the great scholars belonged to one or other of these orders, and a quite surprising number of them were connected with Oxford. S. Thomas had two precursors: Alexander of Hales in Gloucestershire, and Albertus Magnus, whose pupil S. Thomas was. Of those that came after, many were Oxford men: Duns Scotus, a much wiser man than his later nickname suggests; Roger Bacon, the solitary scientist of the middle ages, struggling gallantly against ecclesiastical censure; Adam Marsh, the first teacher at the Oxford Franciscan School; Archbishop Peckham; Thomas Bungay; and the nominalist William of Ockham, the last of the great schoolmen, who, being an individualist and content to separate faith

---

[1] See David Knowles, *The Evolution of Medieval Thought*, 1962, p. 237 ff.

[2] The essential difference between S. Francis himself and the Order as it developed is well depicted by Prof. Knowles in his short essay on the saint in *Saints and Scholars*, 1962. See also his chapter on Thomas of Eccleston: 'He alone shows us the leaven of Francis at work in a distant country.'

and science by an impassable gulf (as perhaps many do today), had his influence on the thinking of both Wyclif and Martin Luther.

Of all the people who were associated with the work of the early Franciscans in England, the greatest and in some ways the most interesting was Robert Grosseteste, the effective founder (along perhaps with S. Edmund Rich, Archbishop of Canterbury) of the University of Oxford, and its first Chancellor. He was born about 1168 of humble parents at Stradbrook in Suffolk, and was sent by his friends to study both at Oxford and Paris, returning afterwards to become *rector scholarum* at Oxford. After various preferments he was elected in 1235 to succeed Hugh de Wells as bishop of Lincoln, in which diocese Oxford then lay. He was a commanding figure in the England of his day; a scholar, a great pastoral worker and a saint, for his whole life was devoted to the re-awakening of religion and the revival of true learning; although he was never canonized, all the chroniclers agree in calling him 'Saint Robert of Lincoln'. He had a big literary output; over sixty substantial treatises remain, besides many smaller works. Unlike many medieval scholars, he never failed to stress the need to return to original sources; he had a truer appreciation than most of the importance of science and mathematics, and Roger Bacon himself paid tribute to his eminence on this score. His interest in original sources led him to learn some Greek, at a time when few English scholars were familiar with that language. In this he had the help of two men: a Greek named Nicholas, who was a clerk at St Albans; and John of Basingstoke, Archdeacon of Leicester, who was the first Englishman to acquire a genuine knowledge of Greek. John of Basingstoke had studied at Athens, where (according to Matthew Paris) he was taught by a girl of nineteen who was said to have been the daughter of Michael Acominatus, the Archbishop. It is not likely that Grosseteste ever acquired a real mastery of Greek, and unlike his friend Roger Bacon he never learnt Arabic. He did however learn Hebrew, as both Bacon and Adam Marsh also did; though Bacon states that Grosseteste's knowledge of neither Greek nor Hebrew was sufficient to enable him to translate effectively without help. There was a general ignorance of Hebrew at the time, in spite of the number of Jews in the country. Anti-Jewish prejudice probably accounts for this; contact with Jews was not encouraged by the Church, and indeed it was expressly forbidden by the Cistercians.

It might seem from this that Grosseteste was rather an inspirer of scholarship than a scholar himself. This may be unfair, in view of the tributes which so eminent a scholar as Roger Bacon paid him. In the physical sciences, Bacon asserted that Grosseteste superseded Aristotle, and that his work was far more intelligible than Aristotle, being based on the experimental method which Bacon himself used rather than on tradition; moreover, Grosseteste, according to Bacon, was the only living scholar who had a true appreciation of the significance of scientific knowledge, and especially of the supremacy of mathematics in explaining the real causes of things.[1]

Bacon's admiration for both Grosseteste and Adam Marsh is beyond doubt. Equally certain is the fact that Grosseteste not only placed Oxford firmly on the map, making it for a time at least the premier university of Western Europe, but inspired and encouraged a long line of famous scholars whose work won recognition throughout the medieval world.

In addition he was a bitter opponent of ecclesiastical abuses such as the appropriation of benefices by monasteries, and of royal and papal exactions. He was a close friend of Simon de Montfort, whose sons he had educated; he was intimate with the queen, and not without his influence over the king; and he won praise from such different sources as Wyclif and Gower (who praised him as 'beyond Aristotle') and even from Matthew Paris, who, though he regarded him as a persecutor of the monks, yet acknowledged his virtues. 'He was,' wrote Matthew, 'a manifest confuter of the pope and the king, the blamer of prelates, the corrector of monks, the director of priests, the instructor of clerks, the support of scholars, the preacher to the people, the persecutor of the incontinent, the sedulous student of all scripture, the hammer and despiser of the Romans. At the table of bodily refreshment he was hospitable, eloquent, courteous, pleasant and affable. At the spiritual table devout, tearful and contrite. In his episcopal office he was sedulous, venerable and indefatigable.'

[1] The best short account of the scholarship of Grosseteste and Bacon is in David Knowles, *The Evolution of Medieval Thought*, 1962, pp. 282–88.

Both the Dominicans and the Franciscans on their arrival in England sought Grosseteste's protection, and his active encouragement was responsible for their rapid expansion. He was particularly interested in the Oxford Greyfriars, and he became their first rector and divinity lecturer in 1224. It was largely his influence that guided them forward from their founder's rejection of learning and books into the paths of academic studies, and it was at Adam Marsh's suggestion that Grosseteste bequeathed his own books to the convent library. When these books were added, the convent must have possessed a quite remarkable collection of contemporary scholarship: Oxford's first great library indeed, for the University Library in S. Mary's Church must at this date have been small and limited in comparison, and the College libraries were still in the future. Grosseteste's books were still in the convent library in the fifteenth century, when Thomas Gascoigne noted their presence, but it seems as though even then they were being dispersed. One—Grosseteste's copy of S. Augustine *De civitate Dei*, full of his own marginal notes, was given by the friars to Gascoigne, and afterwards transferred to Durham College; it is now in the Bodleian. Some are believed to have been taken to Durham itself, possibly by Richard de Bury. When Leland visited the convent in 1535, its great library had all but vanished.

Not a great deal is known of the organization of the Oxford Greyfriars' library. The convent lay in the parish of S. Ebbe's, near the Castle and the city wall, but nothing remains visible today. The cloisters were as usual on the south side of the church; the chapter house and dormitory were on the east of the cloisters, the refectory on the south, and the library may have been on the west, but no evidence of this survives. The church is believed to have measured seventy-nine yards from east to west,[1] and if the rest of the buildings were on this scale, the library may have been very spacious indeed. There were indeed two separate libraries, one for the friars and one for secular students, but no description of them remains. Each of the friars was provided with a *studium*, i.e. a combined desk and bookcase. At first only the minister and the lector had cells of their own, but later those friars who were Doctors of Divinity were given their own chambers. The first

[1] A. G. Little, *The Greyfriars at Oxford*, 1892, p. 24.

large accession to the library was probably the collection of Adam Marsh, who had inherited the library of his uncle, Richard Marsh Bishop of Durham. He joined the order c. 1237, and was the first of the great Franciscan teachers at Oxford. He became one of Grosseteste's closest friends, and much of the correspondence between these two men relates to their books; in one of his letters Adam Marsh urges that a certain young friar should be allowed to study at Oxford, for at no other place are such aids to study so readily accessible. Grosseteste's bequest of his own library came in 1253. Other bequests are said to have included many Hebrew books, acquired when Edward I expelled the Jews in 1290. In the fifteenth century bequests became rarer however, and the influence of the convent declined. There were indeed scarcely any books bequeathed to the mendicant libraries in the fifteenth and sixteenth centuries, though many were left to the new college libraries. Some of the Greyfriars' books were sold, and moreover in 1412 the friars were excluded from the University Library. Shortly before the dissolution Leland reported that 'at the Franciscans' house there are cobwebs in the library and moths and bookworms; more than this—whatever others may boast— nothing, if you have regard to learned books. For I, in spite of the opposition of all the friars, carefully examined all the bookcases of the library'. If any works of value still remained, the friars may well have taken care that Leland did not see them. The destruction of the convent by Cromwell was complete; none of their records survived, and only a handful of their books have been identified. This is grievous because the convent must have been particularly rich in the works of Grosseteste himself, of Adam Marsh, and his great pupil Roger Bacon, and of other famous Franciscans such as John Wallensis, whose very popular writings are specially illustrative of the practical side of Franciscan teaching. And there would doubtless have been many examples of that bibliographical innovation for which the mendicant orders were particularly responsible. Continually travelling from one university to another, or between village and village, they needed pocket-size books that were light and portable: tiny Bibles, collections of sermons, breviaries, missals, perhaps six inches by five, with fifty or more lines to the page and five hundred or more leaves. These 'little Bibles' grew popular in the thirteenth century, and examples of many can be seen in the British Museum. Some of the finest were made in Paris in the period 1270–1320. They were written on a new sort of vellum almost as fine as India paper, possibly made from rabbit or squirrel skin. Books of this type were a necessity to the peripatetic friars, in a way that they had never been to the older orders. Thus in Robert Greene's play, Friar Bungay draws out his 'portace' to marry Lord Lacy and Margaret, but is struck dumb by Friar Bacon before he can begin. This was his pocket breviary. The medieval Latin was *portiforium*, and the Middle English *porthors* (which occurs in Chaucer) developing into 'portas', 'portess', or 'porteous', i.e. a book that can be conveniently carried about out of doors.

Textbooks as well as service books were of course needed in this handy portable form; the Dominican Richard Fishacre, the bosom friend of Robert Bacon (possibly the uncle of the more famous Roger) was accustomed to carry about with him a copy of Aristotle which must obviously have been a kind of pocket edition. These small books were not made by the friars themselves but by professional scribes; the friars wrote some of their own service books and lecture notes, but they maintained no large scriptoria.

Of the other Greyfriars' libraries in England, the best known is perhaps that of the London Greyfriars, which was on the site later occupied by Christ's Hospital in Newgate Street. John Stow in his *Survey of London* describes how Richard Whittington founded it in 1429. This was the period when so many of our cathedrals and religious houses, as well as the colleges at Oxford and Cambridge, were for the first time establishing separate library buildings or rooms to house their collections. The London Greyfriars' library lay on the north side of the great cloister, 129 feet long and 31 feet broad, 'all sealed with wainscot, having 28 desks and 8 double settles of wainscot, which in the next year following was altogether finished in building, and within 3 years after furnished with books, to the charges of £556. 10s; whereof Richard Whittington bore £400; the rest was borne by Doctor Thomas Winchelsey, a friar there; and for the writing out of D. Nicholas de Liva, his works, in two volumes, to be chained there, one hundred marks, etc.'. This must surely have been one of the handsomest of English fifteenth-century libraries, and quite possibly one of the best equipped. Like the Greyfriars' libraries at Oxford and Cambridge it would have been particularly rich in scholastic works and in contemporary literature in general. The only rival to these amongst the monastic libraries would have been the later foundation of the Brigittines at Syon, which before its dissolution had amassed a greater collection of contemporary works, including printed books, than any other English house; Miss Bateson's catalogue of their library reveals nearly 1,500 volumes, in addition to the separate library of the nuns.

An illustration of the London Greyfriars' library, as it appeared in 1700, is given by R. A. Rye, *Students' Guide to the libraries of London* (3rd ed. 1927, p. 12); one wall of the library, badly mutilated, survived as late as 1834.

Raymond Smith suggests[1] that Winchelsey himself influenced Whittington to make this endowment. The London Greyfriars had a famous school of theology in the fourteenth century. It was a *studium particulare*, as opposed to the *studium generale* of Oxford; student friars were expected to spend two or three years at the London School, prior to their studies at Oxford. The London Greyfriars had a library before 1429 of course; they are known to have borrowed at least one of Grosseteste's works for copying.

Of the other libraries of the English friars, the most interesting was that of the Austin Friars of York, collected mainly by John Ergome, who was Prior in 1385. This convent obtained a generous royal endowment from Edward III in 1370–1, and the friars spent much of their money on their library. Its catalogue, on vellum and dated 1372, which is now at Trinity College, Dublin, has been printed by M. R. James. In its original form it contained some 250 titles, many of course being composite works. On Ergome's death, his private collection of some 220 works was added. The original library was of normal monastic pattern, but Ergome's collection was of a much more advanced nature, containing recent works of the Oxford schoolmen, some general literature and classical texts (including the very rare *Commentaries* of Caesar), works on mathematics, medicine, music and astronomy, a few Latin translations from the Arabic, some Goliardic

[1] Guildhall Miscellany No. 1, 1952; No. 6, 1958.

verse and surprisingly some works on black magic and kindred arts.

To return to Grosseteste. Though he deliberately encouraged the Franciscans in the collection of great libraries, and often went out of his way to get rules relaxed to enable individual friars to obtain special books, yet he never lost interest in the pastoral and missionary work of the friars, urging them constantly to cling to the poverty prescribed by their Order, and to the security and freedom from care that poverty confers. He quoted for them a line from Juvenal: *Cantabit vacuus coram latrone viator*; he who travels light will sing in the face of the brigand. But he did admit that, noble as the idea of poverty and mendicancy was, there was a rung of the heavenly ladder that stood even higher, namely, that a man should live by his own labour and not burden the world with his exactions. And his assertion on another occasion that the three essentials of well-being were food, sleep and laughter, reveals the very human side of his character. He wholly approved the vernacular preaching of both friars and parish priests. He himself was accustomed to preach in Latin to the clergy, but to laymen in English, thus following the good example of Abbot Samson of S Edmund's, who did not hesitate to preach in the Norfolk dialect when occasion demanded. Dr Owst, in his *Literature and the Pulpit in Medieval England*, has reminded us how much Chaucerian and Tudor English owes to the form in which our native language had been crystallized in the pulpit, and to the matter of the sermons, homilies, stories and allegories which were the standard fare of the medieval preacher.

In a sense, Grosseteste's patronage of the Franciscans was their undoing. Their founder, pledged to his Lady Poverty, had little use even for service books. 'After that thou shalt have the Psalmbook, thou wilt be covetous and want to have a Breviary, and when thou hast a Breviary, thou wilt sit in a chair like a prelate and wilt say to thy brother "Fetch me my Breviary". No brother ought to have anything but his habit and girdle and hose.' Fortunately or unfortunately, the good Bishop's encouragement, the teaching of S. Bonaventura himself, who inclined towards intellectual discipline rather than the asceticism of the Founder and the example of their friends the Dominicans, whose aim was to establish a school at all their houses and a graduate school at every university, made it impossible for the Greyfriars to keep within the bounds that S. Francis had set. Indeed they developed an insatiable thirst for books. Richard de Bury, sadly confusing his metaphors, likened them to ants and bees, 'ever preparing their meat in summer or continually building their cells of honey ... although they were late in entering the Lord's vineyard, they have added more in this brief hour to the stock of sacred books than all others'.

And so, having tasted the joys of possession, they fell. Their initial success, both in the academic and the religious field, was brilliant; their subsequent failure was correspondingly tragic and inglorious. Their good name lasted little more than a hundred years, and soon in the eyes of many people they had fallen almost into the same category as rogues and vagabonds. S. Francis, seeing the weakness of the monastic system, had determined to break away from it; but in a few years the good brothers were gathering property and building a new monastic system of their own. It was almost inevitable; primitive simplicity and the educated life do not fit easily together. During the thirteenth century the flow of gifts to the monasteries was largely diverted to the friars; but by Chaucer's time their glory had faded and gifts were tending instead towards the foundation of chantries and schools.

Though often popular with the ordinary layman, the friars were, for quite understandable reasons, out of favour with the church authorities. In the latter half of the fourteenth century the controversy[1] over the mendicant orders was raging bitterly, and the leader of the conservative opposition, Archbishop Richard Fitzralph of Armagh, preached a series of sermons at S. Paul's Cross against the friars. The theological arguments do not concern us, but more than theology was involved. The Archbishop claimed that neither poverty nor mendicancy had valid authority in scripture or tradition, and he supported this claim by turning his fire on the hypocrisy of the mendicant orders. 'How can the friars speak of poverty,' he cried, 'when they live in such splendour? They have churches finer than cathedrals, their cellars are full of good wine, they have ornaments more splendid than those

---

[1] For an account of the controversy see Knowles, *Religious orders in England*, vol. II, 1955, ch. V.

of any prelate in the world, save only our Lord Pope. They have more books, and finer books, than any prelate or doctor; their belfries are more costly; they have double cloisters in which armed knights could do battle with lances erect; they wear finer raiment than any prelates in the world ... Is there no ambition in their anxiety to receive privileges as confessors and preachers? Or is it no small honour to count kings and queens, dukes and duchesses, earls and countesses and other noble men and women among your spiritual children?' (For a century the example of the Plantagenets in choosing their confessors from among the friars had been followed by many of the aristocracy.) Fitzralph was the author of *De Pauperie Salvatoris*, a long discussion in seven books of the doctrine of lordship and grace which developed into an attack on the mendicant orders. It was this work which presented Wyclif with the arguments he used in his condemnation of every kind of organized authority in the church, papal and monastic as well as mendicant.

The case against the friars received much publicity. Chaucer's friar was doubtless drawn from life, but he may or may not have been typical in his own period, though it was perhaps natural enough for the Somnour to hold that 'freres and fiendes been but lyte a-sonder'. Chapter and verse for the prosecution are given in *Piers Plowman*, especially in the version known as the B- text which was written about 1377–8, and is in effect an impassioned denunciation of all the mendicant orders; in the closing scenes of the book they appear in the van of the army of Anti-Christ. Much the same charges are implied, though more soberly, in the three letters to the English friars sent at this time from Italy by William Flete, the English hermit and mystic, at Siena; these are printed by Aubrey Smith in his work on the Austin Friars. Far more extravagant and unbridled was the abuse that Wyclif was pouring out in his Lutterworth pamphlets towards the end of his life; all the organized orders roused his wrath, not excluding his one-time friends the friars, who are now described in scurrilous terms as the tools of the devil himself. A good friar is as rare a bird as the phoenix: *rarus est cum fenice*; and with strange prophetic instinct he outlines a scheme for the absolute suppression of mendicants and possessionists alike, and for the return of their wealth to the original donors or to the State. Langland, however bitterly he condemned the present reality, had a devout and humble respect for the ideal of S. Francis. Wyclif's attack on the other hand was indiscriminate and all-embracing.

The case for the prosecution was no doubt well grounded, but it must not be over-stated. Veneration for the founder of the Greyfriars has widened and deepened through the years and the centuries, so that everywhere his life is accepted as the type and pattern of humble sanctity; and it would be incredible if at any period the picture was as black as Wyclif drew it. The figure of John Brackley who figures so picturesquely in the letters of the Paston family has perhaps some affinities with Chaucer's friar. But throughout the three centuries between Adam Marsh and the suppression, there were good and sincere friars as well as others who were neither. Margery Kempe for example, who died c. 1438, was faithfully befriended during her troubled and vivid career by three of them. This point is fully discussed by Dom David Knowles in the second volume of *The Religious Orders in England*, pp. 198–203, and in his third volume he describes the uncompromising dignity with which the great majority of the Observant Friars met their end; some at least achieved martyrdom. By the time of the suppression of the mendicant orders in 1538, there was in fact little left to suppress. The most faithful had already been driven away; a few had betrayed their cause and taken to the 'new learning'; only the remnant survived, to be turned adrift by the renegade visitors Richard Ingworth and John Hilsey who had sold themselves to Cromwell. Their poverty at the end was extreme; neither wealth nor luxury remained, for they had depended on popular support, and this had been withdrawn. One thing is certain: neither those such as Lawrence Stone or John Forest or Anthony Browne, who are known to have suffered the final penalty under Cromwell, nor the great schoolmen of an earlier day such as Adam Marsh, Roger Bacon or Duns Scotus, have anything in common with the 'frere' in the Somnour's Tale, or with the 'friar of orders grey' in the song, except the colour of their habit.

The coming of the friars was dramatic, and their going was sudden and complete. In the words of Dom David Knowles, 'Three hundred years ago they had come, the brethren of Agnellus of Pisa, of Jordan of Saxony, of Haymo of Faversham and of

Simon Stock, the vanguard of a great movement that had covered the land with its fame. From the English friaries had issued forth a wave of learning that had captured the universities and given a decisive wrench not only to the teaching of the schools but to the whole course of European thought. They had seemed to their adversaries, little more than a century before their end, as numerous and as ubiquitous as flies in summer or as motes in the sunbeam. And now they vanished overnight, like flowers of a day.' Like flowers too their great libraries faded away; indeed they had been fading for many years before the end came. Neil Ker (*Medieval Libraries of Great Britain*, 1941) records but thirteen survivals from the Oxford Greyfriars' library, seven from London and nineteen from Cambridge.

Robert Grosseteste, the sponsor and friend of the Oxford Greyfriars and of their scholarship and their library, died in October 1253, and was buried in his own cathedral of Lincoln. Four years later his close friend Adam Marsh was buried beside him. The tombs were destroyed during the civil war in the seventeenth century. There were repeated appeals from the English Church and from Edward I for the canonization of S. Robert of Lincoln, but nothing transpired; perhaps the Bishop's vigorous independence in the face of papal claims was the obstacle. Miracles followed his passing, however, and church bells were heard in the sky on the night of his death. His memory and his work remained; no one, it has been said, had a greater influence on English life and literature in the later middle ages; few books were written in that period that do not refer to his authority or quote from his writings. Roger Bacon's testimony is unambiguous: *solus dominus Robertus prae aliis hominibus scivit scientias.* Even more telling perhaps is the ungrudging tribute from Matthew Paris, quoted above. Matthew was his contemporary—he died six years later; the superintendent of the St Albans scriptorium, one of the greatest of the monastic chroniclers, a wise and critical historian of his own times, an influential observer of events at home and abroad and the close friend of Henry III.[1] The Benedictine tradition made him a natural opponent of the new mendicant

---

[1] Professor Knowles (*Saints and Scholars*, 1962, p. 109) regards William of Malmesbury as a greater critical historian than Matthew Paris. Professor Galbraith (*Historical Research in Medieval England*, 1951, p. 32) inclines to the opposite view.

orders, though the conflict between the mendicants and the possessionists did not rise to boiling point till the time of Archbishop Fitzralph a hundred years later. Nevertheless there was some common ground between Matthew Paris and the Bishop of Lincoln. Matthew shared Grosseteste's impatience of external authority of any kind, whether its source was Rome or Westminster. And Matthew had a proper respect for the University of Oxford, regarding it as second only to Paris among the schools of the Church. Matthew himself was not an Oxford man; he was probably educated at St Albans, which was then at the height of its reputation as a centre of art and scholarly learning. The Benedictine nursery at Oxford, Gloucester College, with which St Albans was closely associated in later years, did not begin to take shape till well after Matthew's death. On the other hand, Grosseteste took his episcopal duties with due seriousness, and these brought him into frequent conflict with the religious houses. In his first year as Bishop of Lincoln, he carried out a visitation of the houses in his diocese which resulted in the removal of seven abbots and four priors, and the monastic habit of appropriating benefices for their own use and often leaving the parishes unserved or ill-served, was a perennial source of friction. This being so, we may the more readily accept Matthew's honest tribute to the saintly character of the Bishop, who was so wise and forceful a patron of the earlier friars and of their scholarship and their libraries.

CHAPTER X

Richard de Bury

SOME thirty years after the death of Bishop Grosseteste at Lincoln, there was born in a village near Bury St Edmunds another man of outstanding stature in the history of English libraries. Like Grosseteste, Richard de Bury was both statesman and scholar. The scholarship of both might have been deeper had their administrative responsibilities been less. There is indeed more evidence of true learning in Grosseteste than in Richard de Bury, but just as we have Bacon's testimony of Grosseteste's achievements, so we have Petrarch's admiration for Richard de Bury; neither Bacon nor Petrarch had need to flatter. Petrarch's words however were more restrained than Bacon's; Richard was '*vir ardentis ingenii, nec litterarum inscius, abditarum rerum ab adolescentia supra fidem curiosus*—a man of burning intellect, not ignorant of letters, an earnest seeker after knowledge from his youth up. The only other near-contemporary evidence is the life of Richard in the Durham Chronicle, which describes him as 'sufficiently educated'—*sufficienter litteratus*. Both these views suggest superficiality rather than depth in Richard's learning.

For all this, there is no doubt that he was an able civil servant and a good administrator. He spent the ten years 1302–12 at Oxford, taking his MA and BD and soon after began his civil service career by becoming a King's Clerk. Later he had various posts at Chester in the service of the future Edward III, becoming in due course one of Edward's Councillors, acting as his Chamberlain from 1320–4, and then as Constable of Bordeaux in 1326, when Edward became Duke of Aquitaine. During these years he was also Edward's tutor, and it is noteworthy that Edward III was the first of our kings who certainly was able to write. Edward became King in 1327, and Richard rose to the positions of first Cofferer, then Keeper and Treasurer of the Wardrobe, and then (1329–33) Keeper of the Privy Seal. At the same time he collected a wide plurality of benefices, culminating with the Bishopric of Durham in 1333. He took part in an embassy to the Pope at Avignon in 1330, and again in 1333; it was probably on the former occasion that he met Petrarch. He impressed the Pope sufficiently to procure a papal chaplaincy, and a promise of the next vacant English bishopric. In 1334 he became first Lord Treasurer and then Lord Chancellor; the latter office he relinquished in 1335. The rest of his career was divided between further diplomatic missions, and the political and ecclesiastical responsibilities imposed on him by his bishopric. Durham was not only the wealthiest of the English sees, but its distance from London and the neighbourhood of Scotland enhanced its importance; its bishops, as Denholm-Young points out, enjoyed a pro-consular or vice-regal status. During the last three years of his life (1342-5) Richard was troubled by illness, and he died soon after completing his *Philobiblon*. There seems little doubt that Richard de Bury, unlike some later book collectors, was a good man of business, a capable administrator, and conscientious in carrying out his episcopal duties. This is shown by his Chancery Rolls, which are the earliest surviving in the Durham archives. Moreover, however zealous he may have been in the acquisition of books, he was a generous and warm-hearted giver of alms.

Two features of his life make him important in the story of English libraries: the *Philobiblon*, and his immense collection of books. Richard de Bury was neither a great scholar nor an original thinker. He was primarily a practical administrator and civil servant, belonging essentially to the age of scholasticism and widely read in that profound, but limited, field. He stood on the brink of English humanism, but was in no real sense one of its prophets; indeed his view was limited on every side by the bounds of scholasticism. Though a friend of Petrarch, he would not have understood Petrarch's devotion to Cicero, Virgil and S. Augustine. The new learning and the excitement of the return to classical standards of writing and thought would have meant nothing to him; his only standards were those of Donatus and the Fathers and the schoolmen. He had no answer to give to Petrarch's well-known enquiry about the location of Ultima Thule; perhaps the question had no interest for him. Even Petrarch himself can have had small interest for Richard, for

Petrarch complains that his letters brought no reply, meeting only with *obstinato silentio*. Richard's unawareness of the ideals of humanism is evident enough in his limited horizons and his laboured style. It would be unfair to blame him for mistakes that were common at that time among greater scholars than Richard de Bury: the reference to Aristotle's *De Pomo*, which was really a translation from a Hebrew treatise, or the attribution of the peculiar hexameters of *De Vetula* to Ovid. The latter was quoted as Ovid's by many of the schoolmen, though Robert Holcot did indeed have the wits to add 'An sit liber Ovidii, Deus novit';[1] but Petrarch would have had no need to refer the question to Heaven.

Though the *Philobiblon* is no masterpiece of scholarship, it is nevertheless important for two reasons; first as a commentary on the literary side of monastic and academic life in England in the first half of the fourteenth century, and secondly as a statement of faith in the solid worth of books and learning. It is an admission of the bankruptcy of scholasticism as a national system of educa-tion, and a declaration of trust in the enduring value of the book as a tool of education. On the basis of this act of faith Richard gathered together from far and wide his own great collection of books, dedicating it explicitly for academic use after his death. Here he was on common ground with Petrarch, who had planned to leave his rich collection of MSS to the city of Venice. Viewed from another angle, the *Philobiblon* is Richard's apologia and justification of a life dedicated to the collection of books for ultimate public use. Never before in English history had any scholar or administrator seen so clearly the importance in our educational life of a great library; none had thrown himself so wholeheartedly into the task of planning a library of this kind. But although Richard saw some of the failings both of the monastic system and of the academic schoolmen, he was not sufficiently detached to be able to propound a genuine remedy. Something more radical was needed than a homily on the reverence due to books as the vehicles of truth.

Yet for all that this homily is a worthy and laudable endeavour, Richard made no extravagant claims for his one published work. It is a *tractatum parvulinum*, a little essay on the love of books,

[1] *Philobiblon*, Shakespeare Head Press, 1960, p. 187.

inspired by the multitude of young scholars whose ability, so full of promise in spring, has withered away before harvest owing to the poverty of their circumstances; friendless, they return to the mechanical arts to gain a livelihood, to the loss and degradation of the Church. We recall how in the past the Church has supported such students in their poverty, and how many of them 'distinguished by no pride of birth, and rejoicing in no rich inheritance, but supported only by the piety of the good, have made their way to apostolic chairs, have worthily presided over faithful subjects, have bent the necks of the proud and lofty to the ecclesiastical yoke and have extended further the liberties of the Church'. And so Richard sets down his purpose of aiding 'this calamitous class of man', and providing for them both the necessities of life and the books so useful to their studies. 'This ecstatic love has carried us away so powerfully, that we have resigned all thoughts of other earthly things, and have given ourselves up to passion for acquiring books.' And to suit his theme, he claims that his little treatise is written *stilo levissimo modernorum*, in the lightest contemporary style for (he says) it is ridiculous to treat a slight matter in a grand style. The reader today, noting the epithet *levissimo*, may perhaps wonder what kind of Latin Richard could have perpetrated in his ponderous moods. Actually by current standards his Latin is straightforward and reasonably correct, and he was a master of the Roman Cursus which, with its *clausulae* or rhythmic terminations originated in the Papal Chancery and distinguished much of the more formal prose of that period. The *Philobiblon*, however elegantly composed, is not an exercise in dialectics. On the contrary it is a very human and personal justification of an ambition that was close to his heart. Critics had accused him of greed and extravagance in amassing his library, and this is his defence. It bears the stamp of a genuine apologia; that is, it is not an afterthought worked up for the occasion.

The first three chapters of the *Philobiblon* expound first the treasure of wisdom enshrined in books; second, the love and respect due to them as the shrines of wisdom; and third, the right view of the cost of books. 'No dearness of price' (he says) ought to hinder a man from the buying of books, if he has the money that is demanded for them, unless it be to withstand the malice of

the seller or to await a more favourable opportunity of buying.
Then follow four chapters on the ill-treatment to which books
are subjected by the Church in its careless use of them, and by
wars. The first three of these are a powerful indictment of the
secular clergy, the possessioners and the mendicants, for their
ignorance and disrespect. The reading of a single set verse from
the psalter was sufficient to obtain benefit of clergy for an accused
man; and although the foundation stone of the whole Church
is a knowledge of literature, yet the love of books has been
replaced by the love of dogs, of horses or of women, and their
books are cast aside to perish and decay. This gives Richard a
cue for one of his purple passages in the grand manner, and he
makes the most of it.

The next victims are the possessioners. The monastic libraries,
once the richest store of wisdom in Christendom, are now
neglected. 'The study of the monks nowadays is the emptying of
cups and not the emending of books.' 'Flocks and fleeces, crops
and granaries, leeks and potherbs, drink and goblets, are nowadays
the reading of the monks, except a few elect ones, in whom lingers
not the image but some slight vestige of the fathers that preceded
them.' Even the canons regular ignore the provision in the
Augustinian rule for the distribution of books at a given hour
each day; scarcely anyone observes this devout rule of study
after prayer. And this charge ends with an appeal to return to the
study of holy books 'without which all religion will stagger'.

The mendicants come next, 'the latest offspring of the ever-
fruitful Church'. Their plight is no better. They have been
seduced by a threefold care of superfluities; of the stomach, of
dress and of houses. They are occupied with the wants of the
mortal body, 'that their feasts may be splendid and their garments
luxurious, *contra regulam*, and the fabrics of their buildings, like
the battlements of castles, carried to a height incompatible with
poverty', For all their extravagant habits and luxurious tastes,
however, Richard acknowledges the value of their acquisitive
instinct when it turned them to book-collecting. 'Although they
lately at the eleventh hour have entered the Lord's vineyard . . .
they have added more in this brief hour to the stock of sacred
books than all the other vine-dressers.'

Yet some saw dangers in the mere accumulation of books, and

there had already been warnings about this, notably from John of Wales, who was himself a Franciscan and was lector at the Oxford Greyfriars c. 1259–62. In his *Compendiloquium*, which was a biographical history of philosophy, John discussed the eight ways in which philosophy could be abused, one of which was over-confidence in the accumulation of books; the reason being that it is wrong to rely on the thinking of others, rather than to think problems out for oneself. This is of course the Socratic attitude towards reading, and perfectly legitimate. It has been suggested however that it was criticism of this kind that called forth Richard's apologia.[1]

When Richard de Bury wrote his bitter condemnation of both possessioners and mendicants, the great days of the monastic age had passed, and the controversies with the friars that reached their climax in the sermons of Archbishop Richard Fitzralph were gathering force. We may think that Richard took too harsh a view of the failings of both. Disrespect for the value of books was not confined to the fourteenth century; and it is a mistake to imagine that a vocation for the religious life and a vocation for scholarship are the same thing. The number of religious in England at any one time during the three centuries prior to the dispersal was perhaps 10,000 or 12,000. In each generation a very few were born scholars. The great majority can have had no natural inclination towards a life of scholarship, and with many their entry into religion was perhaps due to accident or force of circumstances rather than to any profound vocation. For the ambitious young man, the Church was the only channel to high office. The alternative channel of the law was opened in due course; the Inns of Court were the first schools intended for professional lay studies, but not till the Elizabethan period did they win the title of the 'Third Universitie of England'. Long before that, however, law, the *scientia lucrativa*, had drained off many promising students from the religious houses and the universities, to the great injury of both theology and literature. Students were tempted to go straight from Donatus to law, especially civil law, leaving out the classical writers altogether.[2] These however were

---

[1] W. A. Pantin, *John of Wales and Medieval Humanism* in J. A. Watt and others, *ed.*, *Medieval Studies presented to Aubrey Gwynn*, S.J., Dublin, 1961, p. 301.

[2] Helen Waddell, *The Wandering Scholars*, ch. VI.

only the cream on the surface. The ordinary young cleric, whether regular or secular, may often enough have had his full share of humility and piety and self-dedication but he would not be led to equate religion and learning, nor would he necessarily have any inborn respect for the textbooks he was bidden to study. Part of the attraction of the *Philobiblon* comes from the fact that there have been young men in every century down to the present who have committed all the sins that Richard enumerates with scorn and horror; his only mistake was that in blaming the young student, he did not also blame the system of education in which he was entangled.

Next Richard de Bury comes to the 'Complaint of Books against Wars'. Unhappily we have seen worse tragedies than those which Richard was able to cull from the chronicles of the ancients. He was not to know that legend rather than history was responsible for some of the instances he cites. It is perhaps especially in this chapter that the translation of E. C. Thomas takes on a curious similarity to the rhythm of the *Religio Medici*:

'Nay, Aristotle would not have missed the quadrature of the circle, if only baleful conflicts had spared the books of the ancients, who knew all the methods of nature. He would not have left the problem of the eternity of the world an open question, nor, as is credibly conceived, would he have had any doubts of the plurality of human intellects and of their eternity, if the perfect sciences of the ancients had not been exposed to the calamities of grievous wars.'

This is but a pale reflection of Sir Thomas Browne, no doubt; but the reflection is there, though the pregnant thought and the unexpected conclusion is missing. The author of *Religio Medici* would have willingly bartered the lost lines of Cicero and the whole libraries of Alexandria and the Vatican for the perished leaves of Solomon; he wanted a general synod for the benefit of learning, 'to reduce it, as it lay at first, in a few and solid authors', and to condemn all the rest to the flames. This thought would have shocked beyond measure the good Bishop of Durham, who was quite prepared to 'mourn with the grief that they deserve all the various books that have perished by the fate of war', and tearfully to recount 'the dreadful ruin which was caused in Egypt by the auxiliaries in the Alexandrian war, when seven hundred thousand volumes were consumed by fire'. Sir Thomas Browne would have shed no conventional tears over this calamity, nor would he so easily have been persuaded that the ancients 'knew all the methods of nature', and that all the secrets of the universe perished in this 'hapless holocaust, where ink is offered up instead of blood'. Richard here, as elsewhere, is led away by his rhetoric into unthinking fancies.

Next Richard de Bury describes the opportunities of book collecting that had fallen to him. From his youth up he had delighted in the conversation of learned men and in the love of books, but his prosperity and his association with the Court gave him ampler scope for 'hunting as it were certain choice preserves, libraries private as well as public and of the regular as well of the secular clergy'. The news of his hunger for books spread abroad, and clients learnt to choose 'soiled tracts and battered codices' for their bribes rather than jewels and cash. Monastic armaria were opened for him and dead volumes 'covered with litters of mice and pierced with the gnawings of worms' were spread before him. Thus, he says, the sacred vessels of learning came into our control and stewardship; and he admits that if he had loved gold and silver goblets, highbred horses or cash, his treasury would have been rich. But he wanted *libros, non libras*, codices, not coins, pamphlets, not palfreys. All this reads like an attempt to justify ill-gotten gains. He was probably no more scrupulous, and no less, than collectors have been in every age; the acquisitive instinct, though condemned by one of the commandments, is not if reasonably disciplined to be classed with the graver sins; to its operation must be placed the essential value of most of our museums and libraries. It can have its uses in any age, but it may most easily be justified at a time when the will to preserve literary records is at a low ebb. In Richard de Bury's day, no other library in this country was seriously engaged in book collecting as a matter of policy; indeed from Bishop Grosseteste in the thirteenth century to the humanist collectors of the fifteenth century, no scholar apart from Richard de Bury was deliberately building up a large collection, and none of the monastic libraries had ideals of this kind. The inactivity of many monastic libraries, and the attempts of others to reduce their accumulations of manuscripts to manageable limits by summaries and epitomes which tended to outlive the original texts, may go far to justify Richard's acquisitiveness.

He underlines the opportunities of book-collecting which were given to him by his embassies to the French Court, and this leads him to expatiate on the glories of Paris, *paradisum mundi*, which he regarded not without justice as the fountain head and centre of the world of books and libraries; much as, a thousand years earlier, Julian the Apostate, irritated by the scoffing of the people of Antioch, sighed for τὴν φίλην Λευκετίαν, his dear Lutetia, the city which truly understood him and had indeed proclaimed him Emperor. The magic of Paris is powerful in every age. In Richard's time, though Oxford was pre-eminent in the teaching of the schoolmen, she had little in the way of libraries apart from the Greyfriars' collection, and this, important as it may have been, could not rival the Sorbonne; nor could her scribes and booksellers match those of Paris. And it was in Paris that Richard seems to have acquired a fair number of his books: 'there indeed opening our treasuries and unfastening our purse-strings we scattered money with joyous heart and purchased inestimable books, *luto et arena*'—with mud and sand, as he curiously puts it.

Then again he had much help in his collecting from the circle of scholars he gathered round him, from the poor but learned friars whom he cherished 'with munificent liberality of beneficence for the sake of God'. To such he never refused the shelter of his favour, and accordingly he found them 'most special furtherers of our wishes and promoters thereof in act and deed'. The friars especially in their travelling among the universities and schools were invaluable; 'from the body of the Sacred Law down to the booklet containing the fallacies of yesterday (*quaternum sophisonatum hesternorum*), nothing could escape these searchers'. When Richard was raised to the see of Durham, he had several friars, both Preachers and Minors, in his household, and they worked for him zealously in revising, annotating, editing and tabulating (i.e. indexing or cataloguing) books; the Preachers especially are commended for their generosity in giving freely of their stores of wisdom. Moreover booksellers all over Western Europe were employed in collecting volumes needed for purchase; and at many schools the schoolmasters were persuaded to surrender obsolete volumes which still had their uses for the student, some being worth cleaning and carefully restoring. In his various manors Richard employed a staff of copyists, scribes, correctors, binders, and illuminators. And everyone, whatever his rank or sex, who had any sort of association with books, knew how to find his way to Richard de Bury's heart.

As to the kind of books that interested him, though the works of the Ancients were preferred, the Bishop protests that he does not condemn the novelties of the moderns (*novitas modernorum*); but he does this in terms which make it plain that he had very little use for the moderns. It is assumed that the ancients were better developed physically than the men of Richard's day, and probably therefore their mental development was better too. It is this kind of attitude that distinguishes Richard's medievalism so sharply from Petrarch's humanism. His thesis is that everything worth saying had already been said by the great writers of antiquity; the only thing left to do was to abbreviate their lengthy works, and he supports this depressing view by quoting the grammarian Phocas:

Omnia cum veterum sint explorata libellis,
Multa loqui breviter sit novitatis opus

Such an outlook is surely calculated to make any student despair. That it did not always have this effect may be due to the fact that most of Richard's students would accept it as a rhetorical conceit rather than a canon of literary criticism; and if in spite of this some consolation is needed, we may reflect that, when Richard died in 1345, the young Geoffrey Chaucer was about five years old. One useful moral Richard does however draw from his respect for the ancient writers, namely, the prime need to study them in the original language; and this meant a knowledge of Greek, Arabic and Hebrew. This was of course something that very few, if any, English students in the fourteenth century would have had. It was a need that was not generally recognized for almost another two centuries, and credit is due to Richard for perceiving it. How much Greek he had himself is uncertain; probably not very much, but presumably sufficient to make him see the need for more. And this led him to include a

Greek and Hebrew grammar and some glossaries and similar textbooks in his collection. Another lesson which Richard drew from his own experience was deliberately to prefer the liberal arts to law in forming his collection. This was no doubt a personal preference, but it was also intended to discourage the 'lucrative practice of positive law', which is the concern of the children of this world rather than the children of light.

The inclusion of the 'fables of the poets' is defended in a typically medieval way; they are the sugar round a necessary pill. In support he quotes Cassiodorus and Bede; if we are ignorant of the poets, we shall lose much of such writers as Jerome, Augustine and Boethius. Let a man's own intentions be upright, and 'he may thus make of any subject a study acceptable to God'. If the question is asked, who should be the chief lover of books? the answer is, the brief answer is, the clergy. It is precisely those who in earlier chapters were particularly condemned for their sins against books, who are 'bound to serve books with perpetual veneration'.

Chapter XV, on the blessings brought by the love of books, may seem to us today little but a rhetorical exercise, graceful but not very meaningful. The love of books has already been shown to be the love of wisdom, called by the Greeks *philosophy*, the mother of all good things. There is no room in a heart filled with the love of wisdom for the love of gold: *nullus igitur potest libris et Mammonae deservire*—no man therefore can serve both books and Mammon. We are expected to assume that in books vice is condemned, the deceits of the devil are exposed and the worship of God is revealed. Books delight us when prosperity smiles; when fortune frowns they comfort us; in books we climb mountains and scan the depths of the abyss, surveying all the wonders of nature; by their aid we communicate with friends and foes and princes, recall the past and foretell the future. This is indeed an ode or hymn in praise of the written word. The succeeding chapter argues the merits of writing new books to replace the old; and as may be expected, he means by this the transcription of ancient books, not the creation of fresh ones. Like many of his period, Richard is haunted by the idea of a golden age at the beginning of the world, when the fruits of the earth were more nutritious, bodily and mental vigour was more enduring and life itself was longer; this was a divine device to enable men to find out the sciences and write them down in books. Man has always dreamt of a golden age, but soon after Richard's time, it was transferred from the past into the future; still only a dream no doubt, but surely a healthier dream.

Now we come to the most human of all Richard's chapters, his homily on the care of books; human, because the sins he gravely enumerates are familiar and common in every age. Undergraduates are much the same yesterday, today and tomorrow, and the careless among them may always be found ill-treating things they value little. It is fair to add that today, library discipline is better organized, and that in the fourteenth century the average undergraduate was three or four years younger than today, indeed little more than a schoolboy. Today's student also probably knows more of hygiene; fingers are cleaner and handkerchiefs are used more punctiliously. His bookmarks are not straws, but whatever he uses, the book if distended will suffer. He underlines with a pencil rather than his fingernail, but the disfigurement is the same. He still may eat his lunch over the book, dropping cheese or fruit or spilling his tea on the pages; he may still fall asleep over the volume, crumpling the pages.

A memory of one of Charles Lamb's letters comes here. It was in November 1802. He had sent to Coleridge a box of books by the Kendal waggon, including some volumes of Milton; and in his letter he explains: 'If you find the Miltons in certain parts dirtied and soiled with a crumb of ripe Gloucester, blacked in the candle (my usual supper), or peradventure a stray ash of tobacco wafted into the crevices, look to that passage more especially: depend upon it, it contains good matter.' With him much will be forgiven, but we would not commend his example any more than Richard would have done; and we are reminded that tobacco is a new evil with which the Bishop did not have to contend.

He found it necessary however to object to the use of books as a flower-press. 'Now the rain is over and gone, and the flowers have appeared in our land'; and the student, *librorum neglector potius quam inspector*, stuffs his pages with violets, primroses, roses and four-leaved clover. This calls up a happy and innocent vision of the medieval springtime, 'whanne that Aprille with his

shoures sote, the droghte of Marche hath perced to the rote'.
But the Bishop saw nothing romantic in this. The scholar's hands
were wet and perspiring, or he was wearing soiled and dusty
gloves, so that the white vellum is smirched, and (sad anticlimax)
a biting flea distracts him and the volume is flung aside still open,
to gather dust for a month or more.

More especially to be condemned are those shameless youths
who canot see a blank margin on a page without trying out their
pen on it and filling it with frivolities; others cut away the margins
or end papers to use for letters if not for worse purposes. Finally
he returns to hygiene. *Praecedat omnino lotio lectionem*; always
wash before reading. Crying children and greasy scullions are to
be kept from books. Clean hands would help still more, if only
skin diseases were not so characteristic of the clergy. The chapter
ends with a warning that torn pages must be repaired at once, to
prevent the damage spreading. It would have been interesting and
useful if some guidance on book repairs had been given at this
point.

Now the Bishop draws towards his conclusion. His zeal in
collecting has been misrepresented and censured, and he publicly
rebuts this calumny. It has been his long-cherished aim to found
and endow a Hall at Oxford for the maintenance of scholars, and
to provide it with a worthy library which would be open not
only to these scholars but to all students at the University. He was
no doubt well aware, though he does not say so directly, that
Oxford was ill-provided with libraries at this time, and we can
only regret that so laudable a design did not come to fruition.

The penultimate chapter outlines the constitution of the proposed Hall and its library. It has often been said that his regulations
for the library were based on those in use at the Sorbonne. This
seems not to be the case; de Bury's rules, which are more detailed
than those of the Sorbonne, represent the normal university
practice of the period. One important difference from the
Sorbonne practice is that Richard makes no reference to the
need for chaining his books.

This chapter, which reads as though it were an extract from his
last will and testament, bequeathes his library to the community
of scholars living in . . . N . . . Hall at Oxford. The Hall was not
yet founded, and its name was left blank. The Master of the

Hall was to nominate five of his scholars to take charge of the library, and the authority of three of these was required for the loan of a book outside the Hall; any copying however had to be done within the library. Loans were to be made against a pledge of greater value than the book, and only books of which the library had duplicates were to be lent. There was to be a register of loans, with names and dates. Books not duplicated in the library could be lent only to scholars of the Hall. There was to be an annual inspection of the books, including volumes on loan. The Bishop notes that he had prepared a special catalogue of his books; this has unfortunately not survived.

The final chapter is an epilogue exhorting his future students to make continual prayer for God's mercy on him, with special veneration for the Confessor Cuthbert, 'the care of whose flock we have unworthily undertaken'.

'This treatise was finished in our manor-house of Aukland on the 24th day of January in the year of our Lord one thousand three hundred and forty-four, the fifty-eighth year of our age being exactly completed, and the eleventh year of our pontificate drawing to an end. *Ad laudem Dei feliciter et Amen.*'

Three or four months after these words had been written, Richard was dead. His death was not sudden, and according to the biographical note by the Durham historian, William de Chambre, he had been ill for some time, *longa infirmitate decoctus.* He may therefore have known, while writing the *Philobiblon*, that the end was near. Moreover, he died in debt, and being an able administrator he must surely have realized that his estate could not endow the new Hall and library at Oxford which he had planned. In the penultimate chapter of the *Philobiblon*, the name of the Hall is specified by a capital N, which was equivalent to leaving it blank; when this was written, neither Hall nor Library had been founded, and indeed the library never was founded. The scheme was not entirely new, however, for seven years earlier, in 1338, the Bishop is known to have concluded an agreement with the King, part of which provided for the founding of a Hall at Oxford for a prior and twelve monks of Durham; this was indeed carried out by his successor Bishop Hatfield, who founded Durham College on the site of the present Trinity College. No library was however established; Richard's books were scattered; his special catalogue has not survived; his tomb in due course was despoiled; the *Philobiblon* is his only remaining memorial. Uncharitable critics have even queried his authorship of this work, which some later manuscripts ascribe to the Dominican Robert Holcot, who was one of Richard's chaplains. Though Holcot may indeed have transcribed and edited it, there seems no doubt now however that it is Richard's own book, much of it being autobiographical. This is indeed generally accepted today. If the authorship is genuine, however, was the plan to found a new Oxford library equally genuine? Or was it perchance a last-minute device to justify his life's interest in book collecting by a scheme which, as he must have known, had little chance of realization? There are no grounds for such suspicions, and charity can have only one answer to give.

Beyond all doubt we can be certain that pre-Reformation England produced no book collector comparable in status with Richard de Bury. If some of his acquisitions came as gifts or bribes, this was in an age when gifts to high officials were part of the accepted machinery of advancement; and if such gifts are blameworthy, a gift of books is surely more pardonable than most. The story of his dealings with the Abbot of St Albans is well known. The Abbot purchased Richard's favour by a present of four volumes (Terence, Virgil, Quintilian and Hieronymus against Rufinus), and by the sale of thirty-two others for fifty pounds of silver. Richard apparently had qualms about this transaction, and when he became Bishop of Durham he returned some of the volumes; others (including a folio manuscript of John of Salisbury which is now in the British Museum, and two others now in the Bodleian) were bought back at a low price from Richard's executors.

The Durham chronicler tells us that the Bishop's books would easily have filled five carts. If this is correct, a fair estimate of the size of his collection would be about 1500 volumes. William de Chambre's account underlines his delight *in multitudine librorum*. He possessed more volumes than all the other bishops put together, and there was a separate library at each of his residences. Wherever he was living, volumes were piled so plentifully in his bedchamber that it was difficult to move without stepping on them. All the time he could spare from administrative business or religious offices was devoted to his books. Whenever he dined, a book was read aloud to him, and a discussion of it followed. There was always a circle of scholars around him to share in these discussions: men such as Richard Fitzralph, afterwards Archbishop of Armagh, Thomas Bradwardine, the mathematician, afterwards Archbishop of Canterbury, Walter Burley the Aristotelian scholar, Robert Holcot the Dominican, John Mauduit, the astronomer, and many others. Some of these were doubtless greater scholars than Richard, but none so far as we know had collections of anything like this size. Amongst other fourteenth-century prelates, Archbishop Simon Langham, for example, who died in 1376, left his collection of 116 volumes, along with most of his great wealth, to his old Abbey of S. Peter's, Westminster. The Benedictine Cardinal Adam Easton, who died in 1398, left his library of about 200 volumes to his monastery at Norwich; he died in Italy where part of his library was collected, and it reached England in 1407, packed in six barrels. An inventory of the books of Richard de Gravesend, Bishop of London, who died in 1303, lists eighty volumes valued at £116 14s 6d. Even these would be large collections for the period, though Richard's must have been many times as large. Few scholars holding episcopal office at this time would indeed have had either leisure or opportunity to collect books, and any works they had written themselves would in general have been completed before they were raised to high office. National and local administration took up most of their time, and much of their lives was spent in nomadic fashion, moving from one manor to another, or travelling on diocesan visitations. In these circumstances, Richard de Bury's achievement stands out as all the more notable.

Time has seen to it that next to nothing of this great collection should survive. The *Philobiblon* alone survives to remind us of the first and greatest English medieval book collector, and his vain hope to establish a great library to serve not only Durham College but the whole University of Oxford.[1]

[1] For further study, see the edition of the *Philobiblon*, with text and translation of E. C. Thomas, and bibliographical postscripts and foreword by Michael Maclagan. Oxford, Shakespeare Head Press, 1960. See also N. Denholm-Young, *Collected Papers on Medieval Subjects*, 1946 (articles on *Richard de Bury* and *The Cursus in England*); and for William de Chambre, see the Surtees Society edition of the *Scriptores Tres*, and *The Birth of a Chronicle*, Bodleian Quarterly Record, vol. VII, no. 80.

CHAPTER XI

Evidences of Literacy

THE historian of libraries must note the evidences of literacy, particularly in periods when it is developing from the mere ability to read, to the formation of the habit of reading; and he will look also for signs that this habit itself is developing from the uncritical absorption of matter that makes little or no demand on the intelligence, to the selective and critical appreciation of creative work in which reader and writer can meet on more or less equal terms. When the habit of reading is established, the habit of collecting books will follow, and nothing will reflect the mental character of the reader so clearly as the books he gathers about him, reading some, perhaps re-reading some, leaving others unfinished or not even attempted, yet setting on all of them a value of some kind which makes them seem worth preservation. Although the expansion of literacy was a notable feature of English life in the fifteenth century, the habit of reading did not take firm root till the eighteenth century. A brief discussion of the evidences in these two periods was included in the previous work,[1] but a further examination of the problem can usefully be inserted at this stage, for it is fundamental to the progress of libraries and scholarship.

The extent of literacy in the ancient period is difficult to estimate, but wherever book-production was widespread and schools and bookshops existed, one must conclude that there was a fair proportion of literacy amongst the population; at least as high a proportion for example as in Elizabethan England, and sometimes higher. This is implied not only by the general familiarity with the written works of Greek, Latin and Jewish literature,[2] but by the development of foreign trade and industry, of highly organized

[1] *Origins*, pp. 150-9, 191-7.
[2] Jewish education was largely based on memorizing, but various passages in the Gospels suggest that literacy was fairly general. See Daniel Rops, *Daily Life in Palestine at the Time of Christ*, 1962, pp. 272-3.

administration, and of religious, legal, medical and other systems of knowledge, all of which involve written communications and records. Further confirmation of the spread of literacy among the general population can be found in the prevalence of public notices, election propaganda and scribbled verses on the walls of Pompeii and on tiles and other artefacts everywhere in the Roman world.

A high level of literacy survived in Constantinople through most of the Byzantine period, certainly till the thirteenth century. Popular education was widespread and by no means confined to the clergy; and the successful administration of the Eastern Empire depended largely on the body of highly trained civil servants educated at the Imperial University; the administrative ability of the bureaucratic class was the main reason for the survival of the Empire for a thousand years. Even in the closing centuries of the period, the literary, encyclopaedic and historical productions of Byzantine scholars reached a much higher standard than Western Europe at that time could boast, and in fifteenth-century Constantinople and Trebizond lay literacy may still have been fairly general. Beyond the limits of these cities however the picture was darker. Even in the twelfth century, Eustathius, Archibshop of Thessalonica, had to beg the monks of his diocese to preserve their books for future generations that might know how to value them better than they did, and Michael Acominatus, Archbishop of Athens was complaining of the illiteracy of this once-glorious city; sheep grazed amongst the columns of the Painted Porch, and the congregation at the Parthenon, which was now his cathedral, could not understand his preaching; the only library in the cathedral (and perhaps in the city) was two presses beside the altar, and the Archbishop had to console himself with the books he had brought from Constantinople: copies of Homer, Thucydides, Nicander, Galen and Euclid. According to Matthew Paris, it was from the daughter of the Archbishop, a girl of nineteen named Constantina, that John of Basingstoke, Archdeacon of Leicester, acquired his knowledge of Greek during his sojourn in Athens; he may have been the first Englishman to have mastered the Greek language. The citizens of Athens were however no more illiterate than the Franks who captured Constantinople in 1204; Michael's brother,

Nicetas Acominatus, described them as unlettered and uneducated barbarians who scoffed at the city of clerks and bookworms. After 1453, Greek scholarship disappeared from Constantinople, and the Orthodox Church, so far as it survived under Turkish rule, became a largely uneducated and illiterate body.

In the West from the sixth century onwards lay literacy vanished, and the world of books became almost exclusively an ecclesiastical preserve. The word *clericus* stood for clerk as well as clergy; they were the same thing. Even the royal courts were illiterate, as Professor Galbraith has reminded us,[1] though there were two or three exceptions to prove the rule: Sigbert, king of the East Angles and Aldfrith, king of Northumbria, both of whom Bede describes as *doctissimus*, and of course Alfred the Great. Aldfrith, the pupil of Adamnan, was perhaps the first English king to own a royal library, to which Ceolfrith presented a 'beautiful volume of the Geographers'. With the possible exception of Athelstan, no English king after Alfred could claim to be literate, till Henry I (Beauclerk), or more probably Henry II, whose learning was beyond suspicion. Through all this period, literacy (which must here be equated with a knowledge of Latin) was a clerical monopoly in which the clergy had a vested interest.[2] No more illuminating proof of this monopoly could be quoted than the privilege known as 'benefit of clergy', which was extended not only to all clerical grades, but to all who could read their Latin. A psalter was given to the prisoner, and the judge then put the question, *Legit ut clericus?* to the bishop's officers, if the answer was in the affirmative, he was handed over to the ecclesiastical courts.

If however the layman was regarded as necessarily illiterate, it would be a mistake to imagine that illiteracy signified ignorance; in a true sense kings such as Athelstan and William the Conqueror were highly educated men, even if they could not easily construe their Latin.[3] If kings and noblemen did not write, this was because they had clerical servants trained to do this for them; but this by no means implies illiteracy in the widest sense of the word. Reading and writing were a clerical prerogative, jealously

[1] V. H. Galbraith, *The Literacy of the Medieval English Kings*, 1935.
[2] See pp. 163–4 *supra*.
[3] Galbraith, *op. cit.*, pp. 5, 12.

guarded by the Church and beneath the proper dignity of the aristocracy. The clergy were in a real sense professional readers and writers. It is worth remembering that, in medieval times far more than today, books were commonly intended for reading aloud; the punctuation, which marked breathing pauses rather than grammatical construction, indicates this, and much other evidence confirms it.[1]

The translations of Alfred and Aelfric reveal some progress towards lay literacy in the sense of being able to read English. Alfred speaks in the preface to his translation of the *Cura Pastoralis*, of English as 'the language which we can all understand' and he looked forward to the education of all the youth of free men wealthy enough to devote themselves to it, first in English, and later in Latin for those destined for high office. The use of written English, though not Latin, prospered after Alfred's time, and the more polished Anglo-Saxon prose of Aelfric and Archbishop Wulfstan in the early eleventh century, confirms this. There seems no doubt that some of these works, especially the school books, homilies and Biblical translations of Aelfric, were definitely written for laymen who found Latin unintelligible and so had nothing but Alfred's translations to read. There is indeed one example in this period of lay writing in the chronicle of Ethelwerd the Patrician, written for his kinswoman Matilda, though both his grammar and scholarship are elementary, and the content is brief and derivative.

Such lay literacy as there was came to an end with the Norman Conquest, when English was replaced by Latin as the official language of Church and State; henceforward the vernacular became French for all but the humbler classes. There came in consequence a period of clerical illiteracy, illustrated amusingly by the story in John of Ford's *Life of S. Wulfric* describing how Brictic, the parish priest of Haselbury, quarrelled with S. Wulfric because the saint, in curing a dumb man, had caused him to speak fluently in French as well as English; the miracle seemed quite unnecessary to the unfortunate Brictric, who had no French, and when called to appear before the Bishop was compelled to be silent like a dumb man.[2] In the twelfth and thirteenth centuries

---

[1] On this, see *Origins*, p. 94.
[2] Lady Stenton, *English Society in the Early Middle Ages*, 1951, p. 211.

there were continual efforts to improve the educational standard of the parish clergy, and many presentations to livings were rejected owing to the illiteracy of the candidate, or accepted subject to the priest receiving some education.[1]

English began to come into its own again as the vernacular language in the fourteenth century, and French began to disappear except in the form of Law French. The school belonging to the Queen's College, Oxford, founded in 1340, was the last school at which the boys were enjoined to speak always in Latin or French; at Merton College School, founded about the same time, English was substituted for French.[2] John de Trevisa in his *Polychronicon*, 1385, observed that forty years earlier, i.e. 1345, two Oxford grammar masters, John Cornwall and Richard Pencrich, had decreed that their boys should henceforward construe their Latin into English instead of French, and that this custom had become general. In 1362, a statute was enacted that pleas in the law courts should be conducted henceforward in English, 'since French is unknown in the realm'; and in the following year the Chancellor for the first time used English in opening Parliament. By 1404, English ambassadors to France were begging the Grand Council of France to address them in Latin, 'French being like Hebrew to them'. About this time also the king's personal correspondence under the signet began to be in English.

The production of both original work and of translations in the vernacular is the first direct evidence of the spread of literacy among laymen. Bishop Grosseteste's allegorical romance, the *Chasteau d'Amour*, was written in French for laymen in the thirteenth century, but it was translated into English early in the fourteenth century, and was widely read in both versions. Two of the earliest translations came from John de Trevisa, an Oxford don who suffered expulsion and became vicar of Berkeley and chaplain to the fourth baron Berkeley; his translations included versions of Higden's *Polychronicon*, finished in 1387, and of Bartholomaeus Anglicus' *De proprietatibus rerum*, finished in 1398. Chaucer himself, who more than anyone gave form and discipline to English as a written language, translated Boethuis' *De consola-*

[1] See *infra*, pp. 250-1.
[2] A. F. Leach, *The Schools of Medieval England*, 1916, p. 196.

tione. Lydgate's voluminous works include translations from French. Gower, a country squire and, like Chaucer, a widely read layman, was at this time writing happily in Latin, French and English.

The translations of the Bible by Wyclif and his colleagues had a wide underground circulation, and must have encouraged many folk of humble stock, especially in the West Country and East Anglia, to learn the art of reading. The first lay convert to Lollardry was a certain William Smith of Leicester who had been rejected by the young woman of his choice. Far from drowning his sorrows in drink, he became a teetotaller and a vegetarian; and then, still unsatisfied, he set himself to learn reading and writing. Other men crossed in love have sought solace in study, but whether it brought solace to Smith is doubtful. He kept a Lollard school, and spent eight years writing books, but this ended only in his public humiliation and the destruction of his literary efforts, so that the fruits of this early example of self-help are lost. Other lay adherents of Lollardry are known to have been literate: Stephen Bell, the friend of William Swinderly; the Welshman, Walter Brute, who was a good Latinist; Thomas Compworth of Kidlington; and John Smith, the shoemaker of Thaxted. The few aristocratic adherents of Lollardry were doubt-less educated men. These included the wealthy Sir Thomas Latimer, who had a considerable Lollard library at Braybrooke, where Czech scholars transcribed Wyclif's treatise *On Lordship*, and where Thomas Ile copied and circulated Sir John Oldcastle's tracts. Lollardry however spread mainly among the craftsmen of the newly emerging industrial population, and it has been noted that the tendency to heresy was strongest in those crafts where some degree of literacy could be expected. 'Ecclesiastics who mis-trusted the possession of vernacular literature as evidence of depravity were not entirely wrong.'[1] It may be noted that one medium of Lollard propaganda was the distribution of handbills, which were in use long before the invention of printing. Nicholas Hereford and John Aston are said to have distributed handbills in the London streets during their examination by the Blackfriars Council in 1382. It is reasonable to assume that the 'man in the

[1] K. B. McFarlane, *John Wycliffe and the Beginnings of English Nonconformity*, 1952, p. 180.

street' of that period was likely to understand the purport of these leaflets.

Translations into English did indeed form a substantial and significant part of the literature of the fifteenth century, for they indicate the spread of reading among people not very familiar with the Latin tongue. The long list includes Benedict Burgh with his *Major Cato*, *Parva Cato* and the *Secreta Secretorum*, John Capgrave with his verse translation of the life of S. Katherine of Alexandria, Nicholas Love's *Mirrour of the Blessed Lyf of Jesu Christ*, Richard Misyn, Sir Richard Ros, Stephen Scrope, John Tiptoft Earl of Worcester, Caxton himself of course, and many anonymous translations such as the *Golden Legend*, the *Imitation*, and *The Book of the Knight of La Tour-Landry*. All these in the main were designed for the non-clerical reader.

Further evidence of lay reading in the fifteenth century can be found in the popularity of books obviously intended for reading at home. The production of religious and devotional works in this respect has already been discussed;[1] their importance as gateways to the wider world of literature continued through the succeeding centuries. Another popular type of work compiled for domestic use included the courtesy books, the manuals of etiquette, the guides to health, home management and the education of children, large numbers of which still survive.[2] In this class also can be included the romances, both new and old, many of which had a wide circulation.[3] In contrast to the manuals of personal religion, which circulated largely among the new middle classes, the Anglo-French romances, such as the *Romaunt of the Rose* and Malory, appealed to the wealthier, aristocratic classes. Wace of Jersey, whose *Roman de Brut* was dedicated to Queen Eleanor, declared that he addressed himself to the wealthy who possessed revenues and silver, since those were the people for whom books were made in his day (the twelfth century). Nevertheless the earlier romances (e.g. of Wace, Marie de France and Geoffrey of Monmouth) must have had a wide circulation; the *Roman de Brut* for example survives complete in eighteen manuscripts. By the fifteenth century the popularity of the older romances

---

[1] See pp. 140, 166 *supra*.
[2] H. S. Bennett, *Chaucer and the Fifteenth Century*, 1947, pp. 156–160.
[3] *ibid.*, pp. 311–18.

may have been waning. There were only two printed editions of Malory in the fifteenth century, compared with fifteen of the *Golden Legend*; the saints were more popular than the knights. The new reading public was drawn from the rising mercantile classes, and the craftsmen, such as those that appear in the Paston and Cely letters.

The basic fact behind the emergence of literacy among laymen of the poorer classes in the fifteenth century is perhaps the gradual emancipation of serfs. In 1350 over half the population were unfree; by 1600 no serfs were left in England. Emancipation by manumission or by escape brought a movement of the population towards the larger villages and towns where wages could more easily be earned, and for many this produced a new awareness of the economic value of literacy and at least elementary education. There was opposition to this from some quarters, but Richard II refused the well-known petition that villeins should be forbidden to send their sons to school 'to learn clergee'. (Note the synonymity of 'clergy' and 'learning'; this persisted till the end of the seventeenth century). In 1406 Parliament established the right of every man or woman 'to send their son or daughter to take learning at any school that pleaseth them within the realm.' Walter Map complained of the tendency of serfs to educate their 'ignoble and degenerate offspring' in *De nugis curialium* (*c.* 1200); and two centuries later Langland was remarking on the spread of this tendency in his own day.[1] Another feature of this period was the creation of new boroughs by the grant of charters of burgess rights, thus changing villages into urban communities. Not all the new boroughs prospered or even survived, but they played their part in the spread of literacy both in the new towns and the surrounding countryside.[2] Throughout the later medieval centuries there was a steady infiltration from the peasant class into positions of local and even national importance. Sir William Paston cannot have been the only fifteenth century squire whose parents or grandparents had risen from the ranks, and a quite remarkable number of bishops and archbishops came of lowly origins.

The fifteenth century is well known to have seen the founda-

[1] *Piers Plowman*, C. VI 63–81.
[2] H. S. Bennett, *Life on the English Manor*, 1938, pp. 275–317.

tion of many famous schools from Eton downwards, and this of itself reflects the wider spread of education. Even more significant for our present purpose is the first appearance of teaching for the emergent lay professions, sometimes by lay teachers. This was a considerable innovation. In the latter half of the fourteenth century, at least one of the 'halls' that were springing up in Oxford in the role of grammar schools or cramming establishments was definitely designed for students reading for the lay professions. It was kept by a married master named Thomas Sampson and his wife Isabel. Sampson was employed by the University for some years as a scrivener, but his main occupation during the period 1350–1409 was the conduct of a sort of secretarial school, with a curriculum which included accountancy, estate management, conveyancing, heraldry and business methods, as well as letter-writing in Latin and French. He was the author of several popular text books in these subjects.[1]

The school at Sevenoaks which later became Queen Elizabeth's Grammar School owed its foundation, c. 1433, to Sir William Sevenoke, Lord Mayor of London, whose will stipulated that the headmaster was to be 'by no means in holy orders'; a remarkable provision for the period.[2] The College of Jesus which Archbishop Rotherham founded in 1483 at his native town of Rotherham was intended partly as a grammar school, partly as a choir school and partly to teach writing and reckoning to boys who needed instruction 'in the mechanic arts and other worldly affairs', and a third master was to be appointed to take charge of the commercial side of the school.[3] There was evidently a growing need in the mercantile world for clerks with some knowledge of writing and accountancy, and instruction in these arts would often be given during apprenticeship, either by the master or at a convenient school. A case is recorded of a boy apprenticed in 1442 to a merchant who undertook to send him to school for a year and a half to learn grammar, and half a year to learn to write.[4] A large number of petty schools teaching the three R's came into being during this century.

[1] Emsden, *Biographical Register of the Univ. of Oxford*, III; *Amer. Hist. Rev.*, 1941, XLVI, pp. 259–80; *Bull. of John Rylands Lib.*, 1939, 23, pp. 452–4.
[2] A. F. Leach, *op. cit.* See also *D.N.B.*
[3] A. F. Leach, *op. cit.*, p. 275 and *D.N.B.*
[4] C. L. Kingsford, *Prejudice and Promise in Fifteenth Century England*, 1925, p. 35.

The practice of lay teaching was deliberately adopted at Colet's foundation of S. Paul's School in 1509, which has been taken, not without justice, as the date of the introduction of humanism in English education. The new school was entrusted to the Mercers' Company rather than to any ecclesiastical body. In the words of Erasmus, 'he set in charge, not a bishop, not a chapter, not dignitaries, but married citizens of established reputation'. It was expressly provided that the masters might be married men. William Lily, the first high master was himself married, with fifteen children, and the sur-master, John Rightwyse, married his daughter Dionysia, and succeeded to the high mastership on Lily's death in 1522; ten years later when Rightwyse died, Dionysia married the then sur-master, John Jacob. The school did not, like Rotherham, provide a commercial education. Its curriculum embodied the humanist ideals of Erasmus and Colet, specializing in theory on the Christian poets both of antiquity and the classical revival, but in practice on the pagan works of the classical period.[1]

With the appearance of lay schools and the lay professions, there came naturally the first lay scholars and writers. The contribution of the fifteenth century in this respect was modest. Sir Thomas More belongs rather to the succeeding century, but two or three not undistinguished figures can be noted, Thomas Hoccleve the civil servant, for example; John Gower the country squire and poet; Sir Reginald Bray, the statesman and architect who designed Henry VII's chapel at Westminster and S. George's chapel at Windsor; and William of Worcester, who shares with John Rous the honour of being the earliest English antiquary. William, who appears in the Paston Letters as Sir John Fastolf's secretary, was a layman by choice and the first of a long line of English country gentlemen with an interest in topography and antiquities. Though he is perhaps remembered chiefly for his *Itinerary*, with its detailed description of his native city of Bristol, his interests extended in many directions, including medicine and the classics, and he knew something about the dating of MSS by the handwriting. Something is known of his own library; he possessed various medical treatises, some travel books, Poggio's translation of *Diodorus Siculus*, and some plays of Euripides and

---

[1] Frederick Seebohm, *The Oxford Reformers*, 1869, p. 463; M. L. Clarke, *Classical Education in Britain, 1500–1900*, 1959.

Sophocles. He had tried to learn Greek from William Celling of Canterbury, but seems to have made little progress with it.

William of Worcester may have been exceptional among fifteenth-century laymen, but the endeavours of the Paston family to collect a small domestic library at their Norfolk manor may not have been untypical of other country squires in Southern and Eastern England.[1] A considerable body of evidence from fifteenth-century wills testifies to the ownership of books, the titles of which are often specified, and many of the testators belong to the mercantile class, such as Andrew Horn for example, fishmonger and chamberlain of London, who in 1328 left some of his library to the Guildhall.[2] John Carpenter, Common Clerk to the City (1417-38), and Thomas Walyngton, a London draper (1403) are later examples.[3] The lists of private collections in Sears Jaynes *Library Catalogues of the English Renaissance* (1956) are based very largely on evidence from wills, and there is little doubt that further research on fifteenth-century wills would produce much useful information on lay reading in that period.

Much of the evidence for the literacy of the population in the fifteenth century has been carefully assembled and examined.[4] Quite evidently, no statistics of literacy are possible for the period, and no firm conclusions can be reached. Sir Thomas More's estimate in 1533[5] that roughly fifty per cent were illiterate is too uncertain to support any precise figures. In general however More was a most trustworthy commentator, and the *Apology* (in which this estimate was made) was a carefully written treatise that is most unlikely to contain exaggeration or loose thinking. Note also that in this passage he is asserting not the literacy but the illiteracy, of a great part of the nation. Far more than four-tenths of the people (he says) could not read the scriptures even if they had them in English. Doubtless if he had felt that he could have made it more than 'four tenths', he would have done so to improve his argument; 'far more' must imply less than half, otherwise he

---

[1] *Origins*, p. 158; H. S. Bennett, *The Pastons and their England*, 1932.

[2] N. Denholm-Young, *Collected Papers on Medieval Subjects*, 1946, pp. 168-74.

[3] *Origins*, pp. 157-8; C. L. Kingsford, *op. cit.*

[4] See especially J. W. Adamson, 'The Extent of Literacy in the Fifteenth and Sixteenth Centuries', *The Library*, 1930, 10, p. 163; H. S. Bennett, 'The Production and Dissemination of Vernacular MSS in the Fifteenth Century', *The Library*, 1946, 1, p. 175, and *English Books and Readers, 1475-1557*, 1952.

[5] H. S. Bennett, *English Books and Readers*, 1952, p. 28.

would have said 'five tenths', Our surprise therefore is that the remaining six-tenths could read English early in the sixteenth century. In the circumstances we can be reasonably safe in accepting More's figure as the considered view of a wise and clearheaded man who met people of every class in the course of his work, remembering of course that it must apply in the main to London, where literacy was certainly higher than in other parts of the country.

Only one other contemporary estimate has been quoted, and this occurs in a letter from Stephen Gardiner, Bishop of Winchester, in 1547, in which he asserts that 'not the hundredth part of the realme' could read.[1] This was in support of the retention of images (which are books for the illiterate) in churches, and it means simply that very many were illiterate and needed the pictorial instruction that images could give. It is much more of a rhetorical figure than More's carefully worded guess, and indeed it helps us not at all.

At this distance we cannot expect any statistical evidence. We can however affirm that literacy was becoming widespread during the fifteenth century, and that it continued to increase steadily from then onwards. Beyond contradiction there was a considerable reading public waiting for Caxton's printed books. To some extent the demand had been awakened by merchant-scriveners such as John Shirley (1366–1456) who were putting manuscript works on the market in almost wholesale fashion, rather than producing them only on commission.[2] The steadily growing production of books during the first hundred years of printing is evidence enough that more books were being read by more people.

The most potent of all the influences in favour of literacy at this time was that of religion. Almost half the titles in the *Short Title Catalogue* (1475–1640) were in some sort religious in content and purpose, and for the first fifty years of this period the proportion was more than half.[3] Apart from officially prescribed works such as the Bible and the Prayerbook, the *Paraphrases* of Erasmus, Foxe's *Actes and monuments*, Calvin's *Institutions* and the works of

---

[1] J. A. Muller, *The Letters of Stephen Gardiner*, 1933, p. 274; H. S. Bennett, *op. cit.*, p. 28.

[2] H. S. Bennett, *Chaucer and the Fifteenth Century*, 1947, p. 116.

[3] Louis B. Wright, 'The Significance of Religious Writings in the English Renaissance', *J. of the History of Ideas*, 1940, I, pp. 59–68.

John Jewel, Bishop of Salisbury, there were many popular works of devotion such as *The Crumbs of Comfort* and William Perkins' writings which had very large circulations for the time, and were translated widely into many European languages as well as Latin; his *Armilla aurea* (1590) ran through fifteen editions in twenty years.[1] The shelf of books which was the beginning of a domestic library in countless middle-class homes in the seventeenth and eighteenth centuries was in the main a religious collection.[2]

The indirect or external evidences of literacy become evident in the fifteenth century and increase in later centuries. Certain architectural changes point this way. In the larger parish churches clerestory windows became common in the fifteenth century, suggesting the need for more light in the nave, and gradually all windows began to grow taller and wider. Before this century the nave rarely had any seating, except for some stone benches along the walls for the aged and infirm. Now however pews fitted with book-rests were being widely provided: a revolutionary change, for the pews made the nave unsuitable for the many secular purposes it had served in earlier days, such as church ales, feasting and fairing, plays and dances, and even as a warehouse for the storage of goods placed in sanctuary or received as a pledge by the churchwardens. The book-rests imply that service books were being used by the congregation.

The change in social habits which led to the provision of private apartments for the lord and lady, who even in Langland's day were choosing to dine by themselves rather than in the great hall has been noted elsewhere. This led in due time to the building of houses with ample natural lighting, planned so as to accommodate rooms designed for the many special purposes needed by the new landowners. One of these special rooms was the study or library, and this begins gradually to appear in the larger houses and parsonages in the seventeenth century.[3] The recognition of the need for such a special room can be interpreted as a sign that the habit of reading as distinct from the mere ability to read, is awakening.

The observant eye will note many minor evidences of general

---

[1] *D.N.B.*
[2] Such as for example the Johnson family's collection at Glapthorn. See *Origins*, p. 164.
[3] See *infra*, p. 267 ff. and *Origins*, pp. 123, 155.

literacy, especially from the Elizabethan period onwards. The inscribing of the Ten Commandments on the walls of churches was not unknown in medieval days, but it became common under Elizabeth I. The churchwardens' accounts at S. Michael's, Worcester, record in 1547 the putting up of the Pater Noster, the Articles and the Ten Commandments, and it is to be presumed that most of the congregation could read them. At some churches, e.g. S. Mary's, Devizes in 1555, these were defaced or removed at the beginning of Mary's reign. In 1560-61 Queen Elizabeth ordered that 'the tables of the commandments be comely set or hung up in the east end of the chancell, to be read not only for edification, but also to give some comlye ornament and demonstration that the same is a place of religion and prayer'. That is to say, they were intended to take the place of the banished images and pictures (which Stephen Gardiner described as books for the illiterate). Sometimes the table of prohibited degrees was also put up.[1]

Still another piece of evidence from parish churches is the inscribed gravestone. This did not in fact become general among ordinary people till the eighteenth century. Dated gravestones are very rare before 1600, and are not common in the seventeenth century. Although the expense of an inscription rather than the illiteracy of the family will often have been the limiting factor, nevertheless when the provision of such memorials becomes an accepted custom, it can be assumed that literacy was fairly general. Inside the church, inscribed stone memorials to local notables were replacing the brasses of medieval times, and many members of the congregation must have whiled away the hours of service in deciphering the often elaborate wording of the inscriptions. One sign of illiteracy was the custom of declaiming the 'run-line' before each verse of a psalm was sung. This was established by the Westminster Assembly in 1643 to aid those who could not read. It spread through Scotland, and its disuse a century later caused some Presbyterians to secede. In 1746 the General Assembly recommended its abandonment in public worship.

The appearance of wall mottoes, embroidered or painted on cloth, and of samplers, amongst the new domestic luxuries which

[1] J. C. Cox and A. Harvey, *English Church Furniture*, 1908; J. C. Cox, *Churchwardens' Accounts*, 1913.

began to be popular in middle-class houses in the Elizabethan period is a further sign that children were learning their letters and that their parents recognized the value of this. Horn books became common educational tools during the fifteenth and succeeding centuries. The usual pattern comprised an oak panel with a handle, the lettering and figures on the panel being protected with a transparent horn covering.

The emergence of the habit of reading fairly widely, especially among the male population, during the eighteenth century was marked by a number of signs that bear witness to this change. The lapse of the Licensing Act in 1694, the Parochial Libraries Act of 1708, the Copyright Act of 1709, the spread of bookshops, the expansion of the book market, making literary patronage unnecessary, the fashion of social gatherings, dinner parties and coffee houses which stimulated the interest in literary criticism and intellectual discussion that distinguishes that fruitful period extending from Pepys, Evelyn and Dryden to Addison, Steele and Defoe, and so to Johnson and his circle: all these confirm the new habit and have been discussed elsewhere.[1] With many men (Squire Western is an example) this habit was concentrated on the new game of politics, which found expression in the flood of pamphlets that so astonished Dean Swift; often these had extraordinarily large circulations. Next to religion, politics was perhaps the main stimulus to the formation of the reading habit. The use of the pamphlet form for propagandist purposes, which is so conspicuous a feature of the eighteenth century has a considerable history. The great collection of civil war material which George Thomason had bound in almost 2,000 volumes is well known; it contained nearly 23,000 separate items, collected during the years 1641–62, carefully dated, arranged chronologically and catalogued. Perhaps however the earliest successful use of the pamphlet form for propaganda was the *Supplication for Beggars* by Simon Fish, which was scattered broadcast in London in 1529; it drew a reply from Sir Thomas More, in his *Supplication of Poor Soules in Purgatory*.[2] William Parkes the satirist in his preface to *The Curtaine-Drawer of the World*, 1612, notes the multiplication of pamphlets in London during his own lifetime.

[1] *Origins*, pp. 191–7.
[2] David Knowles, *The Religious Orders in England*, 1959, vol. III, pp. 199–200.

The circumstantial evidence of growing literacy in England throughout this period is convincing and indisputable, but there is little doubt that its spread was mainly confined to London, the South-east, East Anglia, and perhaps the West Midlands, where industry, commerce and administration were concentrated. It was here that the proportion of fifty per cent or more may well have been reached in the sixteenth and seventeenth centuries; and from here there must have been (to use a biological term) a cline of literacy extending west and north.

Further north however in Scotland, literacy had a rather different history, and in Southern Scotland, even in its remoter parts, the ability to read may well have been more general at an earlier date than in England. There is a very human picture at the beginning of Robert Henryson's *Testament of Cresseid* of the poet-schoolmaster of Dunfermline on a wintry night late in the fifteenth century sitting by a warm fire in his study reading Chaucer's *Troylus and Cryseyde*: a picture which at that date would be rare in England. The wide circulation of the writings of Sir David Lyndsay, poet and Lyon king of arms, in the sixteenth century has been noted.[1] His books were said to have been in the library of every castle and on the shelves of many cottages in Scotland, and a proverb arose for anything not worth knowing, 'You will not find that in David Lyndsay'. Side by side with Lyndsay on the shelf there would often have been a copy of Blind Harry's poem on Sir William Wallace, whose popularity is witnessed by the lapse of his unknown surname; there were more printed editions of this poem than of any other early Scottish work. There too might have rested a copy of John Barbour's *Bruce*, which a century earlier had become a national epic, widely remembered as a tribute to Scottish independence. How many Scottish bookshelves in the sixteenth century were as richly furnished as this nobody can now tell; there would certainly have been few in England to match them.

The Scottish divine, James Kirkton, in his *Secret and True History*[2] wrote that, 'At the time of the King's return every paroch hade a minister, every village hade a school, every family almost hade a Bible; yea in most of the country all the children of age

[1] *Origins*, p. 169; *D.N.B.*
[2] 1678; first printed, Edinburgh, 1817.

could read the Scriptures'. This was no doubt an exaggeration, and illiteracy must have been common enough in rural Scotland till the end of the eighteenth century. It is probable for example that fewer families possessed Bibles than in south-eastern England; eighteenth-century Kirk Session records often refer to witnesses unable to sign their names; and inscribed gravestones, which were frequent in eighteenth-century England, were comparatively rare till the nineteenth century in Scotland. On the other hand the focus of culture in rural Scotland has always been the manse and its library. One of the reasons given by James Kirkwood for the scheme of parish libraries which he launched in 1699 was the scarcity of books among the ministers, especially in the Highlands, 'some of them not having so many as are worth twenty shillings'. We may however marvel that most had this amount at the close of the seventeenth century; many English parsonage libraries at that date would have been less well equipped.[1]

On the general question of literacy in eighteenth-century Scotland the following story may have relevance. The tall Tuscan column, erected by Commissary James Smollett on the banks of the Leven between Clyde and Loch Lomond to commemorate the novelist, bears a long Latin inscription revised and partly written by Johnson, who visited Bonhill in 1773 with Boswell. Johnson averred that to use English for this inscription would be a disgrace to Dr Smollett, and Boswell added that Smollett's admirers would understand it, and after all it was not intended to be read by Highland drovers. Austin Dobson gives the right tailpiece to this story.[2] One of the early visitors to the monument was Thomas Bewick in 1776, who paused to admire this tribute to one of his heroes, but his Latin being shaky, he could not make out the purport of the inscription till it was translated for him by a passing Highlander. The cattle dealer or innkeeper with a smattering of Latin at that date may well have been the son of an impoverished laird, or a Jacobite to whom the professions were

[1] See H. G. Graham, *Social Life of Scotland in the Eighteenth Century*, 4th ed., 1937 (which takes perhaps too pessimistic a view of the situation), and the sources mentioned in local histories such as J. A. Russell, *History of Education in the Stewartry of Kirkcudbright*, 1951. For the chapbooks and other volumes on an eighteenth century cottage bookshelf, see Graham, *op. cit.*, pp. 188–90; for Manse libraries, p. 281; and for the somewhat pious library of a Scots lady of 1705, p. 23 *n*.
[2] *Eighteenth Century Vignettes*, 1892, 1st series: *The Topography of Humphrey Clinker*.

barred.[1] No certain conclusion is possible of course, but one has the impression that the progress of literacy and the spread of libraries in castle and cottage in Scotland during these centuries was in advance of the same developments in England, and the credit for much of this early enlightenment must have been due to the lively interest taken by many ministers in their manse libraries; the history and influence of these libraries in Scotland would make a rewarding study.[2]

Something has been said elsewhere[3] about the sudden and wide-spread appearance of the habit of reading among women in the eighteenth century. It has been a common belief that, with certain notable exceptions, women have lagged behind their menfolk in education, letters and learning. The more one explores the field, the more one doubts whether there is much foundation for this belief. It is true that till comparatively recent times they did not contribute much to literature, but this (as Lady Winchilsea and Virginia Woolf have pointed out) was mainly because the opportunity for creative writing was denied them, or at least made so difficult to seize. The almost universal habit of reading did not reveal itself till the circulating libraries in the eighteenth century produced in quantity the food on which this habit could be nourished. But in all periods before that century history produces so many instances of women of considerable intellectual calibre that no easy generalization is possible; no rule can be proved by such a wealth of exceptions. There were many in the ancient world besides Hypatia and Sappho. There were many in the medieval world besides Hroswitha of Gandersheim. One example nearer home would be Leobgatha (Lioba, the beloved), the kins-woman and dear friend of S. Boniface; we have a charming picture of her sending the saint specimens of the hexameters she had composed on the model of S. Aldhelm's awkward verses, with a covering letter begging him to correct her Latinity.[4] She left her nunnery at Wimbourne to become Abbess of Tauber-bischofsheim, where she became a leader in the new German church, and the close friend of Hildegard, the wife of Charles the

---

[1] Graham, *op. cit.*, pp. 34–35.

[2] For early public libraries in Scotland, see Dr. W. R. Aitken's valuable thesis, *A History of the Public Library Movement in Scotland*, University of Edinburgh, 1955.

[3] See pp. 274 ff. *infra*, and *Origins*, pp. 197–209.

[4] G. W. Greenaway, *Saint Boniface*, 1955.

Great. And there were many others in medieval days: Marie de France, for example, who has been called the ancestress of all the great women novelists; Abelard's lover and pupil, Heloise; and Christine de Pisan (1364–1430) who supported herself and her children by writing. Mrs Aphra Behn has been described as the first woman to make a living by writing plays and novels; but Christine de Pisan had earned her living three centuries earlier by more serious writing. She was left a widow at the age of 25, and is notable particularly for her attack on the *Roman de la Rose*, and for almost the first genuine presentation of the woman's view of life and morals. In 1418 she left Paris and retired to a convent.

Before the fifteenth century it is probable that feminine literacy was restricted to aristocratic women and to nuns, who were indeed largely drawn from the upper classes. There was a general feeling that while some education was beneficial for girls of noble birth, it was dangerous for those in a lowlier position; having more freedom than the high-born, they were more susceptible to error.[1] This feeling was echoed by Petrus Godefridus in the sixteenth century, who held that women should be strictly guarded from the temptations that the ability to write will bring.[2] The prejudice lingered long. The captain in Thomas Hardy's *Return of the Native*, offended by the rude words chalked on gatepost and barn door, would have applied the prohibition to men as well: 'If they'd never been taught to write, they wouldn't have been able to scribble such villainy. Their fathers couldn't do it, and the country was all the better for it.' Leaving this aside, however, the exigencies of human courtship have at all times been a considerable stimulus towards literacy. Love letters have to be both written and read, preferably in private. Some it is true (such as for example the young women who sought Samuel Richardson's help in composing their love letters) have at times been compelled to rely on the professional scribe; but few can have been happy about this awkward arrangement. It has been said that the popular novels of the eighteenth century tend to stress the advantages of a little education in women and the great disadvantages of too much; the necessity of humility and conceal-

---

[1] H. J. Chaytor, *From Script to Print*, 1945, p. 109.
[2] *Origins*, p. 198.

ment if their market value is not to be spoilt, and the admission that reading and botany need not make them incompetent house-wives.[1]

There seems little doubt that women as well as men in fifteenth century England were achieving a fair degree of literacy. In the case of women the impulse came from two main sources: religion, and household management. The wide interest in personal religion and in the works of the mystics in this century has already been described.[2] Much of the demand for books of this type came without doubt from women. The cynic might suggest that this was partly due to the fact that there was then no competition from books of the lighter or more frivolous sort. Their interest must often however have been genuine, and it would be fair to reply that some of the books that found favour with them in the fifteenth century are in print today and still commanding large circulations. Books of deportment and of household and garden management were an obvious interest for women whose task it was to supervise the running of a house and the work and welfare of a staff of indoor and outdoor servants: a complicated task requiring not merely a knowledge of accounts, but skill in medicine and all the domestic arts, nearly all the house-hold needs being made or supplied on the estate. The special responsibilities of the women of the family are well revealed in the Paston letters. The Paston women could certainly read, but there is distinct evidence that, if they could write, they neverthe-less found writing difficult and awkward. As Professor Galbraith has pointed out in regard to the medieval English kings,[3] this does not necessarily signify any lack of intellectual capacity. They often had other people to do their writing for them, and if they could command the services of a secretary, there was less need to write themselves. The letters of the Paston women were in fact written by many different hands, and there is no proof that any of them were autograph.[4] None of the medieval books of deportment is more interesting and revealing than the domestic 'enquire within' which Le Ménagier de Paris wrote for his young wife about 1393;

---

[1] J. M. S. Tompkins, *The Popular Novel in England, 1770–1800*, 1932, p. 167. Botanizing was not always regarded as a seemly occupation for women.

[2] See p. 139 *supra*.

[3] *Supra*, p. 199.

[4] Norman Davis, 'The Language of the Pastons', *Proc. Br. Academy*, 1954, p. 120.

though she was only fifteen, she was evidently an able young person, and completely literate.[1]

Eileen Power in *The Legacy of the Middle Ages* (pp. 430–1) quotes several fifteenth-century wills in which books are bequeathed to women. The works specified are 'my boke of the talys of cantyrbury', 'unum librum de Romanse incipientem cum Decem Preceptis Alembes', 'unum librum de Romanse de Septem sages', 'unum librum de Anglico vocatum Gower pro remembrancia', and 'librum Angliae de Fabulis et Narracionibus'; this last was left by a priest of York in 1432 to a woman who had been his servant for many years.

The natural interest of women in religion and in household concerns continued through the sixteenth and seventeenth centuries. It is revealed for example in the diaries of Lady Margaret Hoby and Lady Anne Clifford, both of which give a glimpse of the aristocratic woman's reading at the beginning of the seventeenth century. Lady Margaret Hoby was a puritan whose literary tastes were limited to sermons, theology, the Bible and her herbal. Lady Anne Clifford had a wider interest in poetry, essays, history and religion, and her shelves included copies of Montaigne and Ovid.[2]

A few pre-Reformation convents eked out their finances by keeping schools for girls, those at Barking and Shaftesbury being particularly notable; but the practice was not encouraged by the authorities. The fashion for girls' boarding schools had its origin however in those established by Charles I under the governance of refugee Huguenot ladies. Unlike the Puritans, Charles believed in the education of women; his grandmother, Mary Stuart, was the most charming woman of her age, he said, and no one thought the less of her because she knew Latin and Greek. To one of these schools, Charles sent the equally charming Mary Villiers; but she cannot have made much progress with her education, for when she married James Stuart, Duke of Richmond, she was only fifteen and already a widow, her first husband, Lord Herbert, having died within a month of the wedding. She did however

---

[1] *Traité de Morale et d'Economie Domestique*, Paris, 1846. See also Eileen Power, *Medieval People*, 1924, and for a survey of such works, A. A. Hentsch, *De la Littérature Didactique du Moyen Âge s'addressant spécialement aux Femmes*, Cahors, 1903.

[2] See Mrs. Meads' ed. of the *Diary of Lady Margaret Hoby*, 1930, p. 55, and the *Diary of Lady Anne Clifford*, ed. V. Sackville-West, 1923.

(like many other girls of that time) acquire shorthand, as well as various handicrafts such as toymaking.[1]

Later in that century, about 1680, Josias Priest moved his boarding school from Leicester Fields to Chelsea, where the young gentlewomen performed Purcell's new opera *Dido and Aeneas*, with its libretto by Nahum Tate: a signal achievement on both sides, for the composer was only 22 at the time. At the end of the century Celia Fiennes in her diary noted various 'very fine schooles for young gentlewomen as good as any in London' at Manchester, Shrewsbury and elsewhere. The feminine part of the population was making ready for the advances of the eighteenth century, when the ability of women to read was transformed into a confirmed and widespread habit.

Some further evidence of the reading of women in the sixteenth century is given by Richard Mulcaster, the first headmaster of Merchant Taylors' and later high-master of S. Paul's, in his *Positions* (1581). One of the first English women to claim equality with men in reading and writing seems to have been Margaret Tyler, who translated *The First Part of the Mirrour of Princely Deedes and Knighthood* in 1578. 'Men dedicate their books to us,' she said, 'so we may surely read them; and if we read, why cannot we write too?' A reasonable enough demand, one would think. But Lady Winchilsea a century or more later, making the same claim much more vigorously, found few to support her. Even Dorothy Osborne declared to her husband, 'Sure the poore woman is a little distracted, shee could never bee soe rediculous else as to venture at writeing book's and in verse too, if I should not sleep this fortnight I should not come to that'. But Dorothy was a loyal and tactful wife, and her tongue may have been in her cheek when she wrote this. Margaret Tyler's claim has indeed only won general acceptance in comparatively recent times; though in every generation there has been the occasional voice lifted up in support of it. The *Spectator*, in its discussion of Leonora's library and the books it might contain,[2] could not, for all its charity to the gentler sex, treat the idea very seriously. Three classes of books in such a library were imagined: those proposed by ladies themselves; those suggested by booksellers anxious to

[1] See Margaret Irwin, *The Stranger Prince*.
[2] Nos. 37 and 92.

find a market for their wares; and those recommended by husbands anxious to discipline their wives. It is of interest to note that the first class contained *The Innocent Adultery*, which was one of the books that Lydia Languish later in the century was anxious to conceal from Sir Anthony Absolute, hiding it inside *The Whole Duty of Man*. One of Paul Scarron's novelettes bore this title; several English editions were published from 1665 onwards. It was also the sub-title of *The Fatal Marriage*, Thomas Southerne's tragedy based on one of Mrs Aphra Behn's novels and produced at the Theatre Royal, Drury Lane, in 1694. Leonora's work may have been the one by Paul Scarron, but Lydia Languish may have been reading Thomas Southerne, for Garrick had revived this not long before.

A few years later than the too playful argument about Leonora's library, Dean Swift's friend, Patrick Delany in his Dublin *Tribune* was satirizing hard-drinking squires who had no use for books and suggesting that the lady of the house in such cases 'is generally the better scholar as well as the better Christian of the two'. She will, it was said, have a Bible, a Prayerbook and a *Week's Preparation* for her own use, while her woman 'may happen to have a *Robinson Crusoe*, *Gulliver's Travels* and Aristotle's Master-piece, both for her own Edification and for the Instruction of the young Ladies, as soon as they are grown up, not to mention *Tommy Pots*, *Jack the Giantkiller*, the *Cobbler of Canterbury* and several other notable Pieces of Literature carried about in the Baskets of itinerant Pedlars, for the Improvement of His Majesty's Liege People.'[1]

Later still the egregious Thomas Seward, canon of Lichfield and friend of Johnson, was writing his verses on *The Female Right to Literature*, in which at considerable length he urges a lady named Athenia to let her growing mind take every knowledge in of every kind. This poem (printed in Dodsley's *Collection*, vol. II) is chiefly remarkable for the lines:

> In Rome too liberty once reign'd, in Rome
> The female virtues were allowed to bloom,
> And bloom they did.

[1] *Tribune*, No. 11, Nov. 25, 1729, quoted by R. M. Wiles, *Serial Publication in England* 1957, p. 13.

which were duly noted by D. B. Wyndham Lewis and Charles Lee in their anthology *The Stuffed Owl* (1930).

Not dissimilar examples could be quoted even from the nineteenth century. In *Shirley* Charlotte Bronte, trying to conceal her identity under a masculine pen-name, was doubtless expressing her own feelings when she made Caroline Helstone complain in bitter and forthright terms of the fate that condemns an unmarried girl to a life of sewing and cooking and nothing else. And yet we are left with the firm impression that this 'nothing else' must often have concealed a great deal of intellectual and creative activity, often of a humble sort, often carried out in secret, but none the less important for that. Indeed for much of the period we have been discussing, ordinary women may well have been in advance of the ordinary man in the progress towards literacy and culture. Jane Austen, writing her novels in the sitting-room of her house, kept her occupation secret from servants and visitors. Advertisement of such accomplishments was to be shunned. In *Pride and Prejudice*, Miss Bingley's notion of an accomplished woman comprised a knowledge of music, singing, drawing, dancing and the modern languages; and Darcy insisted that extensive reading must be added to all this. Miss Bingley then declared that no such paragon existed. That was for Darcy's benefit; she knew quite well that such paragons were far commoner than men realized.

In this chapter we have been discussing the condition of literacy which made possible, and even probable, the existence of libraries: small libraries for the most part, unknown to history, their very existence often a matter of conjecture, insignificant if considered by themselves and in isolation from the pattern of society. The importance and interest of such a discussion will be questioned only by the man who fixes his eyes on the high peaks and overlooks the plains and valleys at his feet. The value of this discussion is twofold. These small and unrecorded collections of books, these bedside shelves 'ycovered with a falding reed' constitute no unimportant part of the social background of our race in past centuries; they are eloquent in revealing the thoughts and dreams and aspirations of our forefathers, and the extent to which their view of life was raised beyond the bread and butter needs of daily existence. And though we have in this chapter said nothing of the great collectors and librarians; though Cotton,

Pepys, Harley, Sloane, Heber, Phillipps, Ogden and the rest of the giants have not even been mentioned; yet we feel and know that this is the fertile ground, well-tilled, enriched and in good heart, from which these commanding figures have arisen. Let us not underestimate the significance of the good earth.

CHAPTER XII

The Approach to a National Library in England

THE two hundred years that preceded the foundation of the British Museum saw the gradual awakening of a national consciousness in the English people. The English withdrawal from the Continent, the shift of interest to the 'new found lands' beyond the sea, commercial prosperity and the delayed effects of the Reformation, all tended to encourage the new idea of nationhood. A small but not unimportant part of this long process was the realization of our need for a national library that would be worthy of the ideal towards which the country was feeling its way. There was no sudden achievement of this end. In a typically English way we advanced towards it slowly and hesitantly, making many false steps, and even those moves that were successful had the appearance of being almost accidental. It is of interest to trace these steps one by one.

First a note about the background. The invention of printing and the replacement of parchment by paper led slowly but naturally to the mass-production of books. Religious activity and the expansion of commerce together produced an increase in literacy. Christianity has always depended on books as its most powerful weapons of offence and defence, but never before had these weapons been used with such vigour and such prodigality. Nearly half the titles in *STC* are religious weapons in some degree; the new Bodleian itself was planned as a bastion of the reformed church; and the common domestic bookshelf of the time consisted of religious manuals: the Bible, the Prayerbook, and devotional works such as Michael Sparke's *The crumbs of comfort* which had so wide a circulation that the first six editions have disappeared entirely.[1]

[1] See Louis B. Wright, 'The Significance of Religious Writings in the English Renaissance', *Journal of the History of Ideas*, 1940, I, p. 64. The earliest edition in STC is the 7th 1628)

Apart from religion, the main impetus towards literacy came perhaps from the widening field of commerce and communications, and the interest in the new experimental philosophy which itself derived partly from the desire to apply the results of scientific discovery to the needs of industry and trade. Schools were beginning to train boys for work in the counting houses as early as the fifteenth century; and in the Elizabethan age, such interest as there was in the foundation of a University of London was inspired by the need for men trained in astronomy, geometry and the sciences of navigation, of surveying and cartography. The applications of science were the major concern of most contributions to the Royal Society from its earliest years. The combined stimulus of religion, commerce, communications and science produced a new cultural climate marked by that hunger for information and instruction which is the first result of literacy; the hunger for entertainment came later, as the area of literacy with its widening fringe of semi-literacy, expanded like the ripples from a stone in a pond. The habit of reading took root.

It was against this background of active religion and of science in the making that a steady stream of plans for the formation of a national collection of books with facilities for study and research took shape in the minds of both far-sighted practical men and unpractical visionaries alike. It is typical that none of them was disinterested. The pursuit of knowledge for its own sake had small part to play in them. Indeed the phrase would have meant little to men whose lives were dominated by the pressing needs of the moment: the need to give historical sanction to the reformed church, or to the lineage and inheritance of particular families, the need to inculcate orthodox doctrine and discourage heresy, the need to maintain sea-power and communications within the newly emerging colonial empire, the need to enhance the profits of industry and commerce by using new materials or new processes of manufacture. It is a characteristic of human endeavour that our ideals should at the last transcend the motives that inspired them.

Pre-Elizabethan attempts to fill the vacuum caused by the dispersal of the monastic libraries were few and feeble; the flood-tide of Henry's destruction had to recede before the damage could be assessed and salvage begun. Various people were of course rescu-

ing volumes for their own purposes, whether worthy or un-
worthy, but very few had any vision of a national resting place for
the salvaged books. More valuable things than books were being
destroyed at this time, and it was natural for Latimer to think first
of the needs of education ('it is a pitiful thing to see schools so
neglected . . . very few there be that help poor scholars').[1] John
Bale, in the preface to the 1549 edition of Leland's *Laboryouse
Journey*, wished that the chief monuments and most notable
works of our excellent writers could have been gathered into 'one
solempne lybrary' in every shire. This, he says, would have 'been
yet sumwhat'; and he adds that to destroy all without consideration is and will be unto England for ever a most horrible infamy
among the grave seniors of other nations.

The difficulties of organizing shire libraries of this kind in the
troubled years 1535-40 would doubtless have been formidable.
The only existing institution which could have absorbed even a
small proportion of the monastic volumes was the Royal Library.
John Leland saw this clearly. He was apparently on the staff of the
royal libraries, though not Royal Librarian, nor even King's
Antiquary as the DNB and other authorities imply.[2] Leland
states in his *Antiphilarchia*[3] that Henry had in fact three royal
libraries, at Westminster, Hampton Court and Greenwich, all
devoted to the collection of ancient texts. In 1533 he received a
royal commission from Henry to search the monastic and academic
libraries of the realm 'to the intente that the monuments of
auncient writers as welle of other nations, as of this yowr owne
province might be brought owte of deadly darkenes to lyvely
lighte'. What he was in fact seeking, however, was not 'auncient
writers' as such, but the kind of books that interested him, and
that he thought would please his master—historical evidences of
the ancient and modern glory of the Tudor dominions. The
proper place for the manuscript sources of British history from
the earliest times was he thought, the Royal Library; and his most
prized acquisition was the S. Patrick's Charter from Glastonbury
which proved beyond doubt the antiquity of that famous house.
Not all of Leland's contemporaries thought highly of him; John

[1] Gasquet, *Henry VIII and the English Monasteries*, 7th ed., 1920; p. 472.
[2] Kendrick, *British Antiquity*, 1950, p. 47 n.; British Museum, *Catalogue of the Royal MSS* (Introduction).
[3] Cambridge Univ. Lib. MS. Ee V. 14.

Caius, the Cambridge scholar, and Polydore Vergil regarded him as an empty boaster and an unreliable antiquarian, and even Bale commented on his vainglory. However, he pressed on with his survey of English libraries, and appealed to Cromwell for help in furthering his plan. The appeal seems to have had a very limited result. Many books of value were deliberately and successfully concealed from Leland; some were carefully transferred by abbot or prior to a convenient manor house where they could lie hidden. Moreover, only a proportion of the religious houses were in fact visited by Leland. It is however known that at least one of his lists reached the king, who apparently marked for preservation certain titles which do in fact appear in an inventory of the Royal Library made in 1542. During Henry's last years the number of volumes in the Library rose from 143 to 1,450, and the sudden increase must have been mainly due to the appropriation of monastic books.[1] But the number thus saved was only a small fraction of the total, and many even of these perished or were despoiled as a result of the Order in Council of February 25, 1550-1 for the 'purging of His Highnes Librarie'. It would of course be a mistake to think of the Royal Library at this date as anything but a private collection of books belonging to the king. Not even Leland can have regarded it in any other light. At the time of the suppression however it was the only important collection that had any prospect of stability or security.

The tide turned on the accession of Elizabeth in 1558. Many individual collectors had for some time been seizing whatever spoils they could lay their hands on. In 1568, the well-known Privy Council letter attempted to direct the salvaged volumes into a securer anchorage, and Matthew Parker observed that 'if this opportunity be not taken in our time, it will not be so well done herafter'.[2] The work of private salvage continued, however, and it is our good fortune that so many of the collections made at this time have since found a safe home: Parker's own books for example at Cambridge; those of Henry Fitzalan, Earl of Arundel (who had acquired most of Cranmer's library) and Sir Robert

---

[1] See Dr C. E. Wright's contribution to Wormald and Wright (ed.) *The English Library before 1700*, 1958, pp. 148-75. The best recent account of Leland is in T. D. Kendrick, *British Antiquity*, 1950.

[2] C. E. Wright, *op. cit.*, p. 157, 190.

Cotton in the British Museum; and those gathered for the new Bodleian at Oxford. Neither Parker nor Cecil had in mind any sort of national repository for the books. Their concern was primarily with the safe preservation of the documents on which both Ecclesia Anglicana and the newly emerging English nation depended for their historical continuity and authority.

The one serious and systematic attempt to achieve this aim was made later in Elizabeth's reign by the first Society of Antiquaries. The membership and work of this group of early antiquarians has been described in detail by Dr C. E. Wright, and need not be repeated.[1] Sir Robert Cotton and two fellow members of the Society presented a petition to the Queen requesting a charter for the foundation of an academy of antiquarian and historical studies, 'to preserve old books concerning the matter of the history of this realm, original charters and monuments'. It was 'to be well furnished with ancient bookes and rare monuments of antiquity, which otherwise may perish; and that at the costs and charges of divers gentlemen which will be willing thereunto'. The Society apparently came into existence about 1586, and the petition was presented c. 1602. It had no result, partly perhaps owing to the Queen's death very soon afterwards. This setback must have caused Cotton to redouble his efforts to assemble the magnificent library that bears his name; he began collecting in 1588 and continued steadily till his death in 1631. It is fitting that it should have found its rightful home in our national library, even though it had to wait a century and a half for this.

Two of the schemes put forward in the Elizabethan period bore immediate fruit. It was in February 1598 that Sir Thomas Bodley wrote his famous letter to the Vice-Chancellor, offering at his own expense to restore the Public Library to its former use, 'and to make it fitte and handsome with seates, and shelfes, and deskes, and all that may be needfull, to stir up other men's benevolence, to helpe to furnish it with bookes'. Two years were spent in refurnishing the building. In 1600 Bodley began the task of collecting books, appointing Thomas James as his first librarian; and the Library opened on November 8, 1602.

The early history of the Bodleian is well documented and there

[1] C. E. Wright, op. cit., pp. 176–212.

is no need to tell the story again.[1] It is sufficient to make the point
that from the beginning it was in the public estimation given the
status of a national institution. It was indeed the first attempt in
England to establish a collection of this type with secure and
permanent endowments. There is no doubt that Bodley's contemporaries viewed it in this light. Robert Burton for example
put it at the head of his list of famous English libraries, calling it
'our public library in Oxon'; and 'public library' then meant
national library in effect. King James honoured it with a visit
when it was only three years old, and it inspired him with the
thought that if he were not king, he would choose to be a university man, and to live happily chained and confined within the
library along with so many good authors. Its reputation as our
one national library survived till the founding of the British
Museum. As late as 1767, when Dr Johnson had his famous inter-
view with George III in the Royal Library, the king questioned
him about Bodley, which he described as *the* public library'—
par excellence as it were. Its national status was placed beyond
doubt in 1610, when Thomas James concluded his arrangement
with the Stationers' Company for the free supply of all works
printed by its members. Under James and his immediate successors the library was well administered. Its first printed catalogues of 1605, 1620, 1635 and 1674 were models of their kind,
and in accessibility to readers it compared favourably with other
libraries of the day.[2] It proved at once a magnet for magnificent
gifts of books and manuscripts; and if its administration tended to
slumber in the eighteenth century, gifts nevertheless continued,
and its collections grew steadily in stature and quality. This was
an age in which national libraries were being established throughout Europe: the Royal Libraries in Berlin, Vienna, Copenhagen,
Stockholm, Paris and at the Escorial near Madrid, and academic
libraries such as those at Uppsala and Leyden; and Bodley's
Library is a worthy member of this great company, and if the
libraries at Uppsala and Stockholm were enriched by plunder in
the wars of Gustavus Adolphus and his daughter, Queen Chris-
tina, the Bodleian can match this too in a small way; Sir Walter

---

[1] See J. N. L. Myres' contribution to Wormald and Wright (ed.), *The English Library
before 1700*, 1958, and references there quoted.
[2] J. N. L. Myres, *op. cit.*, p. 244.

Ralegh in 1598, after the victory at Cadiz, carried off the library of Osorius, Bishop of Faro, and presented it to Bodley. If this story lacks good authority, it is nevertheless just what Ralegh might well have done; and in any case, he is known to have subscribed £50 to Bodley's new library in 1603.

In Ireland and Scotland, the library of Trinity College, Dublin, was founded about the same time as the Bodleian, while the Faculty of Advocates in Edinburgh dates from 1682. Deposit rights may perhaps be justly regarded as conferring national status on a library, and we may note therefore that these were conferred on the Royal Library and on the Universities of Oxford and Cambridge by an Act of 1666; in 1709 the four Scottish Universities, the Faculty of Advocates and Syon College were added; Trinity College and King's Inn, Dublin, received theirs later.

One other 'public library' (in the earlier sense of the term) grew to importance about the same time as the Bodleian. The Lambeth Palace Library is based partly on the collection of Whitgift, but no permanent library existed at Lambeth before 1610. In that year Archbishop Bancroft died, and in his will he gave explicit and careful directions for the establishment and continuity of an archiepiscopal library, and to it he bequeathed his own very rich collection of books and pamphlets, dedicating it 'to the service of God and his church, of the kings and commonwealth of the Realme and particularly of the Archbishops of Canterbury'. If the terms of this bequest were not acceptable to his successors, then the collection was to go to 'his Majesties College to be erected at Chelsey; if it be erected within the six years; otherwise I give and bequeath them all to the public library of the University of Cambridge'. Bancroft's successor, Archbishop Abbot, welcomed the bequest, and King James gave approval to its designation as a public library thus awarding it official status as a national collection. The king also 'did, after mature deliberation commend the care and consideration hereof unto Sr Frauncis Bacon ... that he should think upon some course, how the custody of this library might be established, and by the negligence of those that came after, so excellent a worke might not be frustrated, to the hurt of the Church and Commonwealth'. Bacon's advice was that a catalogue of the books should be 'accurately and exquisitely made', so as to provide a permanent record of Bancroft's bequest. This was done, and one copy was deposited at Canterbury, another remaining at Lambeth; both are now at Lambeth.

Bancroft had desired that each Archbishop should be responsible for passing on the collection intact to his successor, but Bacon advised against this. The king had evidently intimated that he proposed to borrow books himself, and it might also happen that volumes were taken out 'for some publicke use of the Church' and not returned, by some accident or default of another; all that was needed was that any avoidable losses should be made good. Archbishop Abbot at his death in 1633 added his own books to the collection. These were in 'the great study'; but the Bancroft library was kept in a gallery over the four sides of the cloister, the inner walls, 75 feet long, being lined with shelving. At this date the whole collection amounted to nearly nine thousand volumes (6,065 from Bancroft's library and 2,667 from Abbot's): a very large collection for the period. About half the works were theological; law, history and topography and classical texts were very well represented in the remainder.

Archbishop Laud did little to enlarge the library, his interests being turned rather to the rapidly growing Bodleian, to which he gave his own collection of manuscripts. While he was in the Tower, however, he used his influence with the House of Lords to ensure its safe preservation. In 1643 the House of Commons appointed a commission, headed by Laud's friend, John Selden, to protect the books from damage or dispersal, and in the following year the House ordered the removal of the Lambeth library to Syon College, at the request of the Fellows of that institution. There is however no record of any such request in the College archives, and the removal was not in fact carried out, either because the College was unwilling to give public access to it, or because a rival claimant emerged in the University of Cambridge. Bancroft had indeed provided for its transfer to Cambridge, in the event of proper security not being given to it at Lambeth; and Selden apparently advised the University to petition for its transfer to their care. Both Houses in due course agreed, and the removal took place in 1647, after a fresh inventory of the books had been made. It was returned to Lambeth after the Restoration, its place in Cambridge being to some extent filled by the library of Richard Holdsworth, whose will in 1649 had expressed a desire for this, though failing its achievement within five years his very large collection was to go to his own Emmanuel College. Restored to its original home, the Lambeth library continued to grow steadily. By the end of the century it had become one of the few very great libraries in England; so much so that (as Macaulay tells us) when Peter the Great visited Lambeth in 1698, nothing in this country astonished him so much as the Archiepiscopal Library, for he had never imagined there were so many printed volumes in the world. Today it numbers about 70,000 volumes, including 3,000 early printed books.[1]

There was no other 'public library' in London during the two centuries prior to the opening of the British Museum: a deficiency which was remarked on by John Evelyn, who considered the West End of S. Paul's to be a suitable place for such an institution, and by Archbishop Tenison, who, while still vicar of S. Martin-in-the-Fields, founded his famous parish library in Castle Street, Leicester Square in 1684, apparently with some help from Wren in the design, and in the hope that it would fill part of the gap. The only notable library in seventeenth-century London at all comparable to the Royal Library or Lambeth was that of Syon College, which was founded under the will of Dr Thomas White in 1630. The library was established five years later. The college was in effect a guild of the clergy of Greater London, and its library was built by Dr John Simpson, rector of S. Olave, Hart Street. The buildings were destroyed in the Great Fire, and much damage was done to the books, but the loss was repaired by many large donations and subscriptions, and a very rich collection indeed was amassed. As is mentioned above, it came near to absorbing the Lambeth Palace Library in 1644, but it did not strictly offer public access to its books. It was however granted deposit rights (and thus a degree of national status) in 1709; these were commuted in 1836 for an annual payment of £363 15s 2d to be spent on the purchase of books. Though the library is general in nature, it has a natural bias in favour of theology; and

---

[1] See especially Ann Cox-Johnson, 'Lambeth Palace Library, 1610–1664', *Trans. Cambridge Bibl. Soc.*, vol. II, 1958, pp. 105–26; and M. R. James, 'The History of Lambeth Palace Library', *Trans. Cambridge Bibl. Soc.*, vol. III, 1959, pp. 1–31.

in this respect it may be compared with Dr Williams's Library which was founded in 1716 to serve a similar purpose in the field of nonconformity.

The second Elizabethan achievement was equally important in its results, though it lay in a different field. If the Royal Society had any direct antecedents from which it sprang, they can be found in the early history of Gresham College. Sir Thomas Gresham, the typical example of Elizabethan big business, and the founder of the Royal Exchange, died in 1579, leaving his house in Bishopsgate as the home of the college that bears his name. The College opened in 1598, and became at once the recognized meeting-place of English scientists. Sir Thomas' fame was sufficient for Thomas Heywood to take him as the hero of his early play *If You know not Me, You know Nobody* (1604-5).

The limitations of medieval science can be ascribed no doubt to many causes, but to nothing so much as the difficulties of communication, and the secrecy under which it was often practised. Scientific progress depends for its life blood on its channels of communication, as every librarian today knows; and it was the advent of the printed word, together with the growth of institutions and learned societies providing opportunities for meeting, that gave the main impetus to seventeenth-century science. The Royal Society was (and still remains) the premier institution of this kind; but Gresham College was the nursery ground from which it sprang. Sir Thomas Gresham's will provided for seven professors of law, rhetoric, divinity, music, physic, geometry and astronomy: a scheme of education devised by a merchant prince, and giving for the first time due weight to the applied sciences needed by commerce and navigation. Neither astronomy nor geometry had as yet achieved academic respectability. It was not till 1619 that the Savilian chairs in these subjects were established at Oxford. They were however the corner stones of the art of navigation on which the Elizabethan sailor depended for his journeys across the Atlantic and back. The first professor of geometry at Gresham College was Henry Briggs, who with William Gilbert, the author of our first great scientific work, the *De Magnete* and Edward Wright, who translated Napier's work on logarithms into English and is believed to have been the actual discoverer of Mercator's principles of projection, was primarily responsible for establishing the College as a meeting place of scientists, and for maintaining close relations with shipwrights, sailors and the navy. The College maintained its importance at least till the birth of the Royal Society, and the circle of scientists associated with it may well have been that 'invisible college' which Robert Boyle describes as having emerged in 1645, to form the nucleus from which the Royal Society grew in 1660.[1] The College indeed became the headquarters of the Royal Society and its library from 1660 to 1710, when the Society acquired a building of its own.

No library is recorded at the College in its early days. The seven professors received a stipend of £50 per annum, and resided in the College. George Vertue's engraving of the College[2] (1739) shows however a large 'reading hall' which may have housed the library, but was probably in the main a lecture hall.

The absence of any formal university in Elizabethan London was made good partly perhaps by Gresham College, but rather more effectively by the Inns of Court, which then bore a closer resemblance to a university than they do today. In the sixteenth century it became common for a lay student, after spending two or three years at Oxford or Cambridge, to proceed to the Inns of Court for further studies in law: a course which had obvious advantages for any aspirant to the government service. Dom David Knowles notes that in this century, 'the Inns of Court harboured and trained the flower of the intelligence and energy and ambition of the country. Of the men who influenced policy and rose to high position and wealth by their wits and personality between 1490 and 1590 perhaps three out of every four were lawyers ... The young Thomas More was brought back by his father from the useless humanism of Oxford to the study of law, and the foreigner Erasmus noted with surprise how young men of good family flocked to the Inns'. Under Elizabeth the four Inns (the Middle Temple, the Inner Temple, Lincoln's Inn and Gray's Inn) were at the height of their prosperity and received the Queen's especial favour. They were in fact a group of colleges designed for legal studies; indeed they were the earliest profes-

[1] See F. R. Johnson, 'Gresham College', *J. Hist. Ideas*, 1940, I, pp. 413–38, and Sir Harold Hartley, *The Royal Society*, 1960.
[2] Reproduced in Sir Harold Hartley, *op. cit.*

sional schools intended expressly for lay students. Though not incorporated into a formal university, they were closely linked together, each with its dining hall, library, garden and chapel, though the two Temples shared the old Church of the Templars. Their libraries were all founded about this time. At Lincoln's Inn the library dates from a bequest in 1497, though it did not become an effective force till early in the seventeenth century; the Middle Temple library was refounded under Robert Ashley's will in 1641; the Gray's Inn library is first recorded in 1555. Though primarily legal, they have good collections in the wider fields of history and topography, but they cannot be regarded as in any sense 'public'. That the Londoner of Elizabethan times regarded them as a University is evident from the account of the Inns in Stow's *Survey*; and Sir George Buc's appendix to the 1615 edition of Stow's *Annales*, in which they are described in detail, is very properly entitled 'The Third Universitie of England'.[1]

In the hundred years prior to the Restoration there must have been a score of other comparable projects and schemes which for one reason or another failed to establish themselves. They are worth recording however, if only because they show which way the wind was blowing, how constant that wind was, and how men's minds were feeling their way towards the setting up of a national institution of recorded knowledge and research. The more important of them are listed here.

First to be mentioned is John Dee, who, on January 15, 1555-6, and rather in advance of his time, submitted a petition to Queen Mary for the preservation of 'ancient writers and monuments' which had been scattered at the dispersal of the monastic libraries. He had in view the building up of a magnificent royal library at trifling cost, and he proposed a commission to report on this to the synod of the province of Canterbury. He undertook himself to procure copies of famous MSS from the Vatican Library, S. Mark's, Venice, Bologna, Florence and Vienna. Nothing came of this, but the attempt is noteworthy in that it antedated the similar campaign launched by Archbishop Parker after the accession of Elizabeth. Dee however has his importance quite apart from this. He has a higher place in the history of science and technology

---

[1] Knowles, *The Religious Orders in England*, vol. III, 1959, p. 5; *Shakespeare's England*, vol. I, p. 408; Rye, *Students' Guide to the Libraries of London*, 3rd ed., 1927, pp. 353-9.

than is sometimes recognized. At his house at Mortlake he gathered round him not only a fine library[1] but a circle of scholars and scientists comparable with the Gresham College circle a few years later: Sir Philip Sidney, Sir Edward Dyer, Lord Burghley, Martin Frobisher, Thomas Digges the astronomer, Sir Humphrey Gilbert and Sir Walter Ralegh. He was the intimate friend of Mercator at Louvain, and he maintained a correspondence with many European scientists which kept him in touch with scientific progress on the continent. Unfortunately he never lived down his reputation as a magician—a common fate of the medieval scientist, who was popularly expected to be learned in astrology and the casting of horoscopes; and in his old age he did indeed become immersed in the mysteries of alchemy. But he had more solid achievements than this to his credit. As early as 1551 he was giving technical advice to the Cathay merchants, and in 1557 he published his *Perfect Arte of Navigation*. It was always the practical applications of mathematics that interested him, and in 1570 when Sir Henry Billingsley, Lord Mayor of London, published the first English translation of Euclid, Dee (who had himself lectured on Euclid in Paris) contributed a lengthy and important preface on the value of mathematics to the artificer and craftsman. This was plainly the work of a far-sighted technologist rather than a magician, and he begs that he will not be misrepresented in this light. He was twice visited at Mortlake by Elizabeth, who must have recognized the importance of his work. His life ended in penury and eccentricity, but there is no justification for the belief that his petition to Queen Mary was based on the hope of finding a market for his own great collection of MSS.

About the same time that Sir Thomas Gresham was working out the constitution of his College, Sir Humphrey Gilbert the navigator and founder of the colony of Newfoundland, with his half-brother Sir Walter Ralegh projected another college to be called Queen Elizabeth's Academy. Unfortunately however, the scheme (reprinted by the Early English Text Society in 1869) had no wealthy financier such as Gresham behind it. Even more than Gresham College, the Academy was to have been primarily a

[1] Some of his books still survive; as many as twenty-one are in the library of the Royal College of Physicians.

technological institute, designed to teach the naval and military arts, navigation, shipbuilding, engineering and the making of maps and charts, as well as history for the sake of its practical value. It would have been the first of our naval and military colleges; but Elizabeth had no funds to spare for its maintenance. The project included a great library under a keeper with an annual stipend of £26, and a yearly book fund of £40. There would also have been a copyright provision requiring all printers to deposit at their own charges one copy well bound of every proclamation and pamphlet printed; and in its library provisions the scheme was in advance of that for Gresham College. But 'the best educational scheme of its day'[1] was never brought to reality. Nevertheless technological studies proceeded, and popularizations of the great scientific works appeared. Both Billingsleys' Euclid and Gilbert's De Magnete were followed quickly by simplified versions intended for the use of sailors and navigators.

It is worth noting that the development of the science of navigation in the Elizabethan period was paralleled on land by the development of more exact cartography and surveying, and by the demand for expert surveyors such as Christopher Saxton, John Norden, Ralph Agas and John Speed. Saxton's survey of the English and Welsh counties was made with royal authority to fill a recognized need, and Norden's local surveys were drawn to satisfy the demands of many new landowners for accurate estate maps to replace the vaguer picture given by the terriers and rentals. Norden's projected Speculum Britanniae, though it had official backing from Burghley, was never completed; if it had been, it would have provided a national reference work of exceptional value, combining atlas, gazetteer, town plans, landed estates, who's who and economic survey for the whole country.[2]

With the turn of the century the flow of projected schemes continued, though except in the case of Bacon's New Atlantis, interest switched from the science of navigation to the defence of the reformed religion. In 1606, William Crashaw, puritan divine and poet and the father of the more famous Richard, published his Romish forgeries and falsifications, and in 1609 he prefixed to a

---

[1] Margaret Irwin, That great Lucifer, 1960, p. 310.
[2] M. Beresford, History on the Ground, 1957, p. 156. See also A. W. Pollard's article on 'Norden' in The Library, 1926, p. 235.

further collection of alleged falsifications of scripture a plea to the king to collect and preserve ancient MSS in their purity, using the Bishops as agents and the Universities as repositories, thus assembling an armoury against the papists. 'Popery,' he wrote, 'will receive such a blow hereby and the truth such a defence as seldome hath been given by the hande of men. Thus shall all the world acknowledge your Majesty to be indeede as you are styled, *fidei defensor*.'[1]

In 1617 a more detailed and more fanciful plan was proposed to the king by Edmund Bolton, the antiquary, poet and friend of Camden. This was a project for a royal academy on a grand scale, under which Windsor Castle was to be transformed into an English Olympus. The academy was to consist of 'tutelaries' (i.e. trustees) who were to be the Knights of the Garter, the Lord Chancellor and the Chancellors of the two Universities; of 'auxiliaries', consisting of the pick of the aristocracy; and of what he terms the 'essentials', these being lay scholars who would do the real work of the institution. Their functions would be (a) to review all translations of secular learning, (b) to authorize the publication of all non-theological works, (c) to provide the 'vulgar people' with indexes 'expurgatory and expunctory' (i.e. censored and purified) of all books of secular learning, (d) to establish a national collection of historical documents relating to England, and (e) to produce a detailed history and a large scale map of London. Like many visionaries Bolton ended his days in prison—in the Fleet and the Marshalsea for debt. His elaborate plan came to nothing, but it is worthy of note that one friend who was associated with it, Sir Kenelm Digby, was also connected with the Royal Society over forty years later; indeed he was one of the twenty-one members of the Society's first Council. There is nothing else to link the two together, and their purposes were of course quite different.

Nor is there much certain evidence of any direct connection between the *New Atlantis* and the Royal Society, though Solomon's House has by some authorities been regarded as a blueprint for the latter institution.[2] Bacon published his work in

---

[1] P. J. Wallis, *Trans. Cambridge Bibl. Soc.*, 1956, pp. 213–28.

[2] The term 'Fellows' for the members of the Royal Society comes for example from the *New Atlantis*, and the early members regarded Bacon as their spiritual father.

1626. Solomon's House was a college of natural philosophy at the centre of the life of this imaginary Pacific island, and dedicated to the study of the works and creatures of God. It was not merely the island's university, but its national library and its D.S.I.R. as well. Though Bacon has been regarded as the father of 'experimental philosophy' in England, he was not himself a scientist but a lawyer, and scientists today are inclined to think that his importance in the scientific field has been over-rated. Nevertheless the librarian will recognize the significance of the *New Atlantis* in his own field. It was the first utopia to boast a genuine national library, and a research institution in which scientific interests outweighed those of humanism. A number of the fellows of Solomon's House were engaged in collecting books and abstracts for its library; indeed this is the first use of the word 'abstracts' in this technical sense. These fellows were termed 'merchants of light' (they might be called documentalists today) and 'depredators' (which seems an unkind expression for a research librarian). The curious may find some amusement in the farcical satire of just such a research institution which Swift a century later included in Gulliver's *Voyage to Laputa*.

Two other academies are to be noted during this period. Chelsea College was founded by Matthew Sutcliffe, Dean of Exeter, with the support of both James I and Archbishop Bancroft. In the words of Fuller, this college 'was intended for a spirituall garrison, with a magazine of all books for that purpose; where learned divines should study and write in maintenance of all controversies against the papists'. The King laid its foundation stone in 1609, gave money and materials for its building, and a charter of incorporation in which the name of 'King James's College at Chelsey' is assigned to it. There were to be a provost and nineteen fellows, nominated by the king, all but two being in holy orders. The first provost was Sutcliffe himself; Camden and Heywood were appointed as historiographers. Only a fraction of the proposed building was ever completed however. Archbishop Abbot attempted to raise funds for it in every diocese, but the small amount collected was swallowed up in charges and lawsuits, and the project lapsed with Sutcliffe's death in 1629. Bancroft's faith in the venture however had led him to insert a clause in his will giving the College a reversionary interest in his own library, in the event of his successors as archbishop not being able to guarantee its safe preservation. When the scheme lapsed, Samuel Hartlib and Comenius discussed its re-foundation, not only to encourage the advancement of learning but also the union of the reformed churches.[1] Nothing transpired, and in 1664 the Royal Society petitioned Charles II for the grant of Chelsea College buildings for their own use. The grant was made in 1667, but in 1681 the Crown resumed possession, and they became an asylum for veteran soldiers. The Royal Society received £1,300 in compensation.

The *Musaeum Minervae* was an academy opened by Sir Francis Kynaston (1587–1642), who gave it a home in his own house in Bedford Street, Covent Garden. It was designed for the education of young men of noble or gentle birth. The site is still marked by Kynaston's Alley, Bedford Square. The founder obtained a licence under the great seal, a grant of arms, a common seal, and £100 from Charles I, and its *Constitutions* were published in 1636. It was equipped with books, manuscripts, musical and mathematical instruments, paintings and statues. Kynaston himself was the Regent, and six professors were nominated, in medicine, languages, astronomy, geometry, music and fencing. In addition to these subjects, law, heraldry, writing, sculpture, dancing and deportment were also taught. The six professors were personal friends of Kynaston, none being of any great distinction. The academy closed down with Kynaston's death in 1642, probably because it had been intended mainly for Royalist youths. With less likelihood it has been suggested that both Chelsea College and the *Musaeum Minervae* were killed by the jealousy of Oxford and Cambridge; there had indeed been similar opposition from Cambridge to the establishment of Gresham College.

The Polish scholar and educationalist Samuel Hartlib also took an interest in other similar academies, including one propounded by John Humfrey, and another by Sir Balthazar Gerbier, the painter and architect. The latter opened at his own house in Bethnal Green in 1649 an academy on the lines of the *Musaeum*

[1] G. H. Turnbull, *Hartlib, Dury and Comenius*, 1947; R. F. Young, *Comenius in England*, 1932; J. Crossley, *Diary and Correspondence of Dr. J. Worthington*, Chetham Society, 1847, vol. I, pp. 69–75.

Minervae to teach philosophy, languages, mathematics, art, dancing and fencing. Many of the lectures were printed, but they are of slight importance.

Still another scheme was propounded by Sir William Petty (later one of the architects of the Royal Society) in a letter to Hartlib in 1648.[1] This was in essence a national plan for technological education. There was to be a network of *Ergastula Literaria*, where compulsory instruction in the rudiments of technology was to be given; and a central institute for advanced research (a 'philosophical college') which craftworkers could attend in place of part of their seven years' apprenticeship. This institute would serve as a technical information bureau, and amongst its functions would be the compilation of an official encyclopaedia of technological information. The urgent need for training in the applied sciences lay behind all these manifold plans except those that were primarily religious.

One other projected scheme remains to be recorded. Abraham Cowley in 1661 published his *Proposition for the advancement of experimental philosophy*. This envisaged the setting up of a 'Philosophical Colledge' or university for scientific research on the riverside within two or three miles of London. There were to be twenty 'philosophers' or research professors, and sixteen young research assistants to serve them. Four of the professors were always to be overseas on travelling fellowships. In addition there were to be various officers, including a library keeper who was also to be the apothecary, druggist, keeper of instruments and engines, etc. No details are given of his library, but we are told that it was to be in the second of the three quadrangles, along with the chapel, hall, art gallery, anatomical museum and laboratories. The library keeper's lodgings were to be close to the library, and a 'mathematical room' equipped with instruments, etc. would be an 'appendix' to the library. The keeper's salary was to be £30, that is, a quarter of the professorial salary of £120. Cowley was intimately associated with the Royal Society, and this essay was issued a year before the Society received its charter.

On the scientific side concrete achievement came with the foundation of the Royal Society in 1662. The detailed story of

[1] The advice of W. P. to Mr S. Hartlib, for the advancement of some particular parts of learning. 1648.

this great event can be read in Sir Harold Hartley's tercentenary volume and in the works there quoted. Here we may just emphasize that its royal and national status as the premier scientific academy was conferred on it from the start by the King. It met the immediate needs of science and technology by providing scientists with the means of communication which had hitherto been lacking: an official meeting place where reports and views could be exchanged, and published papers whereby the results of research could be circulated at home and abroad. Its importance to the librarian needs no stressing. The production of documents and their communication must come before their collection on any scale; and the progress of science with its many specializations during the next two centuries is very largely chronicled in the history of the Royal Society and its derivative associations.

In the latter half of the seventeenth century two Royal Librarians speculated on the possibility of giving their library a wider national status. Neither was primarily a librarian; indeed few men of this period were prepared to give themselves wholly to this newly emerging profession, and if this gave us the services of a genius such as Leibniz, it also accounted for the more perfunctory treatment of their libraries by some lesser men. Patrick Young (Patricius Junius) who had been librarian to James I and Charles I, died in 1651. He was succeeded by John Durie, who held his appointment as keeper of the books and medals at S. James' Palace (where he had his lodgings) till the Restoration. His effective tenure of the office lasted however only from October 1650 to March 1652, after which he spent most of his time travelling on the continent. Durie was a moderate puritan, interested mainly in theology and religious education. He could spare little more than a passing glance, as it were, at the library in his keeping. This glance did however awake in him a more tolerant attitude towards the purposes of a library than was common at that time in puritan circles. He published *The Reformed Librarie Keeper* very soon after his appointment, including a description of the library at Wolfenbüttel (where Leibniz in 1691 became librarian) and a vision of the Royal Library expanded into a truly national collection whose function should be 'to keep the publick stock of learning, to increase it, and to propose it to others in the way which may be most helpful to all'. During his keepership, some reorganization of the library was undertaken, and presses were installed in the 'new chapel' which Charles had originally built for his Spanish bride.[1]

Richard Bentley, the classical scholar and Master of Trinity College, Cambridge, secured the keepership of the Royal Library early in 1694. The office had become vacant late in 1693, and the new librarian was persuaded to withdraw in favour of Bentley, who agreed to pay him £130 a year out of the salary of £200. The Licensing Act was due to expire a few months after Bentley took office, and as the copyright deposit law had been a dead letter for many years, he used the short time remaining to bring all his aggressive energies to bear on the London publishers, who to their great astonishment were made to disgorge nearly a thousand volumes for the benefit of the Royal Library. It was about this time that Bentley's famous quarrel with Boyle over the *Letters of Phalaris* reached one of its bitterest phases; Boyle imagined that Bentley was trying to prevent him from collating the manuscript of the *Letters* in the Royal Library. It is not a happy story, but Bentley comes out of it with far more credit than Boyle.[2]

Bentley realized at once the appalling state into which the Royal Library had fallen. The room in which the library was lodged was 'not fit to be seen'; it was mean and far too small for the purpose; no ordered arrangement was possible in so limited a space; the neglect of years had damaged the volumes; no repairs had been carried out and quantities of books were in unbound sheets; no foreign works had been acquired for a long period. The library's most precious treasure was the Codex Alexandrinus (then regarded as the earliest and most authoritative text of the Greek testament); and Bentley kept this in his own rooms, so that scholars inspecting it might not be distracted by the shocking state of the rest of the library.

The sight of the task awaiting him led Bentley to write, or at least to sanction, an unsigned and undated broadsheet entitled *A Proposal for building a Royal Library, and establishing it by Act of Parliament*, probably during the first year or two of his keepership. This broadside assumed that the Royal Library was '*designed and*

---

[1] G. H. Turnbull, *op. cit.*
[2] R. C. Jebb, *Bentley*, 1889.

founded for public use' (a laudable theory, though lacking any sure authority), and after reciting a long catalogue of its present deficiencies, made a concrete proposal for a new library to be erected in a corner of S. James's Park, with a house for the keeper. There was to be an annual grant from Parliament for its upkeep, the funds to be obtained from a duty on imported paper, English paper at the same time being freed from tax. The new building was to have room for 200,000 volumes, and to provide a convenient meeting place for learned societies, much as the Royal Society had already provided in its own special field.[1] The need for a library to provide not merely the books themselves but facilities for their use both in individual research and in association with other scholars, was dawning on men's minds.

The Treasury is said to have agreed to Bentley's plan in principle, but public business prevented the necessary bill being laid before Parliament, and the scheme (like so many other estimable proposals) was shelved. This discouragement served no doubt to direct Bentley's extraordinary energy into other channels. In 1699 he became Master of Trinity College, Cambridge, and entered almost at once on his protracted, and not always dignified, war with the Senior Fellows. He retained his keepership of the Royal Library however, together with the official lodgings at Cotton House, and the keepership was transferred to his son Richard about 1735. Bentley was in residence at the time of the famous fire at Ashburnham House in 1731, and there is a delightful story of his being seen escaping from the burning library in his nightshirt and great wig, with the Codex Alexandrinus under his arm. Lord Oxford, in a letter to Thomas Hearne soon after the fire, laid the blame on poor Bentley's shoulders, referring to 'the terrible calamity that had befallen the Cottonian Library through the villainy of that monster in nature, Bentley; he must be detested by all human creatures, I mean the civilized part of them'. There was of course no justification for so intemperate a charge.

A word at this stage about another matter, not unrelated. If the idea of a truly national library at the end of the seventeenth century was still embryonic; if the collections that should have been safely preserved in such a library were still largely in the private hands of wise and wealthy collectors; it might be thought

[1] Edward Edwards, *Memoirs of Libraries*, I, p. 422.

nevertheless that the national archives, which had always been in the possession of the State, would by now have been housed in a national repository. This was not the case. The Public Record Office did not in fact come till 1838, eighty-five years after the Museum. Before that there were, in Professor Galbraith's words, 'as many keepers as there were courts or departments, and there were as many record offices as there were keepers'.[1] Lord Langdale, who became Master of the Rolls in 1836, noted that the national archives were dispersed in upwards of sixty different places of deposit, all more or less under different management, and having as many rules and regulations for their governance.[2] Not only this, but they were for the most part in a lamentable state of neglect. The seventeenth-century antiquarians had made a brave start at the labour of introducing some order and care in the repositories at Westminster and the Tower. Arthur Agarde (1540–1615), who was a member of the Elizabethan Society of Antiquaries and deputy Chamberlain in the Exchequer, prepared catalogues, lists and other guides which still have their value. The office of General Remembrancer was established in 1627, partly to give some help to students of the records. In 1661 William Prynne became keeper of the records in the Tower, and spent the last few years of his life struggling with the confusion and dirt in which the records were lying. At the beginning of the eighteenth century a House of Lords Committee, with Halifax, Harley and Somers among its members, began to investigate the problem of the records in the Tower and the State Paper Office and the Westminster Chapter house. These preliminary efforts at least made possible the work of those two great historiographers-royal, Thomas Rymer and Thomas Madox in the period 1693–1727. In 1767 Parliament authorized the printing of the Rolls of Parliament, and in 1783 of Domesday Book—the first two official publications of the kind. In the period 1800–37 six Commissions on the Public Records were appointed, and much miscellaneous publication was carried out, and in 1838 came the Public Record Office Act.

To no small degree it was the influence of the great aristocratic collectors, which lay behind both the re-organization of the

[1] V. H. Galbraith, *Introduction to the Use of the Public Records*, 1934, p. 1.
[2] D. C. Douglas, *English Scholars, 1660–1730*, 1951, p. 269.

national archives and the establishment of the British Museum.

In the first half of the eighteenth century the preliminaries that led to the foundation of the British Museum were taking shape. In 1701 the Cottonian collection was bequeathed by Sir John Cotton, the grandson of its founder, to the nation, and in 1707 the Royal Library joined it in Cotton House. The two libraries were moved later, first to Essex House, then to Ashburnham House (where the fire occurred in 1731), and afterwards to Westminster School, finally reaching their home in the new Museum in 1753. Before this two other solutions of the problem had been put forward. John Anstis, Garter King of Arms, had in 1718 proposed their removal to S. Paul's. It was not a new idea that S. Paul's should have its 'public library'; a generation earlier John Evelyn, as has been noted above, had suggested the establishment of a public library within its precincts. Then in 1743 Thomas Carte the historian had proposed the refounding of the Guildhall Library by assembling the two collections at the Mansion House. Ten years later, with the purchase by the nation of the collections of Sir Hans Sloane, the British Museum came to birth at Montague House.

It is a curious fact that the life of Sir Hans Sloane spans exactly the ninety-three years that elapsed between the foundation of the Royal Society and that of the British Museum. He was for many years one of the Secretaries, and for many years President, of the former; and of the latter he must be regarded as one of the chief architects. He took pains to see that his vast collection of books, manuscripts, prints, coins, and his antiquarian and scientific material, should be not only accessible to scholars during his lifetime (no collector could have been more hospitable to visiting students), but should be placed in trust after his death under terms which would ensure its permanent use in future generations. His will thus brought about the immediate establishment of the Museum, and made possible, in Sir Gavin de Beer's words,[1] that 'progress in scholarship and natural history which would never have been accomplished had it not been for the provision of such an incomparable working tool'. Here indeed was a collection great enough in quality and quantity (it included almost 50,000

[1] Sir Gavin de Beer, *Sir Hans Sloane and the British Museum*, 1953.

printed books for example)[1] to form a substantial foundation stone on which the edifice of the Museum could be erected. Over and above all this the world owes many debts to Sir Hans: notably for his encouragement of the use of quinine and inoculation for smallpox, and for his discovery of milk chocolate, which he found a more digestible beverage than the plain variety. But his fame rests squarely on his huge, though systematic, library, his herbarium (which fills 337 folio volumes) and his scientific collections, comprising some 80,000 specimens, which Linnaeus described as an 'incomparable museum'. All these were arranged, first at Nos. 3 and 4 Bloomsbury Place and later at Chelsea, in a series of rooms whose walls were lined with cabinets containing the natural history specimens, with bookshelves above them; many of the specimens were carefully and elegantly displayed in glazed show-cases. The library and museum became widely known amongst scholars and scientists from the beginning of the eighteenth century, and, as Sir Gavin says, 'quickly acquired the reputation of being something which all distinguished foreigners were advised to see'. In 1710 it received a visit from the German traveller Zacharias von Uffenbach, who had found little to commend and much to criticize in the libraries of Oxford and Cambridge; he was however full of praise both for Sloane himself and his magnificent collections. Sir Hans Sloane died on January 11, 1753, and the Act for the Establishment of the British Museum, with the Sloane and Cotton libraries and the Harleian manuscripts as its foundation collections, received the Royal assent on June 7th. The Sloane collection was acquired for £20,000, which then was regarded as a quarter of its value.

The nature of the Sloane collection, with its great assemblage of scientific specimens, reminds us that from the start the British Museum was much more than a library of printed and manuscript books; and it may be appropriate to glance at the steps that led to the formation of a national museum as well as a national library. There is indeed no clear division between the two ideas, especially in the early period. The collection of museum objects or 'cabinets of curiosities' began to make their appearance in sixteenth-century

---

[1] By way of comparison, the Harleian library in 1741 contained 50,000 printed books, 350,000 pamphlets and 7,618 volumes of MSS; the books were dispersed and only the MSS reached the Museum. See Dr C. E. Wright's 'Portrait of a Bibliophile: Edward Harley', in the *Book Collector*, vol. II, No. 2, 1962, pp. 158–74.

Italy. By the seventeenth century, many of the larger private libraries were in part also museums, exhibiting a variety of objects of curiosity or interest side by side with the books. The new zeal for history and antiquities led to the collection of antiquarian objects of every sort; and interest in the new experimental philosophy inspired the collection of mathematical and scientific instruments and apparatus, and anatomical and botanical specimens. Evelyn's accounts of his visits to the Bodleian Library and to Sir Thomas Browne's library suggest more interest indeed in the curios than in the books;[1] the former would no doubt catch the eye of the casual visitor more readily than the latter. Sir Thomas Browne's collections are described as consisting of 'medals, books, plants and natural things' in that order; and it is perhaps natural to associate all these varying objects together.

Evelyn also records visits to other notable collections. In November 1644 he inspected the famous museum of Father Kircherus in his study at the Jesuits' Church in Rome, and was shown his 'catoptrics, magnetical experiments, models, and a thousand other crotchets and devices, most of them since published by himselfe or his industrious scholar Schotti'. Then in 1686–7, he went several times to see the collection of Mr Charleton at the Middle Temple. This consisted of biological and geological specimens of every kind, together with medals, miniatures and drawings, and including 'bookes of birds, fish, flowers and shells, drawn and miniatur'd to the life'. It was valued then at £8,000, and Evelyn regarded it as 'doubtless one of the most perfect assemblage of rarities that can be anywhere seene'. In April 1691, Evelyn visited Sloane's collections, then consisting mainly of the minerals, plants, anumals and insects he had brought back from France and Jamaica. A little later, in 1702, Sloane acquired the Charleton collection for his own rapidly growing museum. About this same time (in 1695) a former servant of Sloane's, James Salter, opened a curious museum of his own in Chelsea which became known as 'Don Saltero's Coffee-house'. It became one of the sights of Chelsea; Steele describes it in a number of the *Tatler*. Some of his specimens came from Sloane himself, but it was

---

[1] So also Celia Fiennes, in recording her visit to Chetham's Library in 1698, was more interested in a six-foot rattlesnake and the 'anatomy of a man wired together', than in the 'two long walls full of books'.

really nothing but an astonishing collection of oddities, designed to attract a gullible public.

The founding of museums was indeed almost as distinctive a feature of the seventeenth century as the collection of books. Both were intimately related to the progress of scholarship, the evidence of the printed word being as necessary as that of the natural objects on the observation of which scientific discovery rests, and the instruments needed for their observation and measurement. Robert Hooke, the curator of the Royal Society's repository, gave an admirable definition of the true functions of a systematic and comprehensive museum of the natural sciences, and of its value to research workers. 'The use of such a collection,' he wrote, 'is not for divertisement, and wonder, and gazing, as 'tis for the most part thought and esteemed, and like pictures for children to admire and be pleased with, but for the most serious and diligent study of the most able and proficient in natural philosophy,'[1] thus sensibly separating the genuine collection from caricatures such as Don Saltero's Coffee-house.

The great German historiographer, D. G. Morhof, in his *Polyhistor* (1688) recognized the value of systematic libraries as well as systematic museums: 'as in acquiring knowledge of the sciences we have need of books, so in experimental science we have need of this one book, the epitome of which can be furnished for us by a *Museum rerum naturalium.* In providing these both men of learning and entire societies have been solicitous, and there exist not a few of them in various places which have been brought together with no small labour.' Leibniz, the greatest librarian of the century, himself planned in 1675 a scientific museum which he intended to launch with a great popular exhibition, accompanied by all the sideshows likely to attract the man in the street. He intended it to become self-supporting, and to endure as a permanent academy of scientific invention. The exhibition was to reveal all the wonders of the world in the arts as well as the sciences, and it would include an art gallery, library, lecture theatre and concert hall as well as scientific displays and novelties. It was to become a clearing house for all inventions, with its own zoo, astronomical observatory, anatomical theatre and displays representing the achievements of military science, physics,

[1] Quoted by Sir Gavin de Beer, *op. cit.*, p. 109.

mechanics and medicine. Scientists everywhere would act as correspondents, and knowledge of scientific progress would be circulated to all interested. A central purchasing office and a 'register of catalogues' would be added, so that up to date bibliographical information could be supplied. This may sound like an elaboration of Solomon's House in the *New Atlantis*, but Leibniz was a much more far-sighted and realistic visionary than Bacon.[1]

Our own first public museum was established in Oxford in 1683, by one of the founders of the Royal Society, Elias Ashmole, who with the help of his second wife's fortune, made a considerable collection of astrological, alchemical, medical and magical MSS, and of coins and archaeological specimens. This was reinforced with the collection of natural history and ethnology made by the Tradescant family at Lambeth; both father and son had been gardeners to Charles I. The family presented their collection in 1659 to Ashmole, who later offered it to the University of Oxford, where the Old Ashmolean Building was erected to house it. It was primarily a scientific institution, with a large lecture theatre, a well-equipped chemical laboratory (the first in Oxford) and a library of chemical and 'philosophical' volumes.[2] During the nineteenth century the collections were transferred to the University Museum and the Pitt Rivers Museum, while the books and coins went to the Bodleian. The Ashmolean was but the first of countless museums and exhibitions, small and large, permanent or temporary, systematic or trivial, culminating in such national landmarks as the opening of the British Museum in 1753, the Fitzwilliam Museum at Cambridge in 1816, and the Great Exhibition in 1851, which itself produced, at the suggestion of the Prince Consort, the Science Museum in South Kensington in 1857.

---

[1] See the paper by P. P. Wiener, *Journal of the History of Ideas*, I, 1940, pp. 232-40.
[2] See the chapter on Ashmole by C. H. Josten in Sir Harold Hartley, *op. cit.*

CHAPTER XIII

Parish Libraries

FROM the earliest times the churches of Christendom have felt the need to possess at least a small collection of books. They were required not merely to regulate the order of the services, but to instruct the faithful and to controvert unorthodoxy and heresy. They have been in fact the most powerful weapons in the armoury of the Church, employed to enforce a disciplined form of worship, to defend the faith and to attack the enemy. From at least AD 200, when Christians were first allowed by the Emperors to own land and build churches, it must have been normal practice for a Christian community to keep a collection of books in its church. A library of this type evidently existed at Constantine in Algeria, which was a centre of the Donatist heresy; during the persecution of AD 303-4 when Diocletian's officers visited the church, they reported that they found the library empty. S. Jerome has several references to church libraries (e.g. *Ep* 49. 3 and 112. 9). S. Augustine made provision on his deathbed for the maintenance of the church library at Hippo (*Ep* 231. 7; *De Haeres* 80), and in the epistle which laid the foundations of the Augustinian Rule there are careful stipulations about the use of the library (*Ep* 211). S. Paulinus of Nola described the basilica which he had built at Nola as having a threefold apse, with recesses to right and left, that on the right being used for the sacred vessels, and that on the left for the holy books.

Although the main tradition of Christian scholarship was passed down to the medieval universities through the monastic libraries and the later cathedral schools, the pastoral and liturgical work of the churches has always involved some dependence on books. The extent of this dependence has no doubt varied with the literacy, first of all of the clergy and secondly of the lay congregation. There has indeed at all times been a necessary relation between clerical literacy and pastoral work; if one is at a low ebb, so also is the other. There is little certain evidence of either in the Anglo-Saxon period, so far as the greater part of the country is concerned. The known schools and libraries were mostly associated with episcopal or monastic centres such as Canterbury, Dunwich, York, Rochester, Malmesbury, Glastonbury, Jarrow and Wearmouth. Alfred's famous letter to Bishop Werferth emphasizes the illiteracy of his period, but he claims that though the knowledge of Latin had decayed, yet many could read English; and it was for such no doubt that he planned his translations into English. The establishment of schools by Alfred is a matter of inference only, but schools are known to have been associated with the collegiate churches and forts set up by Edward the Elder and his son Athelstan in Mercia and Northumbria. The school maintained by Aelfric Grammaticus about AD 1000 is believed to have been a Sunday school for boys of every kind, free and otherwise. He wrote various school books, including a grammar based on Donatus and Priscian dedicated to the boys of England; and his famous Homilies were translated for the many who could not understand Latin, there being little else available for them except Alfred's translations. Aelfric's translations from the Bible and other works were apparently intended for laymen, but the schools of this period (such as Aelfric's and the more famous school at Ramsey over which Byrhtferth presided) were monastic, not parochial.

In the Norman period there is little real evidence of the state of parish life, but many of the secular priests were English and many must have been illiterate.[1] John of Ford's life of the anchorite Wulfric of Haselbury gives a picture of two parish priests of the early twelfth century, Brictric and Segar, both worthy men, but neither with much education. Brictric, having no French, could not speak the same language as his bishop and archdeacon, and he took it ill when the anchorite cured a dumb man who at once began speaking in fluent French as well as English. An uneducated parish priest, however holy he may be, argues an illiterate congregation. The first three centuries after the Conquest saw continual, if not always very successful, efforts to raise the intellectual standard of the parish clergy. The work of Hugh of Wells, Bishop of

[1] On the illiteracy of medieval clergy, see H. S. Bennett, *Life on the English Manor*, 1938, pp. 325-8.

Lincoln (1209–35) in the institution of vicarages for appropriated benefices was particularly effective. Nearly 300 vicarages, with security of tenure, and a house and glebe land for the vicar, were established in the Lincoln diocese, and many presentations to livings were refused owing to the illiteracy of the candidate, or accepted subject to the priest receiving some education. Not until the priest has reasonable security and a reasonable standard of education can any sort of library, whether belonging to the priest himself or to his church, be expected.

J. H. R. Moorman notes only two instances in the thirteenth century of the ownership of books by a parish priest. It was the priest's duty to maintain the service books at his church, but in the fourteenth century this responsibility was gradually transferred to the churchwardens, and the churchwardens' accounts, which begin to occur about 1350, contain many references to the acquisition of books. These in general would be either service books or doctrinal manuals for the instruction of the laity.

Churchwardens were first appointed under a canon of the Council of London, 1127; their civil duties were not imposed on them till the time of Henry VIII and Elizabeth, and they were to begin with strictly church officers. The oldest surviving church-wardens' accounts are at S. Michael's, Bath, where a series of seventy-seven rolls (sixty-seven in Latin and ten in English) covers the period 1349–1575. These, like other accounts of this period, record expenditure on the purchase and binding of many service books (missals, breviaries, processionals, manuals, etc.). An inventory in the accounts at S. Edmund, Sarum, in 1472, records the possession of 5 missals, 9 grayles, a gospeler, and epistoler, 4 breviaries, 6 antiphonors, 14 processionals, 3 legends, a Legenda Aurea, a psalter, an organ book and other volumes. A copy of the Vocabularium of Hugotio of Pisa was chained in the Lady Chapel, and later two copies of the Life of S Osmund (the founder of Old Sarum Cathedral Church) were added. At S. Laurence, Reading, the accounts show about fifty service books, some bound in silver. Items for the binding or copying of books occur frequently; binding expenses were a heavy and recurring charge for volumes in daily use.

It is reasonable to suppose that many churches had in addition copies of devotional manuals for the instruction of the laity.

Popular works such as the *Lay-Folks Mass-book*, the *Lay Folks Catechism* and *Handling Synne* (in Robert Mannyng's translation) would have been often available. There were also guides to preaching and teaching which were widely circulated in the century preceding the Reformation. Examples are the Instructions for Parish Priests, by J. Mirk (*c.* 1420) the *Quattuor Sermones* (of which many editions appeared between 1483 and the Reformation), and the *Exornatorium Curatorum* which priests in the Ely diocese were in 1528 ordered to read aloud to their congregations each year.[1]

The widespread practice of producing religious plays either within or outside medieval churches makes it probable that many churches possessed acting copies of these plays. Churchwardens' accounts and inventories often reveal expenditure on, or storage of, stage properties and costumes; the plays themselves would be copied or re-copied as required, the life of such material being in general short. At S. Dunstan's, Canterbury there was in 1500 a library of over fifty books, including about a dozen volumes of the cycle of Corpus Christi plays.[2] At S. Michael's, Bath in AD 1402 the church-wardens are said to have been charging twopence a volume for the loan of books from the parish library.[3]

There must have been a not inconsiderable development of parish libraries in the fifteenth century. The diversion of bequests from monastic houses to friars and from friars to chantries and for educational purposes resulted in the foundation of a great number of schools of every kind from Eton downwards. Chantries became a popular object of bequests, and chantry priests every-where were being urged to set up petty schools and song schools. Meanwhile changes were taking place in church architecture which reflect the spread of literacy: perpendicular windows, often with clerestory windows above, gave more light, and pews with book-rests were being provided. A few parish libraries in this period are definitely recorded. Stow describes the library at S. Peter's, Cornhill 'built of stone, and of late repaired with brick by the executors of Sir John Crosby, alderman, as his arms on the south end doth witness. This library hath been of late time, to wit,

[1] See Philip Hughes, *The Reformation in England*, 1952, I, p. 96, and Wordsworth and Littlehales, *The Old Service Books of the English Church*, 1904, p. 285.
[2] J. C. Cox, *Churchwardens' Accounts*, 1913, p. 268.
[3] A. R. Powys, *The English Parish Church*, 1930, p. 155.

within these fifty years, well furnished with books; John Leyland viewed and commended them; but now these books be gone, and the place is occupied by a schoolmaster and his usher, over a number of scholars learning their grammar rules, etc.' The pre-reformation library at S. Mary's, Warwick was founded by the antiquarian John Rous, the compiler and illustrator of the famous Rous rolls: two parchment rolls giving the family history of the Earls of Warwick, the earlier version in English and with a Yorkist flavour, the later one in Latin being Lancastrian. Rous died in 1491 and left his library to S. Mary's, Warwick where he was buried, with provision apparently for the building of a room to hold it. Other recorded examples are S. Margaret's, New Fish Street, London, where the churchwarden's accounts give a list of fifty-nine volumes, all but twelve being service books, and the church at Boston, to which various volumes, including a *Polychronicon* and a book of common-law, were bequeathed. The report of the Central Council for the Care of Churches[1] gives details of many medieval manuscripts still surviving which belong, or formerly belonged, to parish churches, but in only one case has there been continuous ownership from pre-Reformation days. This is All Saints, Bristol, which has five early printed books and three fifteenth-century manuscripts which appear to have escaped disturbance at the Reformation.

Such books would often be kept in chests, but in both pre- and post-Reformation days, the more valuable might be chained. The churchwardens' accounts of All Saints, Derby, in 1525 gives an inventory of about ten works which were chained in the Lady Chapel (service books, lives of the Fathers, and a Legenda Aurea).[2] At the beginning of the sixteenth century, some churches were acquiring printed books. The earliest recorded is a copy of Caxton's *Golden Legend*, bequeathed by Caxton himself to S. Margaret's, Westminster, *c.* 1492.[3] Six printed service books are recorded at Pillon, Somerset, in 1507.

It should of course be remembered that pre-Reformation England was liberally sprinkled with religious houses, most of which had libraries, and that in many cases a genuine student would have been able to obtain access to them. Until the fifteenth

---

[1] *The Parochial Libraries of the Church of England*, 1959, pp. 14, 108–11.
[2] J. C. Cox and A. Harvey, *English Church Furniture*, 1907, p. 331.
[3] *ibid.*, p. 111.

century however there cannot have been many either of the secular clergy or layfolk who would have felt the need of this. At least three houses have been recorded as being willing to lend their books to the local clergy and laiety: the Cluniac monks of Bermondsey, and the Austin canons of Anglesey and Albury.[1] Other houses may well have allowed similar privileges; interlending between one house and another was of course fairly common practice.

Practically speaking every parish church lost all its books at the Reformation. The change in religion was only part of the reason. The new learning in its widest sense, and the new printing in which it was embodied, unhappily made the older books seem out of date and out of fashion. The Act against Superstitious Books and Images in 1550 gave legal sanction to the change, and every church having surrendered its most precious treasures to the flames, made a fresh start with a clean slate. To some extent the gaps were again filled by authority. Injunctions of 1538, 1547 and 1559 required the provision of 'one book of the whole Bible of the largest volume in English', together with the *Paraphrases* of Erasmus. These were to be placed in a convenient place in the church so that 'the parishioners maye moste commodiously resorte unto the same, and reade the same'. The Canons of 1571 ordered churchwardens to provide copies of the Bishops' Bible of 1568, with the Prayerbook and Book of Homilies; in addition the higher clergy were required to instal in their homes, in the hall or dining-room where visitors could read them, Foxe's *Book of Martyrs* and 'alios quosdam similes libros ad religionem appositos', and deans were enjoined to provide these also in their cathedrals. Parish churches often followed suit. At S. Michael's, Cornhill, the vestry minutes on January 11, 1571-2 record the decision 'That the book of Marturs of Mr Foxe and the paraphrases of Erasmus shal be bought for the church, and tyed with a chayne to the Egle bras', at a cost of £2 2s 6d. Foxe's *Actes and Monuments of these latter and perilous Dayes* was published by John Day in 1562-3. It replaced the *Golden Legend*; indeed Catholics dubbed it 'Foxe's Golden Legend'. Nine folio editions were issued between 1563 and 1684, and it must have had as wide a circulation as any book other than the Bible. In many

[1] J. R. H. Moorman, *Church Life in England in the 13th Century*, 1945, p. 364.

churches and in many private homes volumes of Foxe still survive, or survived till recently; some were handed in for salvage in the Second World War. Other books which found their way into churches in Elizabeth's time were Calvin's *Institutions* (translated by Thomas Norton in 1561 and reprinted four times before the end of the century), and the works of John Jewel, Bishop of Salisbury, particularly the *Apologia Ecclesiae Anglicanae*, 1562 (translated under Parker's direction, and re-translated in 1564 by Ann, Lady Bacon, the mother of Francis Bacon) and Fuller's edition of the complete works in 1609. The *Apologia* was regarded as stating the official position of the Anglican Church, and Archbishop Bancroft ordered its provision in churches. The metrical version of the Psalms, many editions of which were issued by the authorized publisher John Day from 1562 onwards, would have been in many or most churches; it was often bound up with Bibles or Prayerbooks.

Except for any volumes chained to lecterns, the few books of this kind belonging to the church would probably have been kept in one of the church chests. Chests were the normal receptacle for books, in private homes as well as churches till the seventeenth century.[1] Iron chests were recommended for churches by an Act of 1812, and usually date from that time.

After the Reformation, the church chest was employed mainly for the parish archives, arising from the use of the parish as a unit of civil as well as ecclesiastical administration. They include the parish registers, the churchwardens' accounts, the vestry minutes, the accounts of the constables, overseers, surveyors of highways, charities and similar documents. The instruction of 1538 which first ordered the maintenance of parish registers has been regarded as the only constructive action on the credit side of Cromwell's public life. In 1597 convocation ordered that the registers should be kept on parchment, and that earlier entries on paper should be re-copied on parchment; it also ordered the annual return to the Bishop of the diocese which became known as the Bishops' transcripts. The parish archives are of course important sources of local and sometimes national history. J. C. Cox observes that 'if the vast store of national muniments at the Public Record Office were to be destroyed and all libraries burnt,

[1] See p. 264 *infra*.

the leading facts of English history since 1538 could be gleaned from the parish records'.

The seventeenth-century parish church might also include a collection of school books, particularly if a school was held in the church—sometimes actually in, or over, the church porch. Thus John Evelyn received his first teaching from a schoolmaster in the porch of the church at Wotton, near Dorking, where his family lived. More often the school would be held in the so-called 'parvis' room over the porch, or a loft over the chantry chapel, where in pre-Reformation days the chantry-priest would have held his petty school.

The seventeenth century brought a considerable expansion of organized parish libraries everywhere. Details of them are given with admirable clarity in the recent survey carried out on behalf of the Church of England.[1] The greatly increased production of printed books, the growth in the size of private collections, the spread of literacy among the more prosperous section of the population, the founding or re-founding of countless schools, all encouraged the gift or bequest of books; and the use of the parish for local government purposes suggested a natural object for such bequests. Various methods were adopted by the founders. Some were given directly to the church, such as the collection left to Grantham by the economist parson Francis Trigge in 1606; this is now kept in a room over the porch. Some were set up in the school, such as that established at Guildford Grammar School under the will of Bishop Parkhurst in 1573, though it was intended to be a town library rather than the school library into which it developed. On the other hand Philemon Holland's library at the Coventry Free School seems to have developed into a town library; this collection was dispersed by the governors in 1913–14. Some libraries on the other hand were left to the incumbent and his successors, and some were kept in vicarage or rectory rather than the church. Others were left to the town itself, such as the collection bequeathed in 1631 by Samuel Harsnett, Archbishop of York to the corporation of Colchester; this was to be held in trust for the clergy of the town and neighbourhood, on condition that a suitable room was provided. In

[1] Central Council for the Care of Churches, *The Parochial Libraries of the Church of England*, 1959.

general libraries were not established in towns where there were
cathedral libraries, the main exception being Norwich, where the
town library was set up in 1608; the books are now in the City
Library. Town libraries were also founded about this time at
Bristol, Ipswich and Leicester. In practice however there was little
distinction in function or use among these different types. All
were academic collections likely to appeal in the main to the
student. Many of the volumes would be in Latin. They were in
fact the type of library that a cleric of the day might collect for
himself. The difference between the Grantham Library, founded
at the opening of the seventeenth century, and a comparable
foundation a century later such as the library founded at Reigate
in 1701 by the vicar Andrew Cranston, 'for the use and perusal
of the Freeholders, Vicar and Inhabitants' reflects the expansion
of the private clerical collection in that period. The latter was a
general library of 1,600 volumes with a fairly wide subject cover-
age; it would have done credit to any eighteenth-century vicarage, though its appeal to the laity of that day would have been
limited. The more famous library founded in 1684 at S. Martin's-
in-the-Fields by Archbishop Tenison, in which Evelyn was much
interested, was on a much larger scale, as befits a library in the
heart of London. It contained about 4,000 volumes, including
many manuscripts of value, and was intended mainly for the use
of the schoolmaster and usher, and clergy of the district. Tenison
explained to Evelyn that 'there were thirty or forty young men in
Orders in his parish, either Governors to young gentlemen or
chaplains to noblemen, who being reprov'd by him on occasion
for frequenting taverns or coffee-houses, told him they would
study or employ their time better if they had books'.

The earliest record of a parish lending library seems to be at
Repton in 1622–3, where about fourteen volumes were deposited
with the churchwardens by a local benefactor. They were all religious or devotional works, and it was stipulated that they were
not to be chained or retained in the church, but available for loan
by the minister and churchwardens under certain specified
conditions.[1]

Towards the end of the seventeenth century, an organized

[1] Cox, J. C., *Churchwardens' Accounts*, 1913. This library is not mentioned in *The Parochial Libraries of the Church of England*.

movement for supplying rather more popular libraries to the poorer parishes began to take shape. It was foreshadowed by the bequest of Humphrey Chetham in 1653; he left £7,000 for the endowment of a hospital for the education and maintenance of poor boys; £1,100 for the endowment of the Manchester library that now bears his name; and £200 for the purchase of 'godly English books, proper for the edification of the common people, to be chained in the parish churches of Manchester and Bolton, and the chapels of Turton, Walmesley and Gorton'. Latin works were thus excluded. For many years before his death Chetham's interests had been turned towards charitable purposes, and in his will he was thinking primarily of the needs of his poorer and less literate neighbours. The countryside still being all but illiterate however, charity turned first to the claims of poor and lonely vicarages, ill-equipped with books. The antiquarian Sir Roger Twysden (1597–1692) is credited with the discovery of this plan; and the royalist divine Barnabas Oley (1602–86) of Clare College, Cambridge, vicar of Gransden, put the plan into action. His will provided that his books should be sold, and the proceeds expended by Bishop Nicholson of Carlisle in purchasing certain specified religious works to such poor vicarages in his diocese as he might select. Sixteen volumes were bought for each of ten vicarages at a cost of £10 10s 8d the set. They were to be kept within the church for the use of the vicar and his successors for ever. No provision was made for their safe keeping, with the inevitable result. The Bishop examined them during a visitation in 1703, and the report was not satisfactory. Later in the century at least one set was removed to the rectory. The only survivors today are four books at Dalston and eight at Ainstable.

The real leader and instigator of this new form of charitable service was Thomas Bray (1656–1730), and it was in a sense incidental to his missionary work in the new province of Maryland. The only clergy who volunteered for service in the colonies were poor, and Bray decided that they must be equipped with books. He worked out schemes for this service both in the colonies and in England, and these were outlined in various pamphlets and broadsheets between 1696 and 1709, when Parliament passed its Act for the Better Preservation of Parochial Libraries. At that date there were over 2,000 parishes in England and Wales where the income was under £30; of these 1,200 were under £20, and 500 under £10. A committee had by then made progress in organizing the service, and 7,000 books had been accumulated. Fifty-two libraries were then nearly ready, and 500 more proposed. The Committee based its work on the results of a questionnaire, the replies to which are in a document known as the *Notitia Parochialis*.[1]

Bray's Committee had been set up by the new Society for Promoting Christian Knowledge, and its history is preserved in the SPCK archives. The driving force behind the movement came from two men in addition to Bray, namely Henry Hoare and the religious writer Robert Nelson who was also a Fellow of the Royal Society; both these gave generously to the funds. When Bray died and the Committee disbanded in 1730, about sixty-five libraries had been established. Each had between seventy and eighty volumes, all theological, devotional or pastoral works, costing (with binding, cupboard and carriage) about £22, of which £5 was defrayed by the parish. Many others had been printed in North America and other countries.

The Committee's place was taken by the Associates of the late Rev Dr Bray, who founded seventy-three new libraries up to the year 1768. The Select Committee on Public Libraries in 1849 heard evidence, mainly from Edward Edwards, that many had decayed; 'the books lie exposed to chance, and liable to be torn by the children of the village'. In one case, at Beccles, it was said that the books had been rescued and 'made the commencement of a Town Library', and the Committee urged this idea on others. The same Committee was told that the S. Martin's-in-the-Fields library had been taken over by the S. Martin's Subscription Library, which used it for reading newspapers and modern popular books and playing chess. The original works were in a deplorable condition, thick with dust, their bindings destroyed by fumes from the gas-lights. Only one 'studious person' in the previous eighteen months had applied to use Archbishop Tenison's books, and after three or four days he had left in despair. The collection of 4,000 volumes was sold by auction at two sales in June and July, 1861, the printed books in 1,668 lots and MSS in ninety-eight lots.

The 1709 Act provided (1) that the incumbent should give

[1] Lambeth Palace MSS., 960–5.

security for the preservation of the library before he is permitted to use it, (2) that he should make a catalogue to be delivered to the ordinary, (3) on the death of the incumbent, the library shall be locked up by the churchwardens, (4) the names of benefactors should be entered in a book, and, most important of all, books shall not be alienated without the consent of the ordinary, and then only if they are duplicates.

This Act is still in force, so that there is no excuse for the sale or alienation or neglect of parochial libraries. The direct prohibition of a sale in the 1708 Act has been amended, so as to give power for a faculty from the Consistory Court of the Diocese to sanction a sale. Several sales of parish libraries did in fact take place while the Committee was sitting, some without any faculty at all. A faculty was given for the sale of the copy of the Caxton *Legenda secundum usum Sarum* from S. Mary's, Warwick to the British Museum, and a parish library in the Ely diocese has been similarly acquired by the Cambridge University Library. Such a transfer will certainly ensure the safe-keeping of the books but the alienation of the library from its parish is a misfortune. The Committee particularly advise that the Consistory Court, or Chancellor, will consult the Diocesan Advisory Committee, before giving a faculty.

It is worth noting here that the Parochial Registers and Records Measure, 1929 of the Church Assembly gives Bishops power to appoint and recognize repositories within their dioceses as appropriate places in which the earlier parish records and registers may be deposited, and to inspect such archives and order their transfer to safe-keeping where it seems necessary. Usually the County Record Office serves as the approved repository for this purpose. Thus the care of parish archives is provided for by legislation, though only the 1709 Act gives a theoretic protection to parish libraries.

About the same time as Bray was working out his scheme in England, a similar plan was being invented for Scotland. The General Assembly of the Church of Scotland approved a scheme, initiated by the Rev James Kirkwood, who later acted as agent for the SPCK in Scotland. Kirkwood outlined his plan in an anonymous pamphlet in 1699: 'An overture for founding and Maintaining of Bibliotheks in every Parish.' The scheme was ambitious. It involved the surrender by the Minister of his own books to the parish; the preparation of union lists;

the appointment of parish bookbinders; or the training of the domestic staff at the Manse in binding; and the setting up of a central fund for buying and printing English and foreign books. This last proposal would (so Kirkwood thought) dispense with any need for foreign travel, and would soon put all the European printing presses out of business. In 1704–9, the General Assembly passed four Acts to administer the scheme. The presbytery libraries did not however survive very long. There were frequent complaints in the Assembly about their neglect. A few continued into the nineteenth century, and one, at Inverness, is still extant. It is worth noting that the first reason given by Kirkwood for establishing parish libraries was the great scarcity of books among the ministers, especially in the Highlands, 'some of them not having so many as are worth twenty shillings'. (We may indeed marvel that most had this amount, or even more, in the Highlands in 1700.)

It is noteworthy too that there are signs of a tolerant spirit in Kirkwood unusual for his times. 'As for Popish books and perhaps some others, tho' they be not fit for the weaker sort of people, yet for the library of a divine they are convenient and necessary, that so they may be the more able to deal with the Adversary.' (Bodley would scarcely have viewed it in this way.)

There was another Scottish scheme a century later, established by Samuel Brown, Provost of Haddington in 1817. This was for county circulating libraries. Collections of fifty books were set up at various centres, moving on in a kind of general post every two years; and a small subscription was charged. One-half to two-thirds of each collection was religious, the rest being history, biography or science.

CHAPTER XIV

The Study and the Sofa

I T is evident that a history of libraries must take into account the social and domestic circumstances under which reading is done; and both the words in our title are significant from this point of view.

Consider the word 'study' first. It probably conveys a picture of a pleasant, book-lined room, comfortable, perhaps rather untidy, possibly in a Regency vicarage, possibly the sanctum of the headmaster at a school. In either case it will reflect the character of the owner; it is as much an extension of his personality as his clothes. As an institution the academic or clerical study has a definite place in our social history and in the development of scholarship and letters, and its origins are worth exploring. Note first however two points about it. First, although the walls are lined with books, it is often today more of an office than a place of study. The books are probably evidence of past academic achievement rather than present research. They are part of the trappings of academic distinction, designed, like academic dress itself, to strike awe into the breast of the visitor, be he pupil, parent or parishioner; and in this they often succeed. Moreover, quite simply, they are pleasant things to have around one, and that is their true justification. As Sydney Smith rightly claimed, there is no furniture so charming as books, even if you never open them or read a single word.[1] Secondly, the room is usually masculine. There are more women today with rooms of their own than when Virginia Woolf wrote her book on this topic, but they rarely furnish them in the true tradition; when the study becomes feminine, it quite rightly changes its character.

The room that we have in mind has an unexpectedly short history. Its value was not fully appreciated till the eighteenth century, when for the first time it became a common feature in

[1] Lady Holland, *Memoir*, 1855, vol. I, p. 241.

English houses. There are scattered examples in the seventeenth century, but scarcely anything of this pattern in earlier periods. This is understandable when we recall its essential characteristics, namely, books in attractive bindings treated as a wall decoration, and a degree of comfort in the general furnishings.

The term 'study' has of course a respectable history. In classical Latin *studium* has a commendable association with the idea of zeal, self-dedication, application. In late Latin it acquires the double meaning of both a course of study and the place where it is carried out; in the latter sense it replaced the term *cubiculum* which Vitruvius had used for the study in a villa.[1] In this double sense the word remained current throughout the medieval period. *Studium generale* was a university, or a university course; *studium particulare* was a preliminary course, prior to admission at Oxford or Cambridge. In addition a *studium* was a monastic carrel, in effect a combined desk and bookcase, set in the side of a cloister and partially screened from the neighbouring carrels.[2] Only the more important obedientaries would be given private cells or studies. At the Oxford Greyfriars for example these were reserved for the minister, the lector and the doctors of divinity. At St Albans a group of studies was built by Abbot Michael (1335–49) between the dorter and the guesthouse chapel, so that scholars might not be distracted by the disturbances in the cloister, which was always the normal place for reading. Neither carrel nor cell has much in common with our own studies, except in purpose and function; study furniture as we know it had not yet been evolved.

There is no reasonable doubt that the kind of study with which we are familiar had its origins in the Italian Renaissance. It would be pleasant to know more of the contents of the room in which Petrarch was working when he died. This was in 1374, and at the time of his death he was in his study at Arqua, in the Euganean hills near Padua, making notes on the *Odyssey* which Boccaccio had translated for him into Latin: the house, with at least some of his furniture, still survives. Illustrations are available[3] of many fifteenth-century studies, mostly ecclesiastical or monastic, including for example Savonarola's (which can still be seen in

[1] Vitruvius, *De Arch.* 6. 4. 1.

[2] For the medieval French terms *estude* and *carole* (carrel) see the valuable article by W. Rothwell in *Medium Aevum*, 1960, XXIX, pp. 102–14.

[3] See J. W. Clark, *The Care of Books*, 1901, pp. 310–14.

Florence), but these were cells or workrooms rather than studies in the modern sense.

In England, the beginnings were simple and austere. We can only picture vaguely the appearance of Chaucer's study in his home over the gatehouse at Aldgate, but it cannot have been luxurious. Equally vague is our picture of Sir Thomas More's library, gallery and chapel at Chelsea, in the new building which he erected for this purpose at a distance from his house, for privacy's sake. I suspect that the library was in the gallery—a convenient place for storing heavy folios that were kept flat on sloping desks or shelves. More's fellow-martyr, S. John Fisher, kept his great library in two long galleries, the books arranged in stalls, with a shelf-list at the end of every stall. But a gallery is not a study, and the real work of studying must surely have been carried out in some smaller room.

Note the effect that the discovery of printing and the evolution of binding fashions have had on the appearance of our studies. In the time of manuscript books, and in the earlier days of printing, very many volumes—not all of course, but a very considerable number—were large and ponderous. They were usually kept, not upright on shelves but lying flat, on lecterns or tables, or in cupboards. As a result binding ornament was concentrated on the side panels rather than on the spines. Such books, lying flat, took up a lot of room, but few scholars had large collections of them. The medieval scribe and binder could produce a volume of great individual beauty, but he had no chance to realize the decorative value of a collection of books, as the main ornament of a library. Nor did shelving have its present importance in library furniture. Most book collections were small; very small indeed by present standards. Shelves were certainly used. Chaucer himself was familiar with the bedside shelf; so was his clerk Nicholas who kept there his copy of Ptolemy, his astrolabe and his counters, concealed by a 'falding reed' (i.e. a woollen curtain). But in the ordinary house the usual receptacle for books not in actual use was either a cupboard or a chest. This was the common method before the seventeenth century—in England perhaps up till the Restoration. Many such chests survive; they are still often seen in antique shops, and most of our older churches possess them. They were indeed part of the required furniture of the medieval church; in 1287 for example, the Exeter diocesan synod ordered every parish to provide *cistam ad libros et vestimenta*. They were usually of oak, or built up of oak slabs, strengthened and sometimes decorated with ironwork, later examples being often panelled and carved. Elm or poplar was sometimes used instead of oak. Cedar and cypress wood (thought to be proof against moths) came into use in the seventeenth century, but these woods were expensive and were used mostly for chests in private houses. The extreme example of a decorative chest is perhaps that made for Sir Julius Caesar (*d.* 1636). This was of oak, 16 in. by 11 in. by 3 in., fashioned in the shape of a folio volume and covered in tooled olive-green morocco. It contains forty-four miniature volumes in white vellum, arranged on three shelves, all classified by the coloured ribbons with which they are fastened: blue for theology, red for history, green for poetry. It was intended as his travelling library.

One difficulty of using chests for book storage of course is that you cannot open the lid without disturbing papers or books resting on it. John Leland in his *Itinerary* describes a library in Wressel Castle, East Riding, which was built in Richard II's reign. This was a stone castle, moated on three sides, with towers at each corner and a gatehouse tower. Leland's description is obscure, but apparently in one of the towers there was an octagonal study called Paradise. It contained eight chests, one to each side (the position of the entrance is not mentioned). Above each chest was a desk which could be raised to the ceiling or lowered to breast height at will. One may guess that the desks had to be raised to enable one to take volumes out of the chests beneath them. I think also the room was a school-room rather than a study. The 'paradise' or parvis" room in churches over the church porch was often used as a schoolroom, and this may well have been a room in the gatehouse tower.

As late as 1632, the library of Henry Percy, the ninth Earl of Northumberland (the Wizard Earl, remembered especially for his circle of scientists and philosophers that was called the School of Night) at Petworth was kept almost entirely in chests. Its size at his death was about 2,000 volumes, and the inventory for probate mentions fifty-two chests; only a few folios and pamphlets were kept in a glazed cupboard of cypress in the Earl's chamber.

However fine the contents, there is little aesthetic satisfaction to be derived from an array of fifty-two chests or boxes. And imagine, if you can, the problem of using such a library, of unpacking each box to find your book. It is hard to imagine any scholar being long content with such an arrangement.[1]

It certainly would not have suited Montaigne, who describes his library in some detail. It was in a tower at the entrance to his house, on the second floor. At ground level was his chapel; on the first floor a chamber and withdrawing room; on the third floor above a 'great wardrobe'. 'The figure of my study is round,' he says, 'and there is no more open wall than what is taken up by my table and chair, so that the remaining parts of the circle present me a view of all my books at once, ranged upon five rows of shelves round about me. It has three noble and free prospects, and is sixteen paces in diameter . . . 'Tis there that I am in my kingdom, and there I endeavour to make myself an absolute monarch, and to sequester this one corner from all society, conjugal, filial, and civil.' Surely he has the true essence of the idea of a study here. And this must surely be the first, and perhaps the best, definition of it. No chests or boxes here; but it would be good to know what the shelves were like, and how his books were arranged. It was the late sixteenth century in France, so possibly they stood erect, spines to the front in the modern manner, for it was in France that this new fashion began.

Isaac Walton gives us a view of John Donne's study before his death in 1631. His books included 1,400 authors, six score of his sermons and a great collection of business documents. The neat French custom of spines to the front on wall shelving had scarcely arrived in England at that time, and we can guess that Donne used all known methods indiscriminately—cupboards, chests, tables, lecterns and shelves—convenient for him no doubt, but it can scarcely make a satisfying picture as a whole.

Fixed wall shelving was sometimes being used in English academic circles at this period on a fairly large scale. An inventory dated 1623 of the rooms of the Oxford antiquary, Brian Twyne, reveals a considerable amount of shelving: nine shelves for folios, six for quartos, fourteen for octavos, eight for 16mos, with a desk against the chimney and a locked cupboard. This would

[1] G. R. Batho, 'The Library of the Wizard Earl', *The Library*, 1960, pp. 246–61.

perhaps accommodate 1,000 volumes: a fairly large collection for the time. Probably the books would be arranged fore-edge outwards.[1] Another Oxford collection of the same period was that of Robert Burton, but it was twice as large as Twyne's. There is no clue as to its arrangement, but it included many pamphlets and news-sheets, and for this reason it may well have looked untidy. Nobody yet has solved the problem of storing pamphlets in a way that is pleasing as well as convenient.

The ordinary manor house of course still had very few books, and special storage was hardly needed. The Elizabethan manor house of the Johnson family at Glapthorn, Northants, possessed for example a single shelf, bearing a copy of Froissart, a Bible and some books of devotion, though the rest of their furniture was comparatively luxurious. This would be fairly typical for the time. The well-known inventory of Sir William More's possessions at Loseley House in 1556 reveals about 140 volumes of printed books and MSS—a large collection for the date. The walls of the library were hung with maps, a perpetual almanack and a picture. A globe and various writing materials are mentioned, but no shelving or other furniture. Not many squires would have possessed a genuine study before the eighteenth century, and not all by any means then. Neither Sir Roger de Coverley, nor Squire Boothby in *Joseph Andrews* could boast such a thing. In both cases their copy of Baker's *Chronicle* lived on the hall window sill—a good place for a folio reference book—and this was in effect their library. Squire Boothby did in fact own two other books—the *Whole Duty of Man*, and the *Imitation of Christ*—both rather unexpected titles.

Obviously the study, as the central feature of the house, the mind and heart of the home as it were, is only gradually emerging in these two centuries. Bacon made no allowance for such a room in his ideal great house. Spenser in the *Faerie Queen* describes more than one palace in some detail; but for him, writing *c.* 1580, the three chief rooms were still the hall, the kitchen and the parlour. On the other hand Bunyan, writing in 1678, found room for a study in the palace called Beautiful. In the morning Piety and Prudence 'had him in the study, where they shewed him Records of the greatest Antiquity'. Domestic architecture was

---

[1] Strickland Gibson, 'Brian Twyne', *Oxoniensia*, vol. V, 1940, p. 101.

very much in the stage of transition. The value and pleasure of privacy was being slowly realized. The day of the great hall was going, or gone; it was being changed from the general living-room into an entrance hall. The solar had given a taste of privacy to the lord and lady, and to the town merchant and his wife, but this was only the beginning of expansion. In Elizabethan and Jacobean times, new parlours, new staircases, new chambers and galleries were being added or built on by everyone who could afford them nobles and yeomen alike. The study was only one of the new rooms that evolved. Space was often found for it in the place once occupied by the domestic offices behind the screens in the great hall; the tendency in larger houses was for the kitchen and service rooms to be removed out of sight of the main entrance, perhaps to the basement; in smaller houses, the hall was some-times downgraded to serve as a kitchen-living-room. If the great hall was open to the roof, it could of course be divided into two storeys, and a chamber in the upper part might be used as a library.[1]

The multiplication of new rooms for special purposes is revealed in the designs of contemporary architects and surveyors. The designs of John Thorpe, at the end of the sixteenth century, which still for the most part show a great hall, often with a dais; of John Smithson, c. 1630; and of John Webb, Inigo Jones' pupil, in the mid-seventeenth century show how new rooms with special functions were appearing in English houses, and how the library or study was slowly being accepted as a feature of domestic planning.[2]

Seventeenth-century probate inventories relate in the main to larger houses and they reveal that though such houses were plenti-fully supplied with bedchambers, the day accommodation was still restricted. The dining chamber still served as the 'hall' and the focus of the daytime life of the household; there might also be a small dining-room for private use, and a parlour. Owen Ash-more's survey of inventories of Lancashire manor houses[3] yields only two examples with studies explicitly mentioned. Rufford in

[1] This possibly happened at Sir Simon D'Ewes' house at Islington, where the library is recorded as being in a chamber over the hall (1629). See A. G. Watson's forthcoming book *The Library of Sir Simonds D'Ewes*, quoting Harl. Charter 49. E. 27.

[2] J. A. Gotch, *The English Home from Charles I to George IV*, 1918, p. 115; *The Growth of the English House*, 1909, pp. 142 ff.

[3] 'Household Inventories of the Lancashire Gentry, 1550–1700', *Trans. Hist. Soc. of Lancs. & Cheshire*, 1958, vol. 110, pp. 59–106.

1620 had two studies, as against twenty-four bedrooms, one parlour (used as a bedroom) and a gallery (used, as often, as a general storeroom). Dunkenhalgh on the other hand in 1679 had a library chamber with a sealed press, and two studies adjoining with presses and shelves, and is thus exceptional. Seven of the manor houses examined had small collections of books, varying in value from £22 to £157; the largest was perhaps the Earl of Derby's in 1651, amounting to 265 volumes, of which fifty-four were gilded. In the great majority however no room had as yet been specifically designated as a library or study.

The appearance of studies in smaller houses was naturally slower; where accommodation is limited there is less temptation to assign rooms to special purposes. As might be expected, such records as there are for the seventeenth century refer almost exclusively to parsonage houses. The development of vicarages and rectories in this period can be traced in M. W. Barley's survey,[1] which is based on a fairly wide examination of sources, especially household inventories made in obtaining probate of wills and the terriers which, after 1571, incumbents were expected to return from time to time, so that the diocesan authorities could have information about the state of the property and (especially in the Lincoln diocese) about the adequacy of the vicarage or rectory. The size of parsonage houses seems to have corresponded closely, according to the value of the living, with the houses of yeomen, either those of moderate means or those of the wealthier sort; the commonest type had between four and eight rooms. The following are the only instances recorded in this survey of parsonage houses with rooms explicitly designated as studies:

Wisborough Green, Sussex. The vicarage in 1584 had two service rooms (kitchen and brewhouse), and three chambers furnished as bedrooms, one of which was used as a study.[2]

Wyberton, near Boston. This was a comparatively prosperous living, and the rectory in 1606 was large, with seven bays, part brick and part mud walls. When the rector died in 1615, the inventory recorded a study, three parlours, hall, kitchen, buttery and milkhouse, with a great chamber upstairs, and outbuildings.[3]

Blisby, Lincs. The vicarage contained a hall (with table, forms

[1] M. W. Barley, *The English Farmhouse and Cottage*, 1961.
[2] ibid., p. 65.
[3] ibid., p. 93.

and stools, two chairs and cupboard), two parlours, sitting-room and study (with living table, counter table and one chair), 'maidens' parlour', three chambers and three service rooms. The vicar in the early seventeenth century possessed books valued at £13 6s 8d.[1]

Guiseley, Yorks. The rectory is a thirteenth-century aisled hall of timber with five bays, rebuilt in stone in 1601. The ground floor rooms included study, hall, dining-room and parlour.[2]

Queenborough, Leics. The parsonage had four rooms: hall, parlour, chamber and study, with books valued at £5; the hall was used for cooking, etc.[3]

Sherrington, Bucks. In 1606 the rectory is described as containing, in the wing on one side of the hall a parlour and buttery, and in the wing on the other side a kitchen and boulting house (i.e. room where flour was sieved). Today the first wing is used for the drawing and dining-rooms; in the other, the kitchen remains, but the boulting house has become a study. The date of the change is not recorded.[4]

Therfield, Herts. The parsonage was a medieval house of some size, partly rebuilt and added to in Tudor and Jacobean days. In 1625, in addition to various parlours, chambers and service rooms, it was described as having two studies, and it must have been unique in this respect. One study was on the ground floor, situated with three parlours west of the hall, the service rooms being on the east; the second study, with four chambers and a turret, was on the first floor above the parlours.[5]

Combeinteignhead, Devon. The large parsonage in 1679 included a parlour chamber and a study within it.[6]

Woughton, Bucks. The parsonage in 1707 included kitchen, hall, two parlours, pantry, cellar, milkhouse, two chambers over the kitchen, one chamber over the milkhouse, one over the hall, one over the great parlour, a 'little dark room' over the little parlour, a garret, a closet and a study.[7]

Fulletby, Lincs. (1707). The parsonage was a thatched clay house

[1] *ibid.*, p. 93–4.
[2] *ibid.*, p. 116 (with plan).
[3] *ibid.*, p. 96.
[4] *ibid.*, p. 105.
[5] *ibid.*, p. 146.
[6] *ibid.*, p. 274.
[7] *ibid.*, p. 273.

with hall, parlour, kitchen, brewhouse, dairy, buttery, pantry, passage and a study. The parlour and study were floored with boards, but they were 'very much decay'd, broke up, and gone'.[1]

Farnham Royal, Bucks (1707). Six ground floor rooms are mentioned, including parlour and study 'new wainscot'd'.[2]

Another authority[3] claims that the provision of parsonage studies gradually became normal from the Elizabethan period onwards, but, using probate inventories as his source, he can only adduce the following two instances in the seventeenth century:

Upton-near-Southwell (1663-4). Hall, two parlours (one a bed-sitting room), store-chamber, kitchen, study, buttery and dairy. The study had a library valued at £1 6s 8d.

Prestwick, Northumberland (1645). A large rectory with twenty-two rooms, including hall, three parlours, great chamber and a study containing 150 books and a chair.

Research would no doubt produce further examples, but it seems plain that the parsonage study was still exceptional in this period. While a few rectories had assumed the size and appearance of a manor house, the majority were still small and poorly equipped. Moreover the amount of reading and 'office work' undertaken by the average parson was limited, so that the need for a special room was not always felt. The parlour often served as living-room, dining-room, sometimes even as bedroom, and no doubt as study as well. This was evidently the case for example with the vicarage at Bucknall, Lincs., in 1614, to judge from the furniture assigned to it.[4] Almost as limited was the accommodation in the vicarage at Dean Prior in Devon, which Robert Herrick describes in his familiar 'Thanksgiving to God for his home'; here there was hall, parlour, kitchen and buttery, but no study, and we can imagine the poet writing in hall or parlour. Rose Macaulay gives us a picture of Herrick's home in her novel *They Were Defeated*.

By the time of the Restoration, it had begun to dawn on men's minds that well-bound books, standing upright on shelves with their spines outward, provided not merely the handiest arrange-

[1] *ibid.*, p. 275.
[2] *ibid.*, p. 273.
[3] A. Tindal Hart, *The Country Priest in English History*, 1959, p. 134.
[4] M. W. Barley, *op. cit.*, p. 94.

ment for the reader, but a decorative feature of considerable beauty for the room. The new fashion had its birth, as I have said, in France. The first great library to be shelved with the spines outwards was that of the historian Jacques de Thou (*d*. 1617). In 1627, when Gabriel Naudé published his *Avis pour dresser une Bibliothèque* it was the general custom there; he notes that 'they do not now place their Books upon Desks as the ancients did; but upon shelves that hide all the Walls'. Evelyn published his translation of Naudé in 1661, and by then the new fashion was becoming general in England. The change can be traced by current fashions in binding. Volumes intended for storage flat had their sides decorated with elaborate panels, or with cameos and bosses. Those intended for upright storage had designs and lettering or labels on fore-edge or spine. Fore-edge decoration gave way gradually to spine decoration in the middle of the seventeenth century, reaching its full development with Samuel Mearne, Charles II's binder; storage with fore-edge outwards was still common in English libraries up to Commonwealth times.[1] It is sometimes said that this is a relic of the earlier custom of chaining books. Normally the chain was attached to the lower fore-edge of the cover (or the top fore-edge if the book was kept on a lectern), and this means that the fore-edge must face outwards. Very occasionally the chain was attached to the joint of the cover and spine, so that the book stood with the spine outwards, but this was rare.[2] However, fore-edge arrangement was so general in pre-Restoration private libraries in England (in which chains would rarely if ever have been used) that I find it difficult to regard it merely as a relic of the chained book. In a small collection, I doubt if people bothered which way the book stood. Fore-edge arrangement may have some slight practical convenience, for it saves turning the book round when you take it down from the shelf. The deciding factor is probably the title label. If this is on the fore-edge, the book is placed with fore-edge showing; if it is on the spine, it is placed with spine to the front. Aesthetically the title fits better on the spine, and it is more legible and convenient thus. The fashion thus became universal.

[1] Fore-edge arrangement continued at Cambridge University Library till 1706; see J. C. T. Oates, *Cambridge Bib. Soc. Trans.*, 1960, vol. III, pt. II, pp. 163–5. See also Graham Pollard, *The Library*, 1956, pp. 71–94.

[2] B. H. Streeter, *The Chained Library*, 1931, p. 276.

The real change in England came, as I say, at the Restoration, as an accompaniment to that flowering of wealth, scholarship and elegance that marked the period 1660–1730. In 1666, Samuel Pepys had the first two of his new presses made by Sympson, his joiner, to shelve his growing library: independent, glazed, movable cases of red oak designed for beauty as well as for use, and the earliest known examples of something that today is a commonplace. By the time he moved into No. 12, York Buildings in 1679 he had seven of these presses. Eventually there were twelve of them, to hold his 3,000 volumes. Two oak cases of similar design are known to have been made by the same joiner, Sympson, for the great hall at Dyrham Park; one of these has been acquired by the Victoria and Albert Museum for its Carolean collection.[1]

These of course were independent cases. Fixed wall shelving was also in the main a seventeenth-century development, found at Bodley early in the century, but the finest examples appear at the end of the century in Wren's work at Lincoln Cathedral and Trinity College Cambridge libraries, and at S Paul's in 1708-9. There were I suppose few seventeenth-century private libraries big enough to justify fittings on this scale. Wall shelving is not in general suited to chained books, and most Oxford libraries (loyal as always to lost causes) kept their books on chains till the eighteenth century.

It is difficult to realize how new this idea was in Pepys' time. Some of his contemporaries had larger collections: Selden for example, and Evelyn. But so far as we know, none gave so much thought to their elegant housing, though Pepys himself had a word of praise for his friend Sir William Coventry's new closet (i.e. study) 'which is very fine, and well supplied with handsome books'.

The study however requires other furniture besides bookshelves; it is a writing room as well as a room for reading, and as well as elegant presses, it needs an elegant writing desk. The desk is basically a development of the lectern, and in its primitive form it appears in many fifteenth- and sixteenth-century pictures, either as an independent article or combined with some shelving. In the sixteenth and early seventeenth centuries the normal desk was a portable box with a sloping front, usually of oak, joiner made, sometimes carved. After the Restoration it was fitted on a stand, with drawers, and was produced by cabinet makers, often veneered with walnut. The earliest known oak pedestal writing desk of the modern kind is the one made for Samuel Pepys about 1680; it still survives with his books. After 1700 the desk slope was increased to its present angle, and a book case was often mounted on top; there was a sudden fashion for bureau cabinets of walnut or lacquer.[1] By this time oak was 'going out', and walnut and mahogany were coming in. With its bureau or desk and its wall shelving the study was now virtually complete as we know it, though the leather armchairs did not arrive till later. For a typical example of the parsonage study at its best, you might take the spacious room with which Sydney Smith provided himself at his rectory at Combe Florey; his library was 28 feet long, 8 feet high, with a large bay window at one end, and the other three walls lined with books.[2]

The eighteenth century however brought a startling change of a different sort. Hitherto, reading and writing books had been a masculine prerogative—mainly an academic or clerical prerogative. In the middle of the eighteenth century it quite suddenly became a feminine interest—indeed a feminine habit. There had of course been women scholars, and a few women writers, before this, but they were rare birds. Many women of leisure had for centuries found comfort in devotional works, few had achieved more than this. Exceptional women, such as Christine de Pisan in the late fourteenth century; Sir Thomas More's daughters, Lady Jane Grey and Queen Elizabeth in the sixteenth century; Lady Winchilsea and Margaret Cavendish, Duchess of Newcastle, in the seventeenth century, stand out because of their rarity. Girls in the seventeenth century were being taught shorthand to help them take down the sermons they heard in church, and Sir Ralph Verney complained that this fostered undue pride in them, to their great injury.[3] It was indeed the very thin end of a very thick wedge. In the early eighteenth century, two numbers of the *Spectator* are given to a discussion of Leonora's library, but even at this date the idea of a woman's library is not treated very seriously. It doubtless seemed as peculiar to the readers of the

[1] 'Origin of the Bureau Bookcase', *The Times*, 1963, Apr. 20.
[2] Lady Holland, *Memoirs*, 1855, vol. I, p. 241.
[3] M. M. Verney, *Memoirs of the Verney family*, 1894, III, p. 72.

Spectator, as the idea of a women's college did to readers of *Princess Ida* in the following century.

The revolution took place about 1740–50, when a virtual epidemic of feminine reading swept through the country. *Pamela* appeared in 1740; *Joseph Andrews* in 1742; *Tom Jones* in 1749. There followed an ever-rising stream of ephemeral fiction, much of which owing to its very popularity has perished completely.

Mark the following points. The population was learning to read for pleasure, and people were realizing that books could have entertainment value, as well as academic value. In the old days a book either improved your mind, or disciplined your soul. Now the word stood also for something which merely killed time. The same word signified two quite different things, and the confusion was worse because there was really no sharp boundary between them. The trouble was that both kinds of book wore the same outer clothes as it were, so that the one could masquerade as the other; this was a blessing to people like Lydia Languish, but a headache to the literary snobs and purists of the day.

Then again, simultaneously with Fielding and Richardson, came the circulating libraries. They sprang up everywhere—in London, in Bath, in resorts such as Brighton and Margate, in almost every town of any size. Many were attached to the shops of milliners or drapers. They served as much for social gossip and the meeting of friends as our cafés do today. They were for the women what the coffee and chocolate houses were for their menfolk.

Now this type of book, that serves mainly in Rose Macaulay's words, 'to kill time for those who like it better dead', is not the kind that people often buy and preserve in good bindings on their library shelves. They were toys rather to fill an idle hour; to pick up and throw aside; that is, to borrow and return to the shop whence they came.

This again meant that the place of reading changed, so far as this kind of book was concerned. It was no longer the study, but the boudoir or withdrawing room. And if you wanted to kill time, you did so in comfort—not at a desk, but preferably lying on a sofa. And again, this meant that these kill-time books must be light to handle, easy to hold in a reclining position, quick to hide in case of alarm at the approach of a disapproving elder. Everyone knows the scene in *The Rivals* when Lydia Languish is surprised by Sir Anthony Absolute. The books she was anxious to hide are thrown under the toilet, into the closet, behind the bolster or beneath the sofa; all except the *Innocent Adultery* which is easily concealed inside the *Whole Duty of Man*. Two other books are left conspicuously on view; Mrs Chapone's Letters on the *Improvement of the Mind*, and the Rev James Fordyce's *Sermons to Young Women*, which was carefully left open at the sermon on Sobriety (in which, as Lydia well knew, the evils of novel-reading are condemned). Almost all Lydia's books (including Fordyce) were duodecimos, featherweights.

And mark finally that Lydia was lying on a sofa. Now if the eighteenth century is remarkable for the spread of reading among women and the new flood of novels, it is equally remarkable for the introduction of the Turkish style sofa. It is not hard to imagine a connection between the two. Leigh Hunt tells us that Thomas Gray's idea of heaven was 'ever to be lying on sofas reading reading eternal new novels by Crébillon and Marivaux'. Crébillon's best known novel was appropriately enough *Le Sopha* (1742), in which an oriental prince, being changed into this article of furniture, was enabled thus to eavesdrop on some interesting conversations.

In a more sober mood Cowper also discovered the comfort of this new luxury. When Lady Austen advised him to try blank verse, he complained of the lack of a subject. 'You can write upon any subject,' she replied; 'Write upon this sofa.' Which he did, beginning thereon *The Task* (though he finished this in his greenhouse). 'I sing the sofa,' he cries, and proceeds to sketch its history:

> 'Thus first necessity invented stools,
> Convenience next suggested elbow-chairs,
> And luxury the accomplish'd sofa last.'

More correctly he could have taken the story back to classical antiquity when couches were common enough, mainly for dining and sleeping. They re-appeared in renaissance times in Italy, particularly in sixteenth-century Florence, where elaborately decorated and carved settees, sometimes combined with a chest, were in vogue. They were familiar in Elizabethan England as day-beds, made of oak, or in Jacobean and Carolean days rather more elegantly of walnut and canework. Shakespeare knew all about day-beds, but he regarded them as slightly effeminate. The earliest surviving English day-bed is in the long gallery at Hardwicke; it dates from the end of the sixteenth century, and is a solid affair of oak, with panelled ends raking outwards, 7 feet 3 inches long, with a mattress of embroidered damask. At that time the long gallery often served as a withdrawing room, but it was uncomfortably furnished by modern standards. Chairs were still rare, and joint-stools or three-legged stools did duty instead. The upholstered sofa is definitely a feature of eighteenth-century furnishing in England, and its connection with the spread of reading among women and the flood of novels in light, portable editions that appeared after about 1750 is obvious.

It may be worth noting that as late as 1825 William Cobbett in his *Rural Rides* was pouring scorn on the sofas that farmers' wives were then installing in their new parlours. His real objection however was to the abandonment of the farm kitchen as the living-room for the family, the servants and labourers, just as in an earlier century the great hall had been abandoned by the lord and lady.

If reading for mere entertainment, or to kill time, calls for relaxation on a sofa, the logical ideal is perhaps to read in bed, where (as they say) an equal strain can be put on all parts. There are in fact difficulties in the way of reading in bed, not the least being the question of light. It did not really become a comfortable method till the coming of electric light. It is of course possible to read in bed with a candle, but not entirely easy; if the bed is a curtained four-poster it is both difficult and dangerous. However, if reading in bed is difficult, dictation is simple. We are told that Margaret Cavendish, Duchess of Newcastle, had a servant always handy at night to take down her sudden inspirations; she would summon him by calling out 'John, I conceive . . .' Both she and Pliny teach us the value of a private secretary.

It should of course be noted that comfort beyond a certain limit does not encourage mental concentration. A slight physical strain tends to keep the mind awake. If therefore you have any object other than the killing of time, a chair and a table are still probably the best furniture for your labours.

One stipulation however has always been made by the best authorities. The study must not be too big, nor must its collection of books be too large. De Quincey demanded a room 17 feet by 12, in which he hoped, rather optimistically to shelve most of 5,000 books. And Leigh Hunt was emphatic about this. 'I hate a grand library to study in,' he wrote, 'I mean an immense apartment, with books all in Museum order, especially wire-safed. I say nothing against the Museum itself, or public libraries. They are capital places to go to, but not to sit in; and talking of this, this, I hate to read in public, and in strange company ... A grand private library, which the master of the house also makes his study, never looks like a real place of books, much less of authorship.' And he returns to this theme again and again. 'We like a small study,' he says, 'where we are almost in contact with our books. We like to feel them about us ... To have a huge apartment for a study is like lying in the great bed at Ware, or being snug on a milestone upon Hounslow Heath.' And elsewhere he describes his own den: 'Sitting, last winter, among my books, and walled round with the comfort and protection which they and my fireside could afford me; to wit, a table of high-piled books at my back, my writing desk on one side of me, some shelves on the other, and the feeling of the warm fire at my feet... I looked sideways at my Spenser, my Theocritus, and my Arabian Nights; then above them at my Italian poets; then behind me at my Dryden and Pope; then on my left side at my Chaucer, who lay on a writing-desk ... I entrench myself in my books equally against sorrow and the weather ... When I speak of being in contact with my books, I mean it literally. I like to lean my head against them ... I like a great library next my study, but for the study itself, give me a small, snug place, almost entirely walled with books ...'

LIST OF SOURCES

The following is a list of the principal sources to which reference has been made. Classical texts are omitted.

ADAMSON, J. W. 'The Extent of Literacy in the Fifteenth and Sixteenth Centuries,' *The Library*, 1930, 10, p. 163.

AITKEN, W. R. *A History of the Public Library Movement in Scotland.* Doctoral thesis, Univ. of Edinburgh, 1955.

ALLEGRO, J. M. *The Dead Sea Scrolls*, 1956.

ASHMORE, OWEN. 'Household Inventories of the Lancashire Gentry, 1550–1700,' *Trans. Hist. Soc. Lancs. & Cheshire*, vol. 110, 1958, pp. 59–106.

BARLEY, M. W. *The English Farmhouse and Cottage*, 1961.

BATESON, M. Catalogue of the library, of Syon Monastery Isleworth, 1898.

BATHO, G. R. 'The Library of the Wizard Earl,' *The Library*, 1960, pp. 246–61.

BENNETT, A. C. *Chaucer and the Fifteenth Century*, 1947.

—— *English Books and Readers, 1475–1557*, 1952.

—— *Life on the English Manor*, 1938.

—— 'The Production and Dissemination of Vernacular Manuscripts in the Fifteenth Century,' *The Library*, 1946, I, p. 175.

BERESFORD, M. *History on the Ground*, 1957.

BOLGAR, R. R. *The Classical Heritage*, 1954.

BOUQUET, A. C. *Comparative Religion*, 4th ed., 1956.

BOYD, C. E. *Public Libraries and Literary Culture in Ancient Rome*, 1915.

BURY, RICHARD DE. *Philobiblon*. Trans. E. C. Thomas, 1960.

CALLUS, D. A. ed. *Robert Grosseteste, Scholar and Bishop*, 1955.

CENTRAL COUNCIL FOR THE CARE OF CHURCHES. *The Parochial Libraries of the Church of England*, 1959.

ČERNY, J. *Paper and Books in Ancient Egypt*, 1952.

CHADWICK, MRS. N. K. *Age of the Saints in the Early Celtic Church*, 1961.

—— *Poetry and Letters in Early Christian Gaul*, 1955.

CHADWICK, OWEN. *John Cassian*, 1950.

CHAMBERS, R. W. 'The Lost Literature of Medieval England,' *The Library*, 1925, pp. 293–321.

CHAPMAN, DOM JOHN. *S. Benedict and the Sixth Century*, 1929.

CHAYTOR, J. J. *From Script to Print: An Introduction to Medieval Literature*, 1945.

CLARK, J. W. *The Care of Books*, 1901.

CLARKE, M. L. *Classical Education in Britain, 1500–1900*, 1959.

CLIFFORD, LADY ANNE. *Diary*, ed. V. Sackville-West, 1923.

CLIFT, E. M. *Latin Pseudepigrapha*, 1945.

COX, J. C. *Churchwardens' Accounts*, 1913.

—— and A. HARVEY. *English Church Furniture*, 1907.

COX-JOHNSON, ANN. 'Lambeth Palace library, 1610–1664,' *Trans. Cambridge Bib. Soc.*, 1958, II, pp. 105–126.

DAREMBERG, CH. and E. SAGLIO. *Dictionnaire des Antiquités Grecques et Romaines après les Textes et Monuments*, 1877–1919.

DAVIS, NORMAN. 'The Language of the Pastons,' *Proc. Br. Acad.*, 1954, p. 120.

DE BEER, SIR GAVIN. *Sir Hans Sloane and the British Museum*, 1953.

DENHOLME-YOUNG, N. *Collected Papers on Medieval Subjects*, 1946.

DICTIONARY OF NATIONAL BIOGRAPHY.

DOBSON, AUSTIN. *Eighteenth Century Vignettes*, 3 series, 1892–6.

DOUGLAS, D. C. *English Scholars, 1660–1730*, 1951.

EDWARDS, EDWARD. *Memoirs of Libraries*, 2v. 1859.

FIENNES, CELIA. *Diary*, 1695–7, 1888.

FOX, L. ed. *English Historical Scholarship in the Sixteenth and Seventeenth Centuries*, 1956.

FREEMAN, K. *Schools of Hellas*, 1907.

FUSSNER, F. SMITH. *The Historical Revolution: English Historical Writing and Thought, 1580–1640*, 1962.

GALBRAITH, V. H. *Historical Research in Medieval England*, 1951.

—— *Introduction to the Use of the Public Records*, 1934.

—— *The Literacy of the Medieval English Kings*, 1935.

GARDINER, STEPHEN. *Letters*, ed. J. A. Muller, 1933.

GASQUET, F. A., *Cardinal*. *Henry VIII and the English Monasteries*, 7th ed., 1920.

GIBBON, EDWARD. *Decline and Fall of the Roman Empire*, 1776–88.

GIBSON, STRICKLAND. 'Brian Twyne', *Oxoniensia*, vol. V, 1940.

—— *Some Oxford Libraries*, 1914.

GISSING, GEORGE. *By the Ionian Sea*, 1901.

GOODRICH, L. CARRINGTON. *Short History of the Chinese People*, 1948.

GORDON, C. H. *Before the Bible*, 1962.

GOTCH, J. A. *The English Home from Charles I to George IV*, 1918.

—— *The Growth of the English House*, 1909.

GRAHAM, H. G. *Social Life of Scotland in the Eighteenth Century*, 4th ed., 1937.

GRAVES, ROBERT. *The Greek Myths*, 1955.

GREENAWAY, G. W. *Saint Boniface*, 1955.

GREG, W. W. *The Editorial Problem in Shakespeare*, 2nd ed., 1951.

HART, A. TINDAL, *The Country Priest in English History*, 1959.

HARTLEY, SIR HAROLD. ed. *The Royal Society, Its Origins and Founders*, 1960.

HENTSCH, A. A. *De la Littérature Didactique du Moyen Âge s'addressant spéciale-ment aux Femmes*, Cahors, 1903.

HESSEL, A. *A History of Libraries*, Translated with Supplementary Material by Reuben Peiss, 1955.

HOBY, LADY MARGARET. *Diary*, ed. Mrs. Meads, 1930.

HUGHES, H. D. *A History of Durham Cathedral Library*, 1925.

HUGHES, PHILIP. *The Reformation in England*, 2v, 1950–52.

IRWIN, MARGARET. *That Great Lucifer*, 1960.

IRWIN, R. *The Origins of the English Library*, 1958. (Cited as *Origins* in the footnotes.)

JAMES, M. R. *The Ancient Libraries of Canterbury and Dover*, 1903.

—— 'The History of Lambeth Palace Library,' *Trans. Cambridge Bib. Soc.*, III, 1959, pp. 1–31.

JEBB, R. C. *Bentley*, 1889.

JOHNSON, F. R. 'Gresham College,' *J. Hist. Ideas*, I, 1940, pp. 413–38.

JONES, A. H. M. *The Greek city from Alexander to Justinian*, 1940.

JONES, H. STUART. *Companion to Roman History*, 1912.

JONES, L. W. *Introduction to Divine and Human Readings* (Cassiodorus), 1946.

KENDRICK, SIR THOMAS. *British Antiquity*, 1950.

KENNEY, J. F. *The Sources for the Early History of Ireland*, 1929.

KENYON, SIR FREDERIC G. *Books and Readers in Ancient Greece and Rome.* 2nd ed., 1951

KER N. R. *Medieval Libraries of Great Britain.* 1941

KINGLAKE, A. W. *Eothen.* 1844.

KINGSFORD C. L. *Prejudice and Promise in Fifteenth Century England.* 1925.

KNOWLES, DAVID. *The English Mystical Tradition,* 1961.

—— *The Evolution of Medieval Thought,* 1962.

—— *The Monastic Constitutions of Lanfranc,* 1951.

—— *The Monastic Order in England,* 1940.

—— *The Religious Orders in England,* 3v., 1948, 1955, 1959.

LAISTNER, M. L. W. 'Bede as a Classical and Patristic Scholar,' *Trans. Roy. Hist. Soc.,* 1933, pp. 69–94.

LANGWELL, W. H. *The Conservation of Books and Documents,* 1957.

LEACH, A. F. *The Schools of Medieval England,* 1916.

LEWIS, C. S. *English Literature in the Sixteenth Century,* 1954.

LITTLE, A. G. *The Greyfriars at Oxford,* 1892.

LOOMIS, R. S. *Arthurian Literature in the Middle Ages,* 1959.

MCFARLANE, K. B. *John Wycliffe and the Beginnings of English Nonconformity,* 1952.

MADAN, F. *Books in Manuscript,* 1893.

MARROU, H. M. *Histoire de l'Education dans l'Antiquité,* 1948.

MOMIGLIANO, A. D. 'Cassiodorus and Italian Culture of his Time,' *Proc. Br. Acad.,* XLI, 1955.

MOORMAN, J. R. H. *Church Life in England in the Thirteenth Century,* 1945.

NAUDÉ, GABRIEL. *Avis pour dresser une Bibliothèque,* 1627, Trans. J. Evelyn, 1661.

OLDFATHER, W. A. 'The Maintenance of Ancient Greek Public Libraries,' *Library Quarterly,* 1938, VIII, p. 287.

OSLER, SIR WILLIAM. *Aequanimitas,* 3rd ed., 1939.

OWST, G. R. *Literature and the Pulpit in Medieval England,* 1933.

—— *Preaching in Medieval England,* 1926.

OXFORD CLASSICAL DICTIONARY, 1949.

PINNER, H. L. *The World of Books in Classical Antiquity,* 1948.

POLLARD, A. W. 'The Unity of John Norden,' *The Library,* VII, 1926, pp. 235–52.

POLLARD, GRAHAM. 'Changes in the Style of Bookbinding,' *The Library,* 1956, pp. 71–94.

POOLE, A. L. *Medieval England,* 2v, 1958.

POWELL, J. U. and E. A. BARBER. *New Chapters in Greek Literature,* 2nd series, 1929.

POWER, EILEEN. *Medieval English Nunneries,* 1922.

—— *Medieval People,* 1924.

POWYS, A. R. *The English Parish Church,* 1930.

REID, J. C. *The Mind and Art of Coventry Patmore,* 1957.

ROBERTS, C. H. *Buried Books in Antiquity,* Esdaile Memorial lecture, 1962. Library Association, 1963.

—— 'The Codex,' *Proc. Br. Acad.,* 1954, pp. 169–204.

ROPS, DANIEL. *Daily Life in Palestine at the Time of Christ,* 1962.

ROTHWELL, W. 'Mediaeval French *Bureau*,' *Medium Aevum,* XXIX, 1960, pp. 102–14.

RYE, R. A. *Students' Guide to the Libraries of London,* 3rd ed., 1927.

SALTER, H. E. *Chapters of the Augustinian Canons,* 1922.

SANDYS, SIR J. E. *History of Classical Scholarship,* 3v, 1900–8.

SAVAGE, E. A. 'Notes on Early Monastic Libraries of Scotland,' *Edinburgh Bib. Soc.*, XIV, 1928.
—— *Old English Libraries*, 1911.
SEEBOHM, FREDERIC. *The Oxford Reformers*, 1869.
SHAKESPEARE'S ENGLAND. 2v. 1916.
SKEAT, T. C. 'The Use of Dictation in Ancient Book Production,' *Proc. Br. Acad.*, XLII, 1956.
SMITH, L. PEARSALL. *The English Language*, 1912.
SMITH, MAYNARD. *Pre-reformation England*, 1938.
STEINBERG, S. H. *Five Hundred Years of Printing*, 1955.
STENTON, LADY. *English Society in the Early Middle Ages*, 1951.
STEVENSON, F. S. *Robert Grosseteste*, 1899.
STOW, JOHN. *Survey of London*, 1598.
STREETER, B. H. *The Chained Library*, 1931.
TAYLOR, JOHN. 'The Monastic Scriptorium,' *The Library*, II, 1890, pp. 237, 282.
TAWNEY, R. H. *Religion and the Rise of Capitalism*, 1937.
THOMPSON, J. W. *The Medieval Library*, 1939, Repr. with supplement, 1957.
THOMSON, S. HARRISON. *The Writings of Robert Grosseteste*, 1940.
THORNTON, J. L. *Classics of Librarianship*, 1957.
TOMPKINS, J. M. S. *The Popular Novel in England, 1770–1800*, 1932.
TSIEN, T. H. *Written on Bamboo and Silk*, 1962.
TURNBULL, G. HARTLIB. *Dury and Comenius*, 1947.
TURNER, E. G. *Athenian Books in the Fifth and Fourth Centuries*, B.C. 1952.
TURVILLE-PETRE, G. *Origins of Icelandic Literature*, 1953.
VAUGHAN, RICHARD. *Matthew Paris*, 1958.
WADDELL, HELEN. *The Wandering Scholars*, 7th ed., 1934.
WALDEN, J. W. H. *The Universities of Ancient Greece*, 1913.
WALLIS, P. J. 'The Library of William Crashaw,' *Trans. Camb. Bib. Soc.*, 1956,pp. 213–38.
WATT, J. A. and others. ed. *Medieval Studies presented to Aubrey Gwynn, S.J.*, 1961.
WEBSTER, T. B. L. *From Mycenae to Homer*, 1958.
WEISS, R. *Humanism in England in the 15th Century*, 2nd ed., 1957.
WHEELER, W. G. *Libraries in Ireland Before 1855*, Thesis for Dipl. in Librarianship, Univ. of London, 1957.
WIENER, P. P. 'Leibniz's Project of a Public Exhibition of Scientific Inventions,' *J. of the History of Ideas*, I, 1940, pp. 232–40.
WILES, R. M. *Serial Publication in England Before 1750*, 1957.
WINCHESTER, BARBARA. *Tudor Family Portrait*, 1955.
WORDSWORTH, C. and H. LITTLEHALES. *The Old Service Books of the English Church*, 1904.
WORMALD, FRANCIS and C. E. WRIGHT. ed. *The English Library before 1700*, 1958.
WRIGHT, C. E. 'Portrait of a Bibliophile: Edward Harley,' *Book Collector*, vol. II, No. 2, 1962, pp. 158–74.
WRIGHT, LOUIS B. 'The Significance of Religious Writings in the English Renaissance,' *J. Hist. Ideas*, I. 1940, pp. 59–68.
—— *Middle-class Culture in Elizabethan England*, 1935.
YOUNG, J. Z. *Doubt and Certainty in Science*, 1951.

Index

283

Date Due